Intercultural Studies in Education

Series editor
Paul W. Miller
School of Education & Professional Development
University of Huddersfield
Huddersfield, West Yorkshire, UK

The book series takes as its starting point the interrelationship between people in different places and the potential for overlap in the experiences and practices of peoples and the need for education to play a larger role in expanding and in these expanding discourses. This proposed book series is therefore concerned with assessing and arriving at an understanding of educational practices in multiple settings (countries), using the same methods of data collection and analysis for each country level analysis contained in each chapter, thereby leading to the production of "Cultures" [of understanding] on different topics. "Cultures" of understanding results from and leads to a deeper appreciation and recognition of educational practices, issues and challenges, (a) within a country (b) between & among countries and (c) between and among traditions and other specificities within and between countries.

More information about this series at
http://www.springer.com/series/15066

Carmel Roofe • Christopher Bezzina
Editors

Intercultural Studies of Curriculum

Theory, Policy and Practice

palgrave
macmillan

Editors
Carmel Roofe
School of Education
University of the West Indies
Kingston, Jamaica

Christopher Bezzina
Leadership for Learning and
Innovation, Faculty of Education
University of Malta
Msida, Malta

Department of Education
Uppsala University
Uppsala, Sweden

Intercultural Studies in Education
ISBN 978-3-319-60896-9   ISBN 978-3-319-60897-6   (eBook)
https://doi.org/10.1007/978-3-319-60897-6

Library of Congress Control Number: 2017952540

Cover illustration: Mohd Bharuddin Naitas Mohd Amin / EyeEm / Getty Stock Images

Printed on acid-free paper

This Palgrave Macmillan imprint is published by Springer Nature
The registered company is Springer International Publishing AG
The registered company address is: Gewerbestrasse 11, 6330 Cham, Switzerland

CONTENTS

LIST OF FIGURES

LIST OF TABLES

Introduction

Carmel Roofe and Christopher Bezzina

We start our Introduction by referring to an article we read over 15 years ago by Nelson, who throws light on the need to ask provocative questions. Whilst Nelson was presenting a framework for thinking about science and mathematics, we feel that this applies to almost every other subject. Nelson states that "[b]efore we can think about the *what* and the *who* of the curriculum, we need to think about the *why*" (2001, p. 13).

> Will the knowledge or skill significantly enhance long-term employment or educational prospects? ... Will the content help citizens participate intelligently in making social and political decisions? ... Does the content have pervasive cultural or historical significance? ... Does the content help individuals ponder on the enduring questions of what it means to be human? (Nelson 2001, p. 13)

C. Roofe (✉)
School of Education, University of the West Indies, Kingston, Jamaica

C. Bezzina
Leadership for Learning and Innovation, Faculty of Education,
University of Malta, Msida, Malta

Department of Education, Uppsala University, Uppsala, Sweden

© The Author(s) 2018
C. Roofe, C. Bezzina (eds.), *Intercultural Studies of Curriculum*, Intercultural Studies in Education,
https://doi.org/10.1007/978-3-319-60897-6_1

1

Five years earlier than Nelson, Cornbleth (1996), in commenting on the purposes of the curriculum, expressed that the curriculum should provide answers to three questions: What knowledge, skills and values are most worthwhile? Why are they most worthwhile? And how should the young acquire them? Answers to these and other difficult questions reveal the underlying tensions in curriculum making.

Curriculum is considered a sociological phenomenon and therefore is influenced by the values, beliefs and understandings that exist within societies. Considering this, we need to define and redefine the curriculum. There are varied definitions of the term "curriculum". Some may look at it as "content" that needs to be transmitted to students through both formal and informal means. Others look at it not from the perspective of a body of knowledge that needs to be transmitted but as a dynamic process of learning through inquiry, co-operative learning, through teacher-learner and learner-learner interaction and co-operation. It is the authenticity of the experience that leads to mastery. Therefore, from a pragmatic perspective, the curriculum can be seen as both a process and a product, one that comprises different forms of learning that take place in different settings, and not only restricted to the school as the place for learning.

According to UNESCO (2015), it is the curriculum that leads all core aspects of education that are known to determine quality, inclusion and relevance. It also represents the core of forging social attitudes and skills, such as tolerance and respect, conflict management, gender equality, justice, self-confidence, motivation, while at the same time contributing to the development of thinking skills that learners need to apply to meet the needs of their daily lives. Furthermore, the curriculum serves as the process that addresses and awakens the consciousness of individuals through the learning it provides.

As a result of globalization, societies today represent a melting pot of cultures that influence the learning provided through the tangible and or intangible outcomes of the curriculum. Within such a context, countries that are perceived as more powerful seem to influence shifts in mental cultures and traditions, which then determine what becomes known as new knowledge. Since curriculum represents the learning that is made available to students, this has implications for how curriculum is theorized and practised. We acknowledge the concern raised by Gershon (2015) that "it isn't so much that there aren't a multitude of educational possibilities about what curriculum might mean or how it can function but rather that educational ideals, ideas, and processes are constantly framed and re-framed along particular narrow visions with equally narrow sets of answers. ...Schooling is always academic and social and all academic content, regardless of topic or delivery is at once necessarily and inextricably about ideas, processes, and ecologies in relation to choice of this over that" (pp. 2–3). The question is therefore not just about what is debated in curriculum but about how we frame the issue(s) under debate.

In a context that includes the challenges of globalization, the phenomenon of contemporary individualism, the dominant economic market-oriented ideology and the influence of social media, the way we view and live learning is extremely important. In *Learning: The Treasure Within*, Delors and associates had argued, back in 1996, that if education is going to succeed "in enabling learners to become not only successful learning achievers at school but also responsible citizens, effective workers, caring community members, and life-long learners, in an increasingly interdependent world" (Nan-Zhao n.d.), then we need to restructure the curriculum to focus on what has been described as the four pillars of learning, namely, learning to know, learning to do, learning to live together and learning to be.

These issues have given rise to the increasing need to undertake analysis of the philosophical, ideological and practical applications of curriculum using an intercultural and cross-cultural lens. For us this book, *Intercultural Studies of Curriculum: Theory, Policy and Practice*, recognizes the central role that the curriculum plays in affecting educational quality and learning. It seeks to provide an opportunity for equitable exchanges and comparisons between and among different cultures.

In this book authors from across five continents provide an intercultural analysis of curriculum theory, policy and practice in 17 different countries. This was achieved through the use of the same data collection methodology across different countries and different continents to explore the same issue. This therefore has produced "cultures of curriculum theory, policy and practice" within a country, between and among countries, and between and among traditions and other specificities within and between countries. This we believe is an innovative feature of the book as those inside and outside of schools continue to grapple with curriculum and its making. This book follows in the series on *Intercultural Studies in Education* initiated in this innovative way by Paul Miller as he encourages researchers to seek understanding of educational practices in and across cultures with particular focus on ensuring equitable recognition of knowledge from different cultures and perspectives. Furthermore,

Intercultural Studies of Curriculum: Theory, Policy and Practice represents a critical approach to the understanding of curriculum by discerning the underlying values and assumptions of curriculum issues as explored by the different authors. Such an approach is significant as Kelly (2004) noted that the "lack of ability to analyse critically and identify the value positions implicit in the forms of curriculum we are exposed to is in the long term inimical to educational development" (p. 21). Moreover, applying an intercultural lens to curriculum provides an understanding of the multiple lens through which curriculum can be viewed, thereby challenging our individual ideologies.

Divided into two sections, the chapters provide empirical research about curriculum across three countries covering a range of issues. Each section begins with an introduction, where we provide an overview of each chapter. Section one, titled *Curriculum as Praxis*, offers a context for reflecting on the inter-sectionality between the planned curriculum, the implemented curriculum and the curriculum outcomes. In this sense, according to Grundy (1987), the curriculum is not merely a plan to be implemented but curriculum as praxis is an active reciprocal process that integrates planning, acting and evaluating which results in informed committed actions. Each chapter in section one therefore presents an examination of curriculum praxis across three different country contexts with the aim of providing understanding of the committed actions that result when the planned curriculum reflective of varying philosophies is acted upon.

Section two, titled *Critical Issues Beyond Pedagogy*, then shifts the intercultural discourse to an analysis of the ideological dimensions of the curriculum. This involves going beyond what is structured in a curriculum to influence knowing and experience. In this context, pedagogy is seen as what is used to influence our knowing about ourselves, others and the world. Each chapter in this section looks at particular philosophies and policies that underpin curriculum theory and policy across three different country contexts. Together they provide critical reflection on how issues and culture of a people are represented in the curriculum when one looks beyond the information that is presented.

Our hope is that this book will stimulate critical dialogue, awaken consciousness and produce innovation in curriculum theorizing, policy and practice within and across different contexts and cultures. We hope that the chapters will help to challenge existing misconceptions that we may hold—whatever form or shape they take—and lead to a recognition that many of these misconceptions stem from environmental factors, such as widespread denial of educational and economic opportunities for minority groups, the social prejudice that still exists and the flawed assumptions (Wolk 2011) that determine our discourse.

In a context where the curriculum reflects the values of society, or part of society, we need to ensure that educators are placed in situations where curricula are debated, challenged and developed through a process of working together (Mitchell and Sackney 2009; Torrance and Humes 2015). It is within such a context that the words of John Goodlad take on added significance.

> The struggle for justice, equity, respect, and appreciation for human diversity has been long and often troubled. It continues to be so. The human race's proclivity for arranging its members in hierarchies of strongly maintained status and privilege is likely to continue as a malaise that can become cancerous.
>
> The answer, we know, is education. But education, despite our honoring the concept, is not in itself good. We must intentionally and even passionately inject morality into education. (Goodlad 2003/2004, p. 21)

If we want to address the injustices that exist in the world that permeate our societies, we must teach students the ideals of democracy and social equality and give our young people opportunities to practise those ideals in their daily lives, both in and out of school, in whichever context we are engaged. To this end multiple perspectives are important in producing curriculum theory, policy and practice that is socially just and provides opportunities for diversity in thinking. This is the principle which this publication upholds.

These chapters are aimed at throwing light on how authors from around the globe are framing and handling issues, issues of social (in)justice through different lenses and perspectives. The intent is to further open and deepen the conversations so as to "better reflect the multiplicities of curricular voices and visions" (Gershon 2015, p. 4).

In the various chapters we see a plea, a call for educators to act from a particular value position, for example, the need to see leadership as a shared activity. The belief that teachers matter is not new to us. The concept and practice of teacher leadership has gained momentum over the past three decades. Empirical literature reveals numerous studies that describe dimensions of teacher leadership practice, teacher leadership characteristics and conditions that promote and challenge teacher leadership. Whilst acknowledging that the construct of teacher leadership is not well defined, conceptually or operationally (see York-Barr and Duke 2004), we do acknowledge that there are conditions that lead towards teachers' powerful learning, which include acknowledging teachers' voice (Frost 2008) where there is collective participation and staff communication (Borko 2004), where teachers play a significant role in the creation of professional knowledge and its transfer within networks and study groups (Spillane 2006; Darling-Hammond and Richardson 2009), where teachers take initiative to question what is, to help us appreciate that we need to go beyond Hoyle's proposition about the "extended professional" (Hoyle 1972) to a commitment that respects Stenhouse's argument for systematic questioning of one's own teaching, to question and to test the theory in practice (Stenhouse 1975, p. 144), to actively engage in the school and beyond so that issues of social justice can be truly addressed. It is here that Fullan's plea for moral agentry, and to pun the phrase "What's worth fighting for …", stands out. This is what educators constantly struggle with and for.

These chapters merely help us to scratch the surface, representing a fraction of what is happening around the globe. We have no doubt that we can find similar work, similar attempts and struggles within other networks seeking to challenge and provoke what is.

References

Borko, H. (2004). Professional development and teacher learning: Mapping the terrain. *Educational Researcher, 33*(8), 3–15.

Cornbleth, C. (1996). Curriculum in and out of context. In E. Hollins (Ed.), *Transforming curriculum for a culturally diverse society* (pp. 149–162). Mahwah: Lawrence Erlbaum Associates Inc.

Darling-Hammond, L., & Richardson, N. (2009). Research review. Teacher learning: What matters? *How Teachers Learn, 66*(5), 46–53.

Frost, D. (2008). 'Teacher leadership': Values and voice. *School Leadership and Management, 28*(4), 337–352.

Gershon, W. S. (2015). Editor's introduction. *International Journal of Curriculum and Social Justice, 1*(1), 1–6.

Goodlad, J. I. (2003/2004). Teaching what we hold sacred. *Educational Leadership, 61*(4), 18–21.

Grundy, S. (1987). *Curriculum: Product or praxis?* Lewes: Falmer Press.

Hoyle, E. (1972). Educational innovation and the role of the teacher. *Forum, 14*, 42–44.

Kelly, A. V. (2004). *The curriculum theory and practice* (5th ed.). London: Sage.

Mitchell, C., & Sackney, L. (2009). *Sustainable improvement: Building learning communities that endure*. Rotterdam: Sense Publishers.

Nan-Zhao, Z. (n.d.). *Four 'pillars of learning' for the reorientation and reorganization of curriculum: Reflections and discussions*. Retrieved from www.ibe.unesco.org/cops/Competencies/PillarsLearningZhou.pdf. Accessed 12 Jan 2017.

Nelson, G. D. (2001). Choosing content that's worth knowing. *Educational Leadership, 59*(2), 12–16.

Spillane, J. (2006). *Distributed leadership*. San Francisco: Jossey-Bass.

Stenhouse, L. (1975). *An introduction to curriculum research and development*. London: Heinemann Educational Books.

Torrance, D., & Humes, W. (2015). The shifting discourses of educational leadership: International trends and Scotland's response. *Educational Management Administration & Leadership, 43*(5), 792–810.

UNESCO. (2015). *Repositioning curriculum in education quality & development-relevance*. International Bureau of Education. Retrieved from http://www.ibe.unesco.org

Wolk, R. A. (2011). *Wasting minds: Why our education system is failing and what we can do about it*. Alexandria: Association for Supervision and Curriculum Development.

York-Barr, J., & Duke, K. (2004). What do we know about teacher leadership? Findings from two decades of scholarship. *Review of Educational Research, 74*(3), 255–316.

Carmel Roofe is Lecturer in Curriculum and Instruction at the University of the West Indies, Mona, Jamaica. She is a member of the Institute for Educational Administration and Leadership-Jamaica and a University Fellow at the Charles Darwin University, Australia. Her career in teaching spans both the secondary and higher education levels of the education system.

Christopher Bezzina is Professor of educational leadership at the Faculty of Education, University of Malta, and the Department of Education, Uppsala University, Sweden. He is both a Commonwealth and Fulbright Scholar and is currently vice-president of the Commonwealth Council for Educational Administration and Management.

PART 1

Curriculum as Praxis

1.1 INTRODUCTION

As borders continue to narrow and societies grapple with catering to diverse needs that arise as a result, the role of teachers has become more critical. Teachers are needed to aid in nurturing the habits and consciousness necessary to create a society where everyone feels valued and respected regardless of cultural context. For this to happen, however, teachers need to be properly prepared. This section therefore opens with a chapter focusing on the preparation of this critical stakeholder group. Roofe, Bezzina and Holness using a social justice lens spotlight teacher preparation as an important area of focus in the curriculum dialogue and the transformation of society. The authors note that teacher preparation should ensure that teachers are prepared in such a way that their practices demonstrate an understanding that each student in the classroom has an indefensible claim to all the benefits, opportunities and resources regardless of gender, socio-economic status, ethnicity or ability. In this sense the teacher preparation curriculum should provide teacher trainees with opportunities to construct their beliefs and identities regarding issues of fairness, equity and power dynamics.

Through case studies of teacher educators in Jamaica, Malta and England, the authors explore the perspectives of teacher educators on a social justice orientation towards how curriculum is developed and enacted in teacher preparation programmes. The perspectives of the respondents are used to provide an analysis of the social justice function of the curriculum in each context.

The respondents though operating in three different country contexts all had a shared understanding of social justice and expressed that for one reason or other students come to educational encounters with different needs and/or disadvantage and resources need to be redistributed. An effective teacher preparation curriculum that nurtures social justice principles and practices is seen as one that develops the learner's relational qualities and skills through both personal and social engagement as prospective teachers engage as learners in relation to other learners. However how this was enacted differed across country contexts. For Jamaica, the theme of social justice was not an explicit concept in teacher preparation curriculum;hence teacher educators in the study expressed the need for this to happen. In Malta and England, explicit notions of social justice underpinned teacher preparation curriculum. However, the teacher educators indicated that the evidence suggested that attempts have not been as successful as expected. Since teaching is not value neutral,we believe the teacher preparation curriculum should be designed to include social justice practices and orientations and be enacted by teacher educators who understand their own interpretations of social justice as well as their students' past and current histories and learning experiences (Lee 2011). This involves teacher educators utilizing pedagogies that are social justice oriented and creating a learning environment that reduces prejudices, incorporates multiple ways of constructing knowledge and takes into considerations individual rights, values and culture to facilitate equity for all (Banks 2008).

Following the chapter by Roofe et al., Cruz, Madden and Asante draw our attention to the complex nature of the curriculum discourse in light of globalization. The authors note that societies no longer have a shared onto-epistemology; instead, there is an increasing diversity of onto-epistemologies in a single context. Cruz, Madden and Asante believe there is a push to globalize what is local to the Global North, as if it were neutral, universal and the best standard that humanity can offer. Citing Marginson and Sawir (2011), Cruz, Madden and Asante stated this creates a case of "othering" that occurs in the assumption that there is a standard or universal way of knowing and being, implying that some knowledges and cultures are better than others.

The study sought to provide a comparative analysis of science education between the Philippines, Ghana and the United States to illuminate a potential model for engaging in anti-hegemonic, cross-cultural curriculum development. To enable this process, Postner's (2004) framework and

Ricouer's (2007) lens of translation were utilized to examine the national science curriculum of each country. The results of the analyses indicated that (1) notions of science education as well as its purposes are subjective; (2) the content of science education between countries is very similar; and (3) the intended delivery and implementation of educational experiences as well as its evaluation are tied to language and culture.

The authors concluded that if we truly want to participate in cross-cultural and more specifically intercultural curriculum development that recognizes and appreciates differences, then stakeholders must first have a curriculum analysis, similar to the one herein, of their local context in order to understand their own philosophical assumptions regarding the subject matter in relation to other contexts.

Continuing the science discourseis the chapter by Sheety, Kapanadze and Joubran where emphasis is placed on the role of the teacher in implementing curriculum initiatives. Using multiple case studies, the study sought to explore high school science teachers' perceptions regarding current practices of inquiry-based science curriculum (IBSC) and teachers' challenges and needs in implementing such a curriculum in three different countries: Georgia (situated on the dividing line between Europe and Asia), Israel (Asia) and the United States (North America). Additionally, the research sought to identify instructional barriers to implementation that might be hampering more widespread adoption of these educational methods. Inquiry-based learning (IBL is)seen as a necessary strategy for providing student-centred learning. The authors note that teachers are the facilitators and mediators between the written curriculum and their students; thus, their beliefs, interpretations and perceptions are of utmost importance in understanding how inquiry-based curricula are implemented in each of the countries.

Findings from the study indicated that similarities and differences among the three countries were found in the four aspects that were studied: perception, implementation, challenges and support. However, there were also differences, even within the same country. For example, in Pennsylvania, USA, differences were noted among teachers who were required to prepare students for a state exam (in Biology) and those teachers who were not (Physics and Chemistry). Differences were also apparent among teachers who worked in private school and public and charter schools, especially with regard to budget and support issues. In Georgia, some of the interviewed teachers have not engaged in inquiry-based teaching because they do not know how to implement it. Not all participant teachers use curricula during their lesson planning. Some use a teacher's guide and consider it more helpful than the curriculum. In Israel, some teachers engage in inquiry-based teaching, despite the difficulties; others have never engaged in inquiry-based teaching because it is not required and they do not perceive that they are well-prepared enough to implement it. Sheety et al. concluded that there is a gap between teachers'desire and capacity to effectively implement IBSC, and professional development of IBL assessment tools was needed to aid teachers in addressing many of the challenges and barriers to the effective implementation of IBSC.

The chapter by Acker and Nyland on music as a platform for intercultural understanding helps us to reflect on the importance of the creative and performing arts in a neoliberal context that we are living in, one that conditions the way we, as educators, engage with education and schooling. In the performativity culture that seems to be engulfing societies, the authors highlight the intercultural potential of music within and across cultures. Acker and Nyland focus on the early childhood years and argue that with increased globalization, with people moving across boundaries, music can serve as a medium to promote social and cultural cohesion. Framed in this manner, the arts become a rights issue. The plea at the end for music teachers to go public reminds us of the work of David Halpin (2003) on hope and that in a context which is becoming more demanding and stressful, especially in contexts of social and economic disadvantage, teachers need to remain hopeful and challenge a reality which can easily lead to cynicism, fatalism, relativism and fundamentalism. This resonates with the writings of Henry Giroux (1988) who argued that teachers need to act as transformative intellectuals in "the struggle to overcome economic, political and social injustices, and to further humanize themselves as part of the struggle" (Giroux 1988, p. 17).

This thread of optimism, of passion and service is also evidenced in the chapter by Blair that explores transformative leadership in the Caribbean islands of the Dominican Republic and Jamaica and the United States. The author acknowledges that in spite of the fact that demands and policies seem to expect that teachers are better qualified and educated to teach, their status and autonomy is low when compared to other professions and that participation in decision-making is limited. Blair argues that transformative teacher leadership"is the mechanism for conceptualizing, implementing and sustaining meaningful change while simultaneously changing the very nature of teachers' work." The author notes that the potential behind transformative teacher leadership lies within a larger framework that encompasses also curriculum theory and practice. Thus, transformative leaders and leadership act within a context which sees teachers engage with the curriculum in a dynamic manner leading to school reform and improvement.

Similar in vein to other chapters in this section, Blair calls for an "interventionist activism" approach by teachers, one imbued with hope and a commitment to advocacy. In a context where outcomes have been disappointing, the challenge is even greater. One of the arguments posited in this chapter is that curriculum and leadership need to come together, highlighting their interdependence, and this can be achieved through a recognition of the central role that teachers can play. The plea is to close the "transformation gap" through the way we view the role of the teacher using the curriculum as a foundation for generating change and doing so through the direct involvement of teachers in collaborative decision-making endeavours.

REFERENCES

Banks, J. A. (2008). *An introduction to multicultural education.* Boston: Pearson.

Giroux, H. (1988). *Teachers as intellectuals:Toward a critical pedagogy of learning.* Westport: Begin & Garvey.

Halpin, D. (2003). *Hope and education –The role of the utopian imagination.* London: RoutledgeFalmer.

Lee, Y. A. (2011). What does teaching for social justice mean to teacher candidates. *Professional Educator, 35*(2), 1–20.

Marginson, S., & Sawir, E. (2011). *Ideas for intercultural education.* New York: Palgrave Macmillan.

Posner, G. J. (2004). *Analyzing the curriculum* (3rd ed.). New York: McGraw Hill.

Ricoeur, P. (2007). *On translation.* London/New York: Routledge.

Social Justice and the Teacher Preparation Curriculum: A Cross-Cultural Analysis

Carmel Roofe, Christopher Bezzina, and Marilyn Holness

INTRODUCTION

In the context of unprecedented change, classrooms have become more diverse and as such educators grapple with understanding how to adapt to a changing and fluid landscape. As classrooms become more diverse, social justice themes ranging from quality of teacher, ethnicity of students, equality of gender, access to resources and distribution of resources continue to occupy discourses surrounding teaching and teacher preparation (Kaur 2012). In order to remain relevant, teacher education institutions need to be responsive by taking action in light of these discourses. The more teacher preparation engages with the realities facing educators on a day-to-day basis, the more adequately teacher educators can review and develop meaningful courses.

C. Roofe (✉)
School of Education, University of the West Indies, Kingston, Jamaica

C. Bezzina
Leadership for Learning and Innovation, Faculty of Education,
University of Malta, Msida, Malta

Department of Education, Uppsala University, Uppsala, Sweden

M. Holness
University of Roehampton, London, UK

© The Author(s) 2018
C. Roofe, C. Bezzina (eds.), *Intercultural Studies of Curriculum*, Intercultural Studies in Education,
https://doi.org/10.1007/978-3-319-60897-6_2

15

The concept of social justice is a complex one, and as a result depending on the context, its practical applications may become elusive in education if not properly understood. According to Rawls (1971), social justice is about assuring and providing equal access to opportunities and human rights and ensuring that there is a fair share of all benefits for the least advantaged group. Shields and Mohan (2008, p. 291) also provide a helpful frame with which to examine the issue of social justice:

> *Our concept of social justice is one that identifies issues of power and inequity in schools and society and that challenges personal and systemic abuses of power as well as alienating and marginalizing beliefs, values, and practices.*

Applying these definitions to the preparation of teachers suggests that teacher preparation should ensure that teachers are prepared in such a way that their practices demonstrate an understanding that each student in the classroom has an indefensible claim to all the benefits, opportunities and resources regardless of gender, socio-economic status, ethnicity or ability. To disadvantage one group of students or an individual over another raises issues of inequity and gives rise to social injustice. Discussions then about social justice in teacher preparation curriculum must be seen in light of opportunities provided to teacher trainees through the curriculum to construct their beliefs and identities regarding issues of fairness, equity and power dynamics. This is necessary as teachers play an important role in influencing student quality (Crowther 2011; Schmoker 2011).

An effective teacher preparation programme should seek to improve the quality of teachers and teaching, thereby improving the standards of schooling and students' achievement (Darling-Hammond et al. 2007). The long-term result of this is that teachers will influence the types of citizens that are produced. The education and training of teachers is a critical component in the intellectual and social transformation of society (Giroux and MacLaren 1986; Rasmussen and Bayer 2014; Evans 2001). To influence teachers' intellectual, social and emotional development in transforming society, teacher preparation should seek to expose teachers to foundational education knowledge, content and pedagogical knowledge and supervised field practice (Kosnik and Beck 2009). In this chapter, we explore the perspectives of teacher educators on a social justice orientation towards how curriculum is developed and enacted in teacher preparation programmes. Case studies of teacher educators in Jamaica, Malta and

England are used to provide cross-cultural analysis of the social justice function of the curriculum in each context.

The Social Justice Function of the Teacher Preparation Curriculum

In any formal education system, the curriculum serves as the means by which the desired knowledge, skills, values and attitudes are planned and delivered to learners. According to Doll (1996), the curriculum of a school is the formal and informal content and process by which learners gain knowledge and understanding, develop skills and alter attitudes, appreciations and values under the guidance of that school. Captured in this perspective is the view that curriculum encapsulates the content that is taught, how it is taught and who teaches it. Therefore, it is through the curriculum that teachers in training will understand the beliefs, values and practices of fairness, power, inequity and marginalisation. Furthermore, the teacher preparation curriculum serves as the means by which pre-service and in-service teachers are prepared to understand the challenges and opportunities that exist within diverse classrooms.

In order to serve its social justice function, it is necessary to embed issues of social justice in the knowledge, skills and attitudes of teacher preparation curriculum design as well as within the actions of teacher educators (Grant and Agosto 2008). This is important in helping to raise the consciousness of student teachers towards theories and actions geared towards addressing issues of inequity as it relates to gender, class, race and the distribution of resources. According to Giroux (1992), social justice should be integrated in teacher preparation curriculum through a pedagogy that allows student teachers to engage in a process of reflection. Student teachers should reflect upon their own actions, those presented by others and reflect on their own practice in relation to the social context. For Cochran-Smith (2004), social justice in teacher preparation curriculum needs to be an outcome of learning to teach. This implies that both reflection and more importantly what Schön describes as "reflection on action" are central to the life of a teacher as s/he engages with others in a context. This context can hinder or nurture a positive culture that allows teachers to reflect and engage in dynamic relationships with others so that issues relevant to social justice can be addressed and lived.

Picower (2012) however argues that most of what student teachers are exposed to in their training about social justice is theoretical and makes the idea of incorporating social justice in their practice overwhelming. This seems to suggest an overhauling of the historical ideologies that underpin traditional teacher preparation curriculum and placing knowledge about culture, context and differences that exists in schools and the wider society at their forefront. Training teachers to teach for social justice needs to combine theory with practice. In other words, social justice needs to be seen as a process and a product (Bell 1997). Extending the narrative of a practical approach to the social justice function of the teacher preparation curriculum, Walker (2003) believes that what is needed is a set of principles or criteria that student teachers and teacher educators can use to determine what actions are socially just or not.

Teacher Educator Teaching for Social Justice

Teaching for social justice is a complex endeavour and one that involves teacher educators having an understanding of their own interpretations of social justice as well as their students' past and current histories and learning experiences (Lee 2011). This involves teacher educators utilising pedagogies that are social justice oriented. These practices should include a learning environment that reduces prejudices and incorporates multiple ways of constructing knowledge and one where teaching takes into consideration individual rights, values and culture to facilitate equity for all (Banks 2008). Teaching is not an activity that is value neutral. Teacher educators bring their own values, perspectives and individual dispositions to their classrooms. The norms and values of the teacher educators may be different from those of the student teachers perhaps as a result of demographics such as the age gap and social background. These differences may create tensions or conflicts. However, a teacher educator teaching for social justice should not see this as a problem but should view these tensions as resources for learning. It is only through engagement, in dialogue that growth can take place.

The role of teacher educator teaching for social justice is an imperative that is based on reducing the disparities that are embedded in the structures of schooling and the curriculum. This imperative is one that challenges teacher educators to ensure the curriculum for their courses is culturally responsive. This requires teacher educators to have intimate knowledge of the contexts within which their student teachers will practise and provide opportunities in these courses for student teachers to have field experiences in varied school contexts.

Teacher Preparation in Jamaica, Malta and England

Across the three countries, key differences exist in how initial teacher preparation is undertaken. While Jamaica and England share similarities in having different types of institutions in which teacher preparation is offered, Malta has only one institution that prepares teachers.

In Jamaica, initial teacher preparation is offered through teacher training colleges and departments within universities. Students enter these institutions to pursue three- or four-year programmes that expose them to foundational education knowledge, content and pedagogical knowledge and supervised field practice (Joint Board of Teacher Education 2012). Upon completion students are awarded a bachelor's degree. Other routes to teacher training in Jamaica include pursuing a postgraduate diploma in education which exposes students with first degrees to pedagogy skills and supervised field practice. Though programme content may vary across institutions, teacher preparation curriculum follows the traditional model where student teachers are exposed to college-/university-based courses prior to concentrated periods of field practice.

Resulting from reports of the National Education Inspectorate regarding the quality of teaching and teachers, teacher education programmes have been facing increased pressure to produce teachers with high quality. Added to this is the fact that students continue to underperform on national and regional examinations. Therefore, there is increased demand for teacher education programmes in Jamaica to produce teachers who can contribute effectively in increasing students' outcome. This requires preparing teachers who are able to evaluate the applicability of instructional strategies learnt in their college or university classrooms in order to respond effectively to the varying school contexts that exist in Jamaica. Given the varying school contexts in Jamaica where schools differ based on students' ability levels, geographical location and socio-economic status of those who attend, teacher education programmes need to prepare teachers to address issues of equity and access which are social justice functions.

In Malta, there is a shift in how teacher preparation is carried out where student teachers learn by working alongside and with skilled practitioners. Student teachers are placed in schools from the beginning of the academic year, and their observation sessions are based on tasks completed through the support and guidance of school-based teacher mentors. Given concerns raised by educational policymakers, leaders and educators in general that student teachers are currently ill equipped to deal with the challenges facing the education of the young in a globalised world, the Faculty of Education at the University of Malta felt that it was essential to review the existing programme and come out with a proposal that would help address current concerns. This has led to the decision to move towards a professional master's degree that would lead to a teaching qualification, hence moving away from an undergraduate programme to a postgraduate programme. This decision led to the commencement of the first Masters in Teaching and Learning (MTL) in the academic year 2016–2017. The aim is to develop prospective teachers engaged with issues that are central to a changing society that presents school leaders and experienced teachers alike with exhausting and psychologically draining experiences (Bezzina 2017).

For prospective teachers to handle issues related to equity and social justice, a direct engagement with school life is needed. Through the new MTL programme, it is expected that teachers will be able to function effectively, efficiently, creatively and innovatively in the schools of today by being reflective, enquiring and adaptive practitioners striving to become quality teachers (Tomorrow's Faculty Today 2015).

In England, following the publication of the Government's White Paper, (2010), which recognises the importance of teaching in improving standards in schools and educational outcomes for young people, policy objectives have focused on putting the talented and best teachers in front of children. The outcome is a proliferation of routes into teaching and a shift towards school-led provision away from university-led programmes. This has resulted in a two-tier system, exemplified by the postgraduate School Centred Initial Teacher Training (SCITT) programme where training is predominately carried out in the classroom by experienced practising teachers, who follow school-led programme tailored towards the needs of the local area, in contrast to university-led undergraduate and postgraduate routes run in partnership with schools where trainees develop practical teaching skills alongside university studies in subject knowledge and pedagogical and professional principles.

Regardless of the route taken, the government is responsible for the teacher education curriculum. This means that the teacher preparation curriculum is fundamentally the same across sectors as all providers have to cover the national curriculum; meet the teachers' standard, the Department for Education Initial Teacher Training Criteria; as well as satisfy OFSTED's initial teacher education (ITE) expectations as set out in the ITE Inspection Handbook. This has resulted in a crowed curriculum and compliance culture where teacher education is better defined as training, where box ticking drives curriculum content and where social justice is relegated to ideology and afterthoughts.

METHODS

Through an exploratory qualitative design, case studies conducted in Jamaica, Malta and England provide a cross national context for exploring the issue of social justice within the context of teacher preparation. The study uses interviews as the main means of data collection. The research conducted in each country adopted purposive sampling where many of the teacher educators were known to the researchers and were selected based on their ability to critically reflect and articulate their experiences having been involved in teacher preparation for the primary and secondary levels of the education system within their country. Except for Malta that has one institution, the teacher educators in Jamaica and England who participated in the study were selected from a variety of teacher training institutions. The researchers were also keen to select participants who had a general understanding of social justice and could respond to the questions asked. Three teacher educators from each country participated in the study, and data was collected through a semi-structured interview entailing the same set of initial questions across each country.

The study was guided by two main research questions derived based on the researchers' interests and the purpose of the study. These were: (1) How can teacher preparation curriculum serve a social justice function? (2) How do teacher educators teach for social justice in teacher preparation programmes?

Altogether nine teacher educators participated in the study. In Jamaica, the three teacher educators were females with varying years of experience and working in different contexts. Donna (JA1) is a teacher educator in a university context and works in a department of education; she is in her mid-50s and has been a teacher educator for 20 years. Wanda (JA2) is a teacher educator in a college that prepares only teachers. She is in her mid-40s and has been a teacher educator for 13 years, while Karie (JA3) is a teacher educator in a university setting and works in a Faculty of Education.

She is in her mid-40s and has been a teacher educator for eight years. All three teacher educators have responsibility for designing courses, teaching and supervising student teachers.

In Malta three respondents have the following pseudonyms: M1, male teacher educator with one-year experience within the Faculty of Education; F2, a female teacher educator with two years' experience; and M3, a male teacher educator with seven years' experience. Two of these teacher educators are in their 30s and one in his early 40s. They have varied and diverse experiences which they have accumulated over the years, both from the way they have furthered their studies with a focus on different learning styles, on inclusion and diversity as part of their portfolio. All three of them have worked directly in schools and/or the community. They conduct research, teach and lead undergraduate and postgraduate courses in the area.

The teacher educators in England were all females, aged 45–60, and were experienced teacher educators with varied experiences of preparing teachers. All worked in a university context. Participant 1, E1, has 10 years of experience as a teacher educator and researcher teaching and leading undergraduate and postgraduate routes into teaching; Participant 2, E2, has over 20 years of teaching and leading teacher education in more than one university; and Participant 3, E3, has almost 20 years of teacher education experience, in both school-led and university-led settings. All three participants have designed courses and supervise student teachers in initial teacher preparation programmes.

The data collected from the teacher educators were transcribed, sorted and coded using attribute and structural coding (Saldana 2013). This was carried out by each country researcher. A summary table entailing codes and narratives from all nine participants was generated. From this, themes were then derived and validated by each country researcher. The data is presented using narrative descriptions from the participants.

FINDINGS

Four main themes are used to share the perspectives of teacher educators on social justice in the teacher preparation curriculum. These are: teacher educators' expressed understanding of social justice, the role of the curriculum in promoting social justice, social justice actions as praxis and teaching for social justice.

Teacher Educators' Expressed Understanding of Social Justice

The teacher educators involved in this study relate to social justice (SJ) as a principle that needs to permeate our thoughts and actions. Though operating in three separate countries, the teacher educators had a shared understanding of social justice. They describe SJ as a belief that "not all children start from a level playing field," that for one reason or other students come to educational encounters with different needs and/or disadvantage and resources need to be redistributed.

> In basic, layman terms, I understand it to be a movement effort for a level of equity to be reached. So, in education, educators engaged in social justice need to be aware that not all pupils start from a level playing field and that they need to take measures, in their teaching, to support those pupils coming from disadvantaged backgrounds or who in some way do not have sufficient access to education and resources. [F2, Malta]

> To me social justice has to do with ensuring that persons are treated equitably and resources are allocated fairly between them. It means that persons have equal access to opportunities and their rights are accommodated. It has to do with human rights and equality as we consider how human rights are manifested in everyday activities. [Wanda, JA2]

> I think social justice, for me, is about ensuring that everyone, particularly minority groups, minority on whatever basis, whether that is ethnicity, race, minority in terms of gender, or minority in terms of cultural religious background, sexual orientations, all the protected characteristics, that they are not disadvantaged, that they have an equal chance to prosper, to do well, to live positive lives and to achieve their full potential. It is also for me about those who are in power, or have power, whether financial power or in terms of authority and control, recognising their responsibility to put in place the systems, the practices, the policies that will allow everyone to have the opportunity to flourish and to live successful lives and to make a positive contribution. [E1, England]

The Role of the Curriculum in Promoting Social Justice

An effective teacher preparation curriculum that nurtures SJ principles and practices is seen as one that develops the learner's relational qualities and skills through both personal and social engagement as prospective teachers engage as learners in relation to other learners. The teacher educators expressed a clear belief and understanding of the importance of the teacher preparation curriculum in helping student teachers to understand their role in teaching for social justice. However how the teacher preparation curriculum has catered for this varies across the three country contexts.

In Malta, while teacher preparation curricula have emphasised the importance of teaching for social justice with a strong emphasis on curricula and pedagogies that prepare and help future teachers work with diverse learners, concern is raised as to how successful these attempts have been. One teacher educator argued that:

In recent years, many teacher preparation programmes have emphasized the importance of teaching for social justice. Initial teacher preparation programmes like ours have emphasized pedagogies and curricula that prepare that help prospective teachers work with diverse learners. Here one has to ask whether we were successful in influencing teacher candidates' perceptions and teaching practices. Looking at our schools and the practices we often witness I would say that we have for the most part of it failed......Therefore, if we are seeking to nurture such attitudes, knowledge and skills in our prospective teachers we need to do much more than simply continue to do what we have done up to now. If we look at our undergraduate curriculum we do find quite a good proportion of the curriculum that is dedicated to knowledge about socio-cultural issues. The students were exposed to quite a dose of literature that deals with social justice issues and ideas. [M7 Malta]

In Jamaica, the three teacher educators noted that student teachers are exposed to the different strategies that are used to cater to different learning styles and working with students of mixed abilities, but the term social justice is not explicitly outlined in the teacher preparation curriculum.

From my observation, I do not think that social justice as a concept is deliberately included in the teacher preparation curriculum. While there is some attempt to introduce student teachers to learning challenges and needs that they might find in the classroom, not enough is done to prepare them to cater to the various types of students which they will encounter in the teaching-learning context, so many students are left behind. Students who operate above or below average in various respects are not accommodated in the classroom context, hence they do not have equal access and opportunities in the education setting. [Karie, JA3]

The situation in England differs, where the three teacher educators agreed that SJ is important in providing the underpinning principles that trainees need to draw on when they are in school to inform their practice, but the requirements for training teachers change over time diminishing the presence of SJ in the curriculum. The need to teach the standards, the requirement of the Office for Standards in Education (OFSTED) and other external pressures, has resulted in drastic reductions in the time allocated to consider SJ issues resulting in it being pushed out, no longer explicitly foreground. They agreed that the least contentious ones like special educational needs and disabilities have tended to remain with a specific focus, while others, considered less important, such as race and ethnicity, is left to permeate the curriculum discussed "as and when" it arises, at the discretion of and depending on the confidence of the staff member. This is illustrated by one teacher educator's account:

> *...teacher preparation curriculum, it is really crucial that it (SJ) is there. I think that a lot of students would not recognise that there is a social justice agenda running through everything, but it would run through everything in terms of curriculum areas: Professional Studies, SEND (Special Educational Needs and Disabilities), EAL (English as Additional Language), PSHE (Personal, Social, Health Education), but also through things like the RE curriculum and into things like the English curriculum and making sure that the literature you use and the kinds of tasks you ask students to do and to work with children to develop their literacy are broad based and not excluding any element of society. So, for instance, in an English curriculum you would make sure that your literature came from different cultures and from different religions, that it included disability, etc. [E2 England]*

Where there was discrepancy between the teacher educators from England was in the extent to which this permeation approach was seen to be sufficient, working and appropriate to effectively address the SJ agenda.

Social Justice Actions as Praxis

For a teacher preparation curriculum to be effective from a SJ perspective, it needs to immerse student teachers in SJ learning experiences. All teacher educators across the different country contexts identified praxis as the main means by which the teacher preparation curriculum can serve a social justice function.

In Jamaica, the teacher educators felt that there needed to be an inclusion of social justice, commitment to preparing teachers in this way and teacher educators who model how to teach for social justice.

There needs to be a commitment to social action; by improving the quality of instructions to all learners, encouraging pre-service teachers to be critical enquirers and socially active practitioners. [Wanda, JA 2]

It now needs to be more explicit because persons can say they were not trained for this and might not be accommodating enough so we have to find ways to facilitate it so it should be a part of the curriculum. [Donna, JA1]

I therefore believe that if the student-centred approach to teaching and learning is adopted in its truest form then a social justice function can be served. This would however mean revising the curriculum to include this approach in a more deliberate way with objectives that speak to social justice in relation to the student centred approach. The approach would also need to be modelled by teacher educators for the student teachers to observe it in action. [Karie, JA 3]

Similarly, in Malta teacher educators expressed that an important starting point is a self-awareness of student teachers' own cultural background.

The first step is to help teachers to perceive of themselves, first and foremost, as learners, and to see that education emerges through a constant dialectic operation between teaching and learning. [M1, Malta]

Student teachers need to be exposed to a number of situations which challenge their beliefs and where they can discuss how social justice can be attained. Social justice needs to be visible in the school's ethos and in every school activity, and the best way to prepare teachers is by allowing them to be engaged in these activities and eventually, to become responsible for some of them. [F2, Malta]

Another argued that:

"the most important attitude that any initial teacher education programme should nurture is an attitude of respect towards the Other – being able to value and respect other worldviews. It is also imperative for prospective teachers to develop a sense of openness to intercultural learning and to people who are diverse from the self. The attitude of openness requires a curios mind that tolerates ambiguity and uncertainty". [M3, Malta]

Similar views expressed by the teacher educators in Jamaica and Malta were found amongst the teacher educators in England.

.... if the curriculum serves a social justice function, it will not only have content that might help new teachers to understand the school system and to understand children who might have a very different background to them and look at the philosophical or even psychological underpinnings, the difference between people and how they learn, but it means engaging with our local communities and so what does it mean in the local community where you are going to become a teacher. ....we should have accountability to our local communities and what we are doing should make sense to them. One of the great wins you can get as a teacher educator is if you have someone who comes on the course, having had one kind of education and knowing one distinct group of particularly academic or financially successful people, who genuinely becomes more interested in the challenges of making sure that people without those advantages can move on and end up having really good lives. [E3, England]

....what we are trying to do is eliminate social injustice from society, so anything and everything that a teacher can do to serve that function has got to be right. It is making sure that students understand on a preparation course that they have a duty to society through all their actions and all their teaching to promote social justice, even with very young children, and that will start in Nursery and Early Years, and go right the way through beyond Primary. [E2, England]

...as a starting point, we need to create more space in the curriculum for student teachers to reflect on themselves, on their histories, on their background, where they are coming from, their own socialisation, their own identities, their own positions...Beginning to unpick who they are and how they see themselves in terms of ethnicity, in terms of social class, even gender. So, getting students to talk about themselves as a starting point...and then much more time for students to really engage in the principles of social justice – what it actually means, what it looks like. Having time to make connections, I suppose, with the challenges that are faced by different groups within society who are not doing well, who are not doing well within education, and begin to unpick the reasons for that. [E1, England]

Teacher Educators Teaching for Social Justice

In Malta responses to teaching for SJ were very much dependant on the teaching and research position of the teacher educator and the background of the teacher educator themselves. All however noted that they do their utmost to identify real-life issues so as to render what is being taught more "tangible, realistic and relevant."

> *Because, inclusion is the focus of my academic research and teaching, engagement with social justice ideals and praxes is essential to my work. Accordingly, the social justice education in my classes are mainly based on three educational operations: first, in generating an awareness of diversity that is different from the self's categories, conceptions, and cognition, secondly, in persevering a possibility for relationality with diversity though different from the self, and thirdly in generating an educational reflection and praxes through encounter and relation with diversity. Since the questions and challenges that diversity brings about, engages the whole class community, my objective is to facilitate the emergence of a community of learners that engages with diversity as an educational experience.* [M1, Malta]

> *My role as a teacher educator should mirror the attitudes, skills and knowledge of SJ. I consider myself as a change agent therefore I seek to be more than just a 'delivery service' of knowledge but seek to help students reflect upon their practice and the contexts in which they practice and inform it with theoretical perspectives embedded in values of social justice.* [M3, Malta]

Likewise, in England, responses to teaching for SJ were very much dependant on the background, teaching, research position and experiences of teaching on the different routes into teaching of the teacher educator. All recognised the challenges involved in teaching for SJ and spoke of the responsibility they had to advocate for SJ.

> *....one of the things about working with other teachers in London involved in teacher education is that a lot of us have a lot in common in thinking that teaching might have a moral purpose and that we need to consider that our values are underpinning a teacher education programme.* [E3, England]

> *...So that is the challenge, of trying to get colleagues and students to recognise that this is important for everyone. That is difficult. I think I have a really important role. And it is something that I have to still keep pushing and fighting for, and trying to help students. ...So, while I see part of my role as trying to educate my peers, my colleagues, I think, actually, at the end of the day, they themselves have to go through the same process. And I suggested that the students need to go through it, where we talk about own identities, and our own baggage, and our own prejudices, and our own unconscious biases, that as teacher educators we have to do that, as a starting point, because, if we don't, how on*

earth are we supposed to do that for our students? I saw my role as quite important in that respect. [E1, England]

Teacher educators play an important role in modelling the practices they want to inculcate in their student teachers. For the teacher educators in Jamaica, social justice as an explicit area of focus has not been a deliberate and conscious aspect of their teaching though they can identify different actions they take in their classrooms as actions aligned with social justice. The teacher educators therefore made some suggestions for making social justice more a deliberate effort in preparing student teachers.

If we are to prepare teachers to be emancipators and to be liberators and to carry that ethic of care into the schools it simply means we have to be explicit in terms of what we are doing. If we say we are preparing teachers for social justice we have to get them to know that education is a tool. It's a vehicle that can be used to liberate a society to liberate a particular social group so we have to teach them to know how to instruct a range of sensitivities from gender issues to social class issues to even the subject areas because some subject areas might be frowned upon and might be seen as only for certain categories of students. [Donna, JA1]

I must admit that promoting social justice was not usually at the forefront of my mind as I have been engaging in the various activities in my courses. However, in my capacity I can bring up matters related to social justice during course/programme review activities to have the leaders and other staff members discuss the issue and consider for inclusion in the curriculum. [Karie, JA3]

DISCUSSION

As societies change, so too should the curriculum. The curriculum is seen as the main vehicle for preparing citizens who are able to respond to these changes. Teacher preparation programmes therefore have to become more and more responsive to changes within the social fabric of society. In a borderless world, issues regarding race, religion, gender and class are contentious. These give rise to the need for inclusion and fairness. Social justice is about ensuring fairness for all and everyone is valued and provided with equal opportunities to access the same resources. All teacher educators in this study had a shared understanding of social justice and believed that the teacher preparation curriculum had an important role to play in preparing teachers who will teach for social justice.

The Social Justice Function of the Teacher Preparation Curriculum

Teachers exude a huge amount of influence in preparing citizens (Giroux and MacLaren 1986; Rasmussen and Bayer 2014); hence they need to be prepared to respond to the issues of social justice that permeate society. Malta and England have made deliberate attempts through their teacher preparation curriculum to prepare teachers for this role. Jamaica has not yet made such deliberate attempts; hence attempts at social justice are based on teachers' own consciousness to do so. While teacher educators in Malta and England were critiquing the results of their attempts, the teacher educators in Jamaica were looking at how they could begin to make social justice a more deliberate focus in the teacher preparation curriculum.

Based on the views of the teacher educators in England, because of ongoing changes in meeting standards and requirements outlined by the government for initial teacher training, time spent on major themes of social justice such as race and ethnicity has been reduced. Given the most recent White Paper (2016) which sets out government plans for the next five years, "to improve educational outcomes through development of a framework of core content for ITT and for behaviour management," this trend is likely to continue. For a multicultural society such as England where diversity abound in race and ethnicity, one would think that issues of race and ethnicity would be given priority attention in the teacher preparation curriculum.

For Malta, research, reflection and dialogue have led to the development of a professional master's degree where the underlying principles guiding the design of the MTL curriculum was to bring theory and practice together, to help prospective teachers cultivate those attitudes that should inform and instigate the knowledge and skills needed to be truly transformed and be able to respond to the needs of all learners. There is a definite belief that SJ depends on such praxis, thus being seen as an intrinsic dimension to teaching and learning. Such an understanding is based on what one teacher educator describes as "an understanding of the human being as a relational agent, who develops both agency and relationality through the educational praxis." Through the MTL programme, the Faculty of Education in Malta believes that for the curriculum to nurture SJ principles and practices, it needs to develop the learner's relational qualities and skills through both personal and social engagement as prospective teachers engage as learners in relation to other learners.

Though the context of each country is different, what is clear from the findings is that if we are to prepare teachers who will teach for social justice, then teacher preparation curriculum should provide opportunities for student teachers to have discussions around race, and ethnicity and around themselves, recognising that some people are subject to multiple disadvantages. Additionally, opportunities need to be provided for them to gain practice in different contexts which means observing and carrying out their field practice in different types of schools; schools, for example, that are co-educational, single sex, rural, urban, under-resourced and so on. One of the noticeable differences of teacher preparation amongst the three countries is that trainees in England have to spend some of their training in a contrasting school placement to help prepare them to teach children from different backgrounds to their own. In doing so, teacher preparation intentionally foregrounds social justice by attempting to prepare teachers to be able to teach all children, wherever they live and whatever their background. Such practices should permeate the teacher preparation curriculum to help student teachers understand that teaching is more than about technical matters such as content, teaching strategies and assessment, but teaching also serves a moral purpose.

The Moral Purpose of the Teacher Preparation Curriculum

Teaching, particularly teaching children and young people, is not only a technical matter of transmitting information but has a moral and ethical purpose (Day and Leitch 2001). As stated by one of the teacher educators in the study, the teacher preparation curriculum should help student teachers understand that education is a tool for preparing students to become liberators and emancipators. Therefore, teaching entails showcasing an ethic of care. Integrating these principles in the teacher preparation curriculum should help teachers generate reflection on deeper questions about underlying issues, educational purposes, values and priorities (Korthagen and Vasalos 2005). Teacher preparation curricula across these three countries did not lack focus on specialised content to a large extent but lacked focus on content that challenged social norms and how content is engaged with—hence the pedagogies used (Rasmussen and Bayer 2014). The teacher educators involved in this study noted that if we are seeking to nurture attitudes, provide knowledge and create opportunities to develop skills in our prospective teachers towards developing a social justice orientation, then more action is needed. There is a definite belief that social justice is an intrinsic dimension to teaching and learning. This dimension is best taught through an inclusion of real-life situations in the curriculum that places the teacher educator and student teachers in the midst of the day-to-day realities of teaching. Understanding these realities require research and enquiry into the lives of the student teachers, teacher educators and marginalised groups to unearth issues of inequity and power dynamics. To achieve this teacher preparation curriculum should be designed to include projects, simulation and other practical activities that encourage student teachers to engage actively with the idea of social justice (Giroux 1992).

As noted in Malta's Faculty of Education reflections (2015), "today's teachers have a very onerous intellectual and moral role to play in supporting the learning of such diverse learners who are learning complex new knowledge through constantly changing learning processes" (2015, p. 10). This belief resonates within the responses given in this study cutting across international boundaries. Through different pedagogies of teaching and learning, prospective teachers can help to redress current SJ issues. It is only through ongoing debate and practice that teachers and prospective teachers can develop a teacher identity based on SJ principles and ideals.

Our societies have become increasingly more complex and diverse, economies are fragile, and inequalities between social and culturally diverse groups are increasing. Knowledge itself and ways of accessing it are changing fast. It is only then going to be within real contexts that prospective teachers (all teachers for that matter) concerns and fears are challenged. Too many of our young are not receiving an education that enables them to overcome early disadvantage, whether this derives from economic, social, cultural, natural or other differences. Social justice is pivotal to an education that seeks to create and restore those relational structures that enhance inclusion and treat human beings as agents of change.

In this study, the data suggests that for teacher educators in England, space is needed in the curriculum to critique and analyse government education policy, to break it down into what it means to provide opportunities for engagement with research and literature in SJ to enable student teachers to be able to apply a critical eye to policy while considering other fundamental issues, like what are the aims of education.

For Jamaica, this study represents an attempt at raising the consciousness of teacher educators who are involved in programme design and the teaching of courses in teacher preparation programmes. The teacher educators who participated in this study have recognised the importance of teacher preparation programmes preparing teachers for their social justice function. In a Jamaican context where government rhetoric on teacher education is largely about certification and the type of teacher needed to meet the challenges in the classroom, teacher educators need to become more critical in advancing the cause of social justice. This becomes even more crucial when one considers the disparities that exist amongst schools given their geographical location and the limited resources available to meet the needs of students who attend the different types of schools.

The Teacher Educator as a Model for Social Justice Principles

According to Darling-Hammond (2010), practising teaching with expert guidance is an essential component of becoming an effective teacher. Therefore, if teachers are to develop the disposition to teach from a social justice orientation, then those who teach them should model this disposition. Consequently, there is an inextricable link between the designed curriculum and those who enact it. In developing the curriculum, considerations need to be given to who as much as the what and the how (Grant and Agosto 2008).

Teaching for social justice does not only require knowledge of the area and the associated strategies, but it also requires that those who prepare teachers review current beliefs and value systems (e.g. how we relate to people/student teachers holding a different faith, coming from a different country). One teacher educator describes this as a journey, an ongoing one. This journey must first begin with the teacher educator who through his or her transformation will help to transform his/her students. This transformation is about the theory-in-use as described by Argyris and Schön which drives actions in their daily lives leading to change agentry.

Teacher educators are called to reflect and act in ways that show that they are able to engage with students as learners whoever they are, wherever they may come from, whatever the learning difficulties they may have. The curriculum therefore represents a critical component in preparing teachers for this undertaking. It is the curriculum that will help to unify the theory, the practice and the individual who teaches (Grant and Agosto 2008; Doll 1996).

CONCLUSION

The responses of the teacher educators in this study indicate that it is important for the teacher preparation curriculum to prepare teachers to teach for social justice. Given that a social justice education perceives the individual as a social and relational being, catering for individual needs and aspirations should complement the development of a society that is diverse, relational and inclusive. It is within such a context that a community of learners is nurtured within and across boundaries. The data presented in the chapter have also helped to highlight that the teacher of today must be able to handle demands that go well beyond content knowledge and pedagogical content knowledge. It sheds light on the need for teacher educators to keep abreast of developments in order to remain relevant in the preparation of future teachers. Ongoing professional development for teacher educators is needed which will help to develop their beliefs, identity and sense of personal mission to serve future teachers. Different teacher educators in this study have articulated that for teacher preparation to be relevant and successful, theory needs to be integrated with practice. Therefore, ongoing field experiences coupled with regular and ample opportunities for reflection and discussion are imperatives in preparing teachers to teach for social justice. Despite the different stages of social justice inclusion across the three countries, teacher educators have articulated the importance of engaging prospective teachers in a context where issues can be experienced first hand; where ideas are debated, and challenged; where values and attitudes are put to the test.

REFERENCES

Banks, J. A. (2008). *An introduction to multicultural education*. Boston: Pearson.
Bell, L. (1997). Theoretical foundations for social justice education. In M. Adams, L. Bell, & P. Griffin (Eds.), *Teaching for diversity and social justice*. New York/London: Routledge.
Bezzina, C. (2017, February 26). Whitewater rafting and the world teachers live in. *The Sunday Times of Malta*, p. 37, 41.

Cochran-Smith, M. (2004). *Walking the road: Race, diversity, and social justice in teacher education.* New York: Teachers College Press.

Crowther, F. (2011). *From school improvement to sustained capacity.* Thousand Oaks: Corwin.

Darling-Hammond, L. (2010). Teacher education and American future. *Journal of Teacher Education, 61,* 33–47.

Darling-Hammond, L., Hammerness, K., Grossmann, P., Rust, F., & Shulman, L. (2007). The design of teacher education programs. In L. Darling-Hammond & J. Bransford (Eds.), *Preparing teachers for a changing world: What teachers should learn and be able to do* (pp. 390–441). San Francisco: Jossey-Bass.

Day, C., & Leitch, R. (2001). Teachers' and teacher educators' lives: The role of emotion. *Teaching and Teacher Education, 17*(4), 403–415.

Doll, R. (1996). *Curriculum improvement: Decision-making and process* (9th ed.). Needham Heights: Allyn & Bacon.

Evans, H. (2001). *Inside Jamaican schools.* Mona: University of the West Indies Press.

Faculty of Education. (2015). *Tomorrow's faculty today: Reflections and proposals,* Faculty of Education, University of Malta.

Giroux, H. A. (1992). *Border crossings: Cultural workers and the politics of education.* New York: Routledge.

Giroux, H., & MacLaren, P. (1986). Teacher education and the politics of engagement. *Harvard Educational Review.* Fall Issue, Harvard Publishing Group.

Grant, C. A., & Agosto, V. (2008). Teacher capacity and social justice in teacher education. *Educational Leadership and Policy Studies Faculty Publications.* Paper 5. http://scholarcommons.usf.edu/els_facpub/5

Joint Board of Teacher Education. (2012). *Aims of teacher training.* Retrieved from http://www.jbte.edu.jm/cms/regulations/aims of teacher training.aspx

Kaur, B. (2012). Equity and social justice in teaching and teacher education. *Teaching and Teacher Education, 28,* 48–492.

Korthagen, F., & Vasalos, A. (2005). Levels in reflection: Core reflection as a means to enhance professional growth. *Teachers and Teaching, 11*(1), 47–71.

Kosnik, C., & Beck, C. (2009). *Priorities in teacher education. The seven key elements of pre-service preparation.* New York: Routledge.

Lee, Y. A. (2011). What does teaching for social justice mean to teacher candidates. *Professional Educator, 35*(2), 1–20.

Picower, B. (2012). Using their words: Six elements of social justice curriculum design for the elementary classroom. *International Journal of Multicultural Education, 14*(1), 1–7.

Rasmussen, J., & Bayer, M. (2014). Comparative study of teaching content in teacher education programmes in Canada, Denmark, Finland and Singapore. *Journal of Curriculum Studies, 46*(6), 798–818.

Rawls, J. (1971). *A theory of justice.* Cambridge, MA: Harvard University Press.

Saldana, J. (2013). *The coding manual for qualitative researchers.* New York: Sage.

Schmoker, M. (2011). *Focus. Elevating the essentials to radically improve student learning.* Alexandria: ASCD.

Shields, C. M., & Mohan, E. J. (2008). High-quality education for all students: Putting social justice at its heart. *Teacher Development, 12*(4), 289–300.

Walker, M. (2003). Framing social justice in education: What does the "capabilities" approach offer? *British Journal of Educational Studies, 51*(2), 168–187.

Carmel Roofe is a lecturer in Curriculum and Instruction at the University of the West Indies, Mona, Jamaica. She is a member of the Institute for Educational Administration & Leadership-Jamaica and a Fellow at the Charles Darwin University, Australia. Her career in teaching spans both the secondary and higher education levels.

Christopher Bezzina is Professor of Educational Leadership in the Faculty of Education, University of Malta, and the Department of Education, Uppsala University, Sweden. He is both a Commonwealth and Fulbright Scholar and is currently Vice President of the Commonwealth Council for Educational Administration and Management.

Marilyn Holness is the Director of Student Engagement at Roehampton University. She has extensive experience across secondary schools and HE teaching, initial teacher education, student engagement, consultancy and senior management. Her services to Teacher Education have been recognised and awarded an Order of British Empire (OBE).

Toward Cross-Cultural Curriculum Development: An Analysis of Science Education in the Philippines, Ghana, and the United States

A.C. Vera Cruz, P.E. Madden, and C.K. Asante

INTRODUCTION

The complexity of curriculum and its development cannot be overstated. It is an innately philosophical activity, reflecting a way(s) of knowing and being of a society. Curriculum development models of the past typically utilize a "democratic" process where various local stakeholders equally provide input into its development (Schwab 1973). Because of this, the resulting curriculum was inevitably rooted in the context's philosophical orientation to knowing and being, something Barad (2003) calls an onto-epistemology, in recognition of the fact that "practices of knowing and being are not isolatable, but rather they are mutually implicated" (Barad 2003, p. 829).

In a globalized society, the curriculum development process is more complex. People from various onto-epistemologies interact with each

A.C. Vera Cruz (✉) • P.E. Madden • C.K. Asante
Lynch School of Education, Boston College, Chestnut Hill, MA, USA

© The Author(s) 2018   37
C. Roofe, C. Bezzina (eds.), *Intercultural Studies
of Curriculum*, Intercultural Studies in Education,
https://doi.org/10.1007/978-3-319-60897-6_3

other on a daily basis. Societies no longer have a shared onto-epistemology; instead, there is an increasing diversity of onto-epistemologies in a single context. In the last 20 years, we have seen a steady rise in "international" schools (ISC 2014) and a larger focus of providing "global" education (British Council 2012).

However, despite its steady increase and government investments, there is little understanding of what "global" education is and what its purposes are. As it currently exists, "global" or "international" education remains largely a distributive mechanism of Western onto-epistemologies (Verger, Altinyelken, and Novelli 2012), thus "localizing" the "global" (Santos 2007). In other words, there is a push and/or pull to globalize what is local to the Global North, as if it were neutral, universal, and the best standard that humanity can offer. Thus, there is a case of "othering" that occurs in the assumption that there is a standard or universal way of knowing and being (Marginson and Sawir 2011), implying that some knowledges and cultures are better than others.

This phenomenon is not novel. For years, countries have been ranked by the Organisation for Economic Co-operation and Development (OECD) based on a Western perspective of science rather than a country's own purposes, understanding, and application of science. Because of this, it is not surprising that countries in the Global South have adopted and adapted scientific curriculum practices from the Global North in order to achieve higher rankings in international benchmarks. Thus, is "global" education limited to the adoption or adaption of a hegemonic Western curriculum or can there be an alternative way of proposing what "global" education can be?

With respect to science education, this issue may seem inapplicable. One may claim the universality of Western science based on its onto-epistemology's almost miraculous ability to predict, control, and/or manipulate the natural world. However, arguments that are justified by their ends or effects are often made and easily rebutted even within Western logic. Others may claim Western science's universality based on its ubiquitous presence globally. However, postcolonial scholars, such as Prashad (2012), have observed that although the Global South has engaged in Western science for the purposes of furthering economic sovereignty, they have not necessarily accepted its onto-epistemological, metaphysical, or cosmological premises. In fact, the diversity of human onto-epistemologies, metaphysics, and cosmologies in science is widely recognized, at least within Global South (Santos 2008), if not critical Global North discourses.

Moreover, critical indigenous scholars, such as Cajete (2000), Grande (2015), Tuhiwai Smith (2012), and Wildcat (2009), have prolifically commented on the particularity of Western science.

Thus, within our discussions of science education, we present Western science as a localized globalism, which although local to the West has been exported and adapted globally (Santos 2008). This is not presented in the desire to replace one hegemonic scientific onto-epistemology for another. Nor is this presented to invalidate Western science's knowledge claims. Rather, it is to position it as a valid, yet embodied and local, onto-epistemology, which orients people to be, think, and create knowledge in a particular way in relation to the natural world. Thus, we call for the development and creation of curriculum development methods that are open to pluralistic definitions of science as well as transformative partnerships (Marginson and Sawir 2011) in the spirit of respect, mutual well-being, and sustainability.

To aid this process, a comparison of national science education curriculums and policies was administered. In analyzing the science education curriculums of Ghana, the United States, and the Philippines, we hope to illustrate the commonalities and differences between these countries' curriculums to illuminate both the presence of and resistance to the localized globalisms of Western science. Moving productively from this, we offer a framework that may offer an interdisciplinary and open-ended methodology that allows for pluralistic discussions about content-based subjects, such as science education. The global problems of our day are too ubiquitous to be limited by the partiality of any knowledge system. We must learn from each other, which, for those of us trained in the West, may mean unlearning that there is one way of knowing. It is our hope that this framework can illuminate a potential model for engaging in anti-hegemonic, cross-cultural curriculum development.

Conceptual Framework

For this study, we engage in a view of globalization that is not simply linked to the global economy but also more sensitive to its social, political, and cultural dimensions. Thus, we utilized de Sousa Santos' (2007) definition of globalization as "the process by which a given local condition or entity succeeds in extending its reach over the globe and by doing so, develops the capacity to designate a rival social condition or entity as local" (pp. 6–7). This definition, like all definitions of globalization, is non-neutral. Of particular merit, this definition calls attention to the legacy and presence of power asymmetries with regard to what is being globalized and what is considered to be the "standard" in knowledge and in culture.

To further follow the understanding and movement of globalization, Santos' (2008) explains "globalized localisms" and "localized globalisms". These terms are used to differentiate the movement and distribution of a more powerful, local onto-epistemology to other contexts (globalized localism) and the adoption of this onto-epistemology in the local context (localized globalism) (de Sousa Santos 2007). This suggests that given the power asymmetries that exist in the world, there are some contexts that are more likely to adopt or adapt ideas rather than provide them, illuminating which knowledge and culture dominates, especially in "global" education.

In acknowledging the onto-epistemological difference within and among countries, we were guided by Ricoeur's (2007) philosophy of translation. Ricoeur (2007) describes language as more than just the words and the sentences—it is also how the meaning is associated with them in its particular culture. Thus, when languages or thoughts are translated from one to another, there is a sense of "faithfulness and betrayal" because, on the one hand, the translator, typically bilingual in both languages, tries to conserve the meaning of one language to another. However, to be able to accomplish this, "creative betrayal" needs to occur because of the impossibility of "perfect" translation due to varying onto-epistemologies. More specifically, Ricoeur (2007) promotes the concept of linguistic hospitality, where culture and context is given more importance than text-to-text translation of languages.

This concept is reflected in the methodology section because despite using English in most government documents, culture and context were given more importance. Thus, the author—local to a particular context, the Philippines, Ghana, or the United States—had the task of "translating" the documents in order to preserve meaning, as opposed to the language. For example, while we are educators in the United States and are fluent English speakers, only one of us grew up in this context. Hence, while we can read and understand the government policies in the United States, two of us are not as familiar of the history, culture, and politics that have shaped them, thus limiting our ability to analyze the document deeply. In order to have a rich understanding of what the documents mean and imply, we individually analyzed the documents and policies from our own respective countries while simultaneously being conscious that the analyses are limited to our experiences and social locations within each context.

In this sense, we believe that each national curriculum in this study (1) implicitly contains meaning that is more than literal and (2) exists in a way that is not necessarily translatable or comprehensible for members outside of its community. Thus, for cross-cultural conversations to occur, bilingual (literate in both local and dominant context) researchers are necessary in order to translate and analyze curricular materials and to bring forward potential concerns for cross-cultural curriculum development.

Finally, we utilized Posner's (2004) framework for analyzing the curriculum. This framework has four general parts. The first is on curriculum documentation and origins. In this section, the governing body responsible for the creation and implementation of the curricula is identified as well as its aims, purposes, and philosophical orientations. The second is on the curriculum proper. In this section, the "content" and organization of the curriculum is identified and explained. Following this, the third section illustrates how the curriculum is used or how it is disseminated to learners. Finally, the fourth section offers a short critique based on the curriculum's strengths and weaknesses.

With these three interacting frameworks, we offer a unique way of (1) illustrating how global education has operated, (2) analyzing different countries' curriculum (as opposed to just test scores), and (3) offering practices for cross-cultural curriculum development that are rooted in both respecting a diversity of metaphysics and onto-epistemologies and learning between contexts.

METHODOLOGY

The methodology for this book chapter is rooted in our conceptual framework, positionality regarding curriculum, and our vision for cross-cultural curriculum development. The researchers for this chapter believe in the political nature and non-neutrality of curriculum and curriculum development. We believe that each curriculum is rooted in and reflective of a particular onto-epistemology. Finally, we recognize the potential power of cross-cultural curriculum development as an opportunity of growth and learning instead of the typical, "uproot-and-plant" unidirectional hegemonic process.

Based on this positionality, we offer our assumptions. First, that each culture has at least one (often multiple) onto-epistemology, but a common metaphysics, that is, shared fundamental assumptions about the nature of time, space, logic, order, and being (Madden et al. in review).

Thus, we assume that each culture experiences and interprets the world differently from other cultures. Second, we assume that the members of the community who speak the local language and have had significant, long-term life experiences in that community are the best interpreters/translators of their own respective educational systems (Ricoeur 2007). Third, we assume that while each country has a diverse set of cultures, national policies and curriculum represent the country's dominant positionality and interpretation of science education. Through these assumptions, we aim to provide as trustworthy of an interpretation, as possible, of local meanings.

Based on these assumptions, we, each member of our respective communities (Philippines, Ghana, and the United States), were responsible for translating (when necessary) and analyzing government policies (retrieved from government websites) for the international reader using our personal experiences and cultural and linguistic understanding in order to provide a description, contextualization, and comparison of STEM education in the three countries.

In order to analyze the curriculum, we utilized Posner's (2004) framework. Because the documents between countries differ in format and structure, we chose questions that can help compare not only the curriculum. For curriculum origins and documentation, we focused on the source of the curriculum, definition of science, as well as the purposes of science education. For the curriculum proper, we focused on scientific subject matter, presented as strands, within it. For the curriculum use, we emphasized the language of instruction as well as the curriculum organization and assessment. Finally, our critique offered an illustration of how the curriculum operates in relation to its purposes as well as how this may affect cross-cultural curriculum development.

Following individual analysis of each context, we presented our findings to each other and engaged in conversation regarding similarities and differences in onto-epistemology as well as implications for cross-cultural curriculum development specifically for science education.

RESULTS

The Philippines, Southeast Asia

The Philippines is an archipelago located in Southeast Asia with a population of over 102 million. It boasts 7107 islands with a wide variety of ethnicities, cultures, and languages. The languages spoken in the Philippines are Filipino and English (Department of Education 2016a). While the Philippines has been colonized by Spain, Britain, Japan, and the United States (Agoncillo 1990), the country is a nonsettler-colonial sovereign state and is a member of the Global South.

The Department of Education (DepEd) is the central governing body for schooling in the Philippines. Its purpose is to

> formulate, implement, and coordinate policies and programs in areas of formal and non-formal basic education. It supervises all elementary and secondary institutions, including alternative learning systems, both public and private; and provides for the establishment and maintenance of a complete, adequate, and integrated system of basic education relevant to goals of national development. (Department of Education 2016a)

Thus, it is responsible for (1) reflecting upon the purposes of schooling and education, (2) relating these to current national goals, (3) creating and monitoring policies on educational experiences, and (4) designing and evaluating assessments.

The values of education and, by extension, science education in the Philippines are four-dimensional (Department of Education 2016b). The first dimension refers to being *maka-Diyos* or God-centered. In that sense, faith in a higher being is first and central in Philippine education. The second dimension refers to being *maka-tao*. This means "for people" but figuratively, this means having an understanding of brotherhood, interdependence, and responsibility. The third dimension is *maka-kalikasan*, or for nature. With respect to being *maka-tao*, this dimension offers the deepest respect for the environment and how we orient ourselves toward the other species or beings in the world. Thus, one of the purposes of education is to protect the environment because we, as humans, depend on it. Finally, the last dimension refers to being *maka-bansa*. This means a sense of love, pride, and sacrifice for one's country. Given the colonial aspect of Philippine's history, Filipinos, over time, have deeply valued freedom and sovereignty (Agoncillo 1990).

Recently, a shift from the traditional Philippine system (kindergarten, grades 1–6, high school years 1–4) to a K-12 system in 2012 led to a similar educational structure in the United States (Santos 2012). Kindergarten and 6 years of elementary schooling comprised of core, typical subject matters such as Math, Science, English, and Filipino. When students attend junior high school (7th–10th grade), they are required to take Technology and Livelihood Education (TLE), which is comprised of agri-fishery arts, home economics, information and communications technology (ICT), and industrial arts, among typical subject matters. Similarly, when students attend senior high school, several "applied" tracks are available to them in addition to core subject matter. These tracks are academic (traditional sciences and humanities courses), technical vocational (agri-fishery, home economics, etc.), (3) sports, and (4) art and design (Department of Education 2016b).

Science education in the Philippines specifically aims to "develop scientific literacy among learners that will prepare them to be informed and participative citizens who are able to make judgments and decisions regarding applications of scientific knowledge that may have social, health, or environmental impacts" (Department of Education 2016b, p. 2). To deliver this aim, teachers are encouraged to take an interdisciplinary, problem-based, and inquiry approach based on the context while using relevant technology. As a whole, the Philippine government believes that when students participate in solving local problems, they gain a deeper understanding of core subject content.

Instead of defining science in a single statement, principles of science were stated instead. The science curriculum revolves around three overarching themes: (1) maintaining good health and living safely, (2) utilizing energy and coping with changes, and (3) conserving and protecting the environment (National Institute for Science and Mathematics Education Development 2011). These themes are based on a complex understanding of science that is rooted in local culture. Links between science and technology and indigenous technology are not only recognized but also encouraged.

For the Philippines, the nature of science is based on the understanding that it serves everyone. It is both a content and a process that contributes to the larger purposes of education. Thus, depth and coherence are considered more important than breadth, and science, as a subject matter and a way of life, should nurture an interest in learning that reflects, influences, and shapes culture (Department of Education 2016a).

To help teachers concretize these aims and goals, teachers are given a scope and sequence for every grade level, in every semester, and in every discipline under "science". The document further organizes the subject into content standards, performance standards, "learning competency" (assessments), learning materials (including textbooks and resources), and necessary science equipment (Department of Education 2016b).

While the purposes and aims of science education in the Philippines are locally defined, an analysis using Posner's (2004) framework illustrates how Western scientific subject matter such as Biology, Chemistry, and Physics has heavily influenced the national science curriculum, as seen in the curriculum provided to the teachers. Moreover, while the educational purposes and aims are indigenous to the Philippines (makatao, makabansa, etc.), the creation, organization, and delivery of the curriculum is largely influenced by Western thought (Biology, Chemistry, Physics). This discrepancy between locally defined aims and Western-inspired breakdown of "science" creates a case of misalignment between purpose and curriculum.

Nevertheless, this view of science, based on globally accepted scientific subject matters such as Biology, Chemistry, and Physics, was intentional. As the Philippines continues to develop its own identity and economy, there is a desire to participate in the "global" arena, learn from other countries especially in terms of developing technology, ICT, and engineering, and adapt to the changing world (Department of Education 2016b).

Ghana, West Africa

Ghana is a nonsettler-colonial sovereign country with a population of about 25 million people (Ghana Statistical Service 2010). It is located in West Africa and borders the Gulf of Guinea to the south. There are 49 local languages spoken, but the official language of the country is English (British). English is also the language of instruction in schools, although recently there have been calls for the use of widely spoken local languages such as Twi, Ewe, and Dagbani. Before the advent of Western education, elders taught the youth of customs, practices, culture, and medicines that helped them thrive. However, this is no longer the case. Instead, the current educational system is an attempt to merge Western education and traditional knowledge.

While the Ministry of Education is the primary government agency responsible for education, its functions are limited to the teaching and learning of science. Within the Ministry of Education is the Ghana Education Service (GES). It is responsible for education from primary to senior high school including a 6-year primary school, 3 years of junior high school which culminates in a high-stake exam called the BECE (Basic Education Certificate Exam), and finally, 3 years of senior high school after which students take another high-stake exam called the WASSCE (West Africa Senior School Certificate Exams) to gain admission to universities.

Ghana's national vision is focused on having "middle-income status of an advanced human society with a better quality of life reflected in all aspects of socio-economic and environmental conditions" (Ministry of Environment, Science, and Technology 2009, p. 12). This is concretized by educational plans that support the effective and efficient use of natural resources with an additional focus on manufacturing in order to compete in the global market. To reach these goals, Ghana guides itself through five basic principles—relevance, cost-effectiveness, realism (realistic in aspiration and efforts), synergy (cross-sectoral and interdisciplinary), and partnerships (conscious efforts for local and international partnerships).

Science has been an integral part of education in Ghana before and after independence in 1957. In the local language of Twi, science is defined as *abodeɛ mu nyansapɛ*, which literally translates into "inquiry into nature". This implies that locals have had an important and unique relationship with science that is different from Western notions and purposes of science. However, in order to reach its national goals, the Ghanaian government is pushing toward bridging local and international views and purposes of science together (Mueller and Bentley 2009).

"Integrated science", a combination of general Biology, Chemistry, and Physics, is required for all students. However, students in high school who major in science are required to take additional, separate Biology, Chemistry, and Physics classes. Science is delivered through classroom instructions and laboratory sessions, and teachers are provided with and required to follow an authorized teaching syllabus that states the content and pedagogy (Ministry of Education, Teaching Syllabus for Integrated Science 2010).

Although the country seeks to merge local ways of knowing with Western science, local knowledge has not been incorporated enough. This is because Ghana has diverse ethnicities with different knowledge systems (Yarrow 2008). However, despite these challenges, there are some documented case studies that exemplify attempts of merging both Ghana and the West. For instance, the curriculum includes a number of local industries such as beer and soap that depend on local technologies (Anamuah-Mensah et al. 2005).

United States of America, North America

The United States (US) is a settler-colonial nation within the Global North comprised of 50 states, including Alaska and Hawaii, which are noncontiguous. Although these 50 states include 566 federally recognized

American Indian domestic dependent nations, these ethnically, culturally, and linguistically diverse nations, given their sovereignty, were excluded from this national science curriculum analysis (NCAI 2016). Despite internal rhetoric about a failing education system and its contribution to the United States' purported economic decline, the United States remains the largest economy in the world by gross domestic product (World Bank 2016). Further, although English is the most commonly used language in education, there is no official language in the United States with "over 300 [non-indigenous] languages...spoken or signed by the population" (USA.gov 2016).

In the United States, decision-making and funding related to education has historically been the responsibility of state and local governments (Duncan 2009). However, since The No Child Left Behind Act of 2001, the role of the US federal government on the local and state level has increased via legislation that ties federal funding to accountability frameworks. As part of the American Recovery and Reinvestment Act of 2009, cash-strapped states and localities welcomed President Obama's Race to the Top program—a competitive grant program that required, among the other key requirements, "adopting standards and assessments that prepare students to succeed in college and the workplace and to compete in the global economy" (U.S. Department of Education 2009). Thus, although national standards were not mandated, the Common Core State Standards were conveniently put into play within this economic context, and currently 42 of 50 states have fully adopted them (CCSS 2016).

Although seemingly separate, The National Research Council's (2012) *A Framework for K-12 Science Education*, a.k.a. Next Generation Science Standards (NGSS), emerged within and in constellation with these standards. Explicitly, NGSS (National Research Council 2012) was developed partially as an update to previous science standards documents that sought national adoption (albeit unsuccessfully), but also in sync with "the opportunity provided by a movement of multiple states to adopt common standards in mathematics and in language arts", that is, the Common Core State Standards (p. 8). Thus, although understandably framed as state developed, given the history of state and local control over educational decisions and the ongoing and controversial debates within the United States over state versus federal power (Duncan 2009), the NGSS was produced with the intention of national adoption. This is further exemplified in an executive summary by a federal agency, that is, the National Center for Educational Statistics (2015), in their comparison of NGSS standards and the content and skills tested on the *National Assessment of Educational Progress (NAEP)*, a.k.a. *The Nation's Report Card*, which their office administers. For in this report, in addition to signifying NGSS' high federal status by placing it in relation to the *Nation's Report Card*, they underscored the report's significance and relevance to educational stakeholders by explicitly labeling the Next Generation Science Standards as "the most recently developed national STEM standards" (p. 1). As stated previously, within the context of the United States, such declarations are nontrivial as they both reveal the federal government's desire for national standards within a political tradition of strife over the balance of federal and state powers.

Not surprisingly within this context, even with attempts at a national curriculum, states have the power to adopt, adapt, consider, or disregard the national NGSS standards. In a systematic curriculum analysis of the 50 states' science standards and related policy documents, Vera Cruz and Madden (forthcoming) found that although only 18 states have formally adopted NGSS, only 6 states, that is, Idaho, Louisiana, New Mexico, Pennsylvania, Virginia, and Texas, have not adopted, adapted, or explicitly or implicitly referenced NGSS or its related foundational documents. However, all six of these states do review or consider science standards documents with national aspirations, that is, the Next Generation Science Standards and its predecessor documents when constructing state standards.

In addition, to the tradition of state control, much of this resistance seems to be related to the polarized debate over whether or not we should present theories regarding climate change and evolution within a curriculum that traditionally treats scientific content as facts. As such, resolution of this polarized debate is unlikely. Thus, although not complete, national standards represented most recently by NGSS (National Research Council 2012) and more broadly by both NGSS and its foundational documents guide what counts as science knowledge in K-12 schooling and thus how science education is assessed and taught within the United States.

While the NGSS (National Research Council 2012) has a clear definition of technology and engineering, the document avoids defining science beyond stating that "in the K-12 context, science is generally taken to mean the traditional natural sciences: physics, chemistry, biology, and (more recently) earth, space, and environmental sciences" (p. 11). Nevertheless, it alludes to definitions of science provided within "*Science for All Americans* and *Benchmarks for Science Literacy* (American Association for the Advancement of Science 1994), developed by the American Association for the Advancement of Science (AAAS), and the *National Science Education Standards* (1996), developed by the NRC" (National Research Council 1996, p. x). In NRC's (1996) national standards, science is portrayed as "a way of knowing that is characterized by empirical criteria, logical argument, and skeptical review" whose goal "is to understand the natural world" (p. 21, 24). In the standards developed by AAAS, science is similarly portrayed as a way of knowing characterized by the assumption that "by working together over time, people can in fact figure out how the world works", albeit with the "implied disclaimers, 'in many cases' and 'in the very long run'". Collectively, this presents a view of science, which although inclusively positioned as an activity that "has been practiced in many different cultures" (NSES, p. 21) has developed in a linear, progressive, and universal way.

Unlike the definition of science, the purposes for science education in the United States is presented as fourfold: (1) address the "reduction of the United States' competitive economic edge", (2) reduce the "lagging achievement of US students", (3) prepare students "for all careers in the modern workforce", and (4) promote "scientific and technological literacy for an educated society" (The Need for Standards n.d.). These purposes present science and technology as central to resolving both individual- and society-level issues, including informed civic engagement, but most especially issues related to maintaining global economic competitiveness.

In the K-12 system, NGSS and its foundational documents promote educational experiences in science within inquiry-based, scientific literacy-focused environments. This mirrors the logic behind the science standards themselves, which are based on the structure of the discipline (Posner 2004). In other words, in science, subject matter and related student experiences are organized based on how experts perceive disciplinary knowledge and practices. Thus, although students are assessed by local standards, most science classrooms in the United States aim for creating inquiry-based and scientific literacy-focused environments.

Finally, while the NGSS (National Research Council 2012) does mention international benchmarking, no nations were specified. Rather, benchmarking, much like the purposes of science education, is framed in terms of maintaining global competitiveness.

Comparative Cross-Cultural Curriculum Analysis

Based on our descriptions of the origins, purposes, definition, and content of science education in each context, we engaged in cross-cultural dialogue, in the spirit of Santos (2008), for the purpose of cross-illuminating our societies' dominant, and often unexamined, culturally mediated philosophical orientations to science. Specifically, we discussed questions such as our dominant cultures' fundamental assumptions about human's relationship to the natural world (metaphysics) and how humans come to understand the natural world (onto-epistemology). Iteratively moving between our country descriptions and our particular understandings of our dominant cultures' philosophical assumptions about the natural world, we sought to understand the similarities and differences between contexts as mediated by power, culture, and purposes.

Resulting from this co-illuminating, cross-cultural discourse were three observations: (1) the purposes of science education vary and are mediated largely by power and metaphysical orientations, (2) the "content" of science education is similar, and (3) the development, delivery, and implementation of science education are tied to language and culture.

In Ghana, in the local language of Twi, science is defined as *abodee mu nyansape*. Although this transliterates as "inquiry into nature", which seems fairly normative within science education discourse, much of its meaning and assumptions about reality (metaphysics) are lost to a cultural outsider. To a cultural insider, this phrase encapsulates a metaphysical assumption that there is a higher being whose creation is composed of both spirit and matter, which we can *seek* to understand through embodied, situated, and empirical observation of the natural world. Thus, when discussing the natural world, there is always an assumption that it is spiritualized. Of course, inquiries that strictly engage with the material nature of creation are possible within this framework. Thus, for Ghanaians, studying physics, chemistry, and biology is simply a much more specific inquiry, coming from a particular onto-epistemology local to the West, but adapted locally for the purposes of developing economic sovereignty from the West.

In the Philippines, although the definition of science is presented similarly to more communitarian definition of science in the United States, its four-dimensional purpose reveals metaphysical assumptions closer to those held by a Ghanaian speaker of Twi. The first dimension, *maka-Diyos* (for a higher being), similarly alludes to the non-duality of spirit and matter present in a Ghanaian conceptualization. The second and third dimensions of *maka-tao* (for being human and the interdependence of beings) and *maka-kalikasan* (for nature as provider of life) both position humans as subordinate to nature and in nonhierarchical interdependence with other beings while, at the same time, recognizing the uniqueness of humans as a species. The fourth dimension, that is, *maka-bansa* (for love of country), similarly positions science as a tool for improving the Philippines ability to compete in and be a part of the global economy in order to advance their economic sovereignty from the Global North.

Both of these definitions and purposes contrast with the United States' metaphysical assumptions implied within their definition and purposes of science. Science as key to global economic competitiveness both assumes that coming to understand nature is about extracting value from nature and/or satisfying human needs. In the former, the Earth is conceived dualistically as material and thus despiritualized and as such knowable, albeit in many cases and in the long run. In the latter science is an anthropomorphic activity that positions nature in service and subordinate to human needs. Humans in this conceptualization are positioned in a superior hierarchical relationship with other beings and our shared habitat. Even environmental studies, although it does much to "protect the Earth", still engages in a materialistic discourse about nature as limited resource, sustainable, and manageable as opposed to shared habitat, mutually reciprocal, and inter-being.

Nevertheless, despite the differences in metaphysical beliefs about the natural world, the "content" in science remains largely the same. Biology, Physics, and Chemistry still remain the hallmark subject matters of general science. However, the difference lies in the "elective" or "track" subjects. For example, science majors (high school) in Ghana are required to take integrated science—a combination of Biology, Chemistry, and Physics—in addition to taking the subjects individually. In the Philippines, students are required to take one or more of the following tracks—academic (traditional science courses and the humanities), technical vocational (agrifishery, home economics, etc.), sports, and art and design—in addition to the core subject matter. In the United States, in addition to Biology, Physics, and Chemistry, there is an increasing presence of Earth, Space, and Environment Science.

Summary of Comparative Analysis

	The Philippines	Ghana	United States
Curriculum documentations and origins	National: Department of Education	National: Ministry of Education, Ghana Education Service	Coalition of government (federal and state) and nongovernment entities
Definition of science	Science understood as content and process, reflective of the culture, and as a service to everyone and the environment	*Abodeɛ mu nyansapɛ*, or inquiry into nature (translated)	Science is "a way of knowing that is characterized by empirical criteria, logical argument, and skeptical review" whose goal "is to understand the natural world" (NRC 1996, p. 21, 24)
Purpose of science education	Develop scientific literacy among learners that will prepare them to be informed and participative citizens who are able to make judgments and decisions regarding applications of scientific knowledge that may have social, health, or environmental impacts (Department of Education 2016b, p. 2)	Promote competitiveness in productive sectors of the economy, creating job opportunities, expanding industrialization, enhancing quality of life through innovation, developing scientific human resources, expanding infrastructure, promoting an information society, optimizing sustainable use of the environment, commercializing research findings (Ministry of Education 2009)	Address reduction of US competitive economic edge, decrease lagging achievement of US students, prepare students for all careers in the modern workforce, educate society through scientific and technological literacy (National Research Council 2012)

	The Philippines	Ghana	United States
Curriculum proper	Biology, Chemistry, Physics, Earth Sciences, and Technical and Livelihood Education	Integrated Science (core Biology, Chemistry, and Physics) and electives (Biology, Chemistry, and Physics)	Physics, Chemistry, Biology, and Earth, Space, and Environmental Sciences
Language of instruction	American English	British English	American English
Curriculum organization and use	Standards-based; national guide for teachers available including scope and sequence, materials, and pedagogy for every grade level for each quarter	Curriculum Division of Ghana Educational Service, National Teaching Syllabus	NGSS standards-based for every level and for each subject matter under science, differences highly visible at the state level
National assessments	National Achievement Test	BECE, West Africa Senior Schools Certificate Exams	NAEP (national) but assessments are also administered at the state level
Potential issues for cross-cultural curriculum development	Misalignment of desired purposes of science and education with Western purposes of science	Alignment with Western science but desire to be independent from the Global North	Benchmarking for the purpose of global economic competitiveness, hyper competitiveness

DISCUSSION

Popular cross-cultural discourse on global education typically involves the comparison of test scores, commonalities between contexts, or the ability of a context to perform on dominant, globalized benchmarks. In this book chapter, we challenged this discourse by re-framing global education by analyzing national curricula from the Philippines, Ghana, and the United States through the lens of translation (Ricoeur 2007) and a focus on differing cultural philosophies. Based on these results, we offer a few recommendations for the first stages of cross-cultural curriculum development: (1) the establishment of a goal that reflects both contexts understandings and ways of being, (2) a conversation regarding the rationale behind the partnership, and (3) space for evolving partnership and goals.

If we truly want to participate in cross-cultural, and more specifically intercultural, curriculum development that recognizes and appreciates differences, then stakeholders must first have a curriculum analysis, similar to the one herein, of their local context in order to understand their own philosophical assumptions regarding the subject matter in relation to other contexts (Vera Cruz forthcoming). We believe that in understanding how local curriculum may be positioned within an outside onto-epistemology, the local context will be able to conserve its purposes and ideologies.

Studies (Mattessich and Monsey 1992) on collaboration suggest that best practices for good partnerships involve the establishment of clear goals between stakeholders. Based on this study, this task is more complex because of the difference in philosophical assumptions. Nevertheless, curriculum development cannot occur successfully without the discussion of a specific goal. Thus, we recommend a detailed conversation regarding the similarities and differences between contexts and stakeholders in order to clarify meanings and establish a goal that can reflect both contexts involved.

Finally, in having these conversations, we expect curriculum development goals and partnerships to change over time. While the adoption and adaption of dominant curricula in local contexts has been occurring for years, there is little evidence of cross-cultural learning. Thus, we suggest stakeholders to be flexible and keep an open mind.

With these suggestions, we believe countries will be able to engage in a more fruitful cross-cultural curriculum discourse that attempts to challenge power asymmetries and participate in a vision for authentic cross-cultural learning rather than competition.

REFERENCES

Agoncillo, T. A. (1990). *History of the Filipino people.* Quezon City: Garotech Publishing.

American Association for the Advancement of Science. (1994). *Science for all Americans: Project 2061.* Oxford: Oxford University Press.

Anamuah-Mensah, J., Savage, M., Quaye, E., & Towse, P. (2005). *Science in action: Student's workbook.* Winneba: SACOST University of Education.

Barad, K. (2003). Posthumanist performativity: Toward an understanding of how matter comes to matter. *Journal of Women in Culture and Society, 28*(3), 801–831.

British Council. (2012). *The shape of things to come: Higher education global trends and emerging opportunities to 2020.* Retrieved from www.britishcouncil.org/higher-education

Cajete, G. (2000). *Native science: Natural laws of interdependence*. Santa Fe: Clear Light Pub.

Common Core State Standards Initiative. (2016). *Standards in your state*. Retrieved from http://www.corestandards.org/standards-in-your-state/

Department of Education. (2016a). *Vision, mission, core values, and mandate*. Retrieved from http://www.deped.gov.ph/mandate

Department of Education. (2016b). *K to 12 curriculum guide: Science*. Manila: DepEd Complex.

Duncan, A. (2009). States will lead the way toward reform: Secretary Arne Duncan's remarks at the 2009 Governors Education Symposium. *US Department of Education*. Retrieved from http://www2.ed.gov/news/speeches/2009/06/06142009.html

Ghana Statistical Service. (2010). *Population and housing census: Summary report of final results*. Accra: Ghana Statistical Service.

Grande, S. (2015). *Red pedagogy: Native American social and political thought*. Lanham: Rowman & Littlefield.

International School Consultancy Group. (2014). New data from international schools suggests continued strong growth. *ICEF Monitor*. Retrieved from http://monitor.icef.com/2014/03/new-data-on-international-schools-suggests-continued-strong-growth-2/

Madden, P. E., Vera Cruz, A. C., Asante, C., Zhang, Z., & Barnett, M. (under consideration). Imagining the future for a future: Concretizing an anticolonial STEM for habitat harmony within the particularized futurity of a youth program in the Global North. *Educational Studies*.

Marginson, S., & Sawir, E. (2011). *Ideas for intercultural education*. New York: Palgrave Macmillan.

Mattessich, P. W., & Monsey, B. R. (1992). *Collaboration: What makes it work. A review of research literature on factors influencing successful collaboration*. Saint Paul: Amherst H. Wilder Foundation.

Ministry of Education. (2010). *Teaching syllabus for integrated science*. Retrieved from http://www.ibe.unesco.org/curricula/ghana/gh_us_sc_2010_eng.pdf

Ministry of Environment, Science, and Technology. (2009). *National science, technology, and innovation policy*. Accra: Ministry of Environment, Science, and Technology.

Mueller, M. P., & Bentley, M. L. (2009). Environmental and science education in developing nations: A Ghanaian approach to renewing and revitalizing the local community and ecosystems. *The Journal of Environmental Education, 40*(4), 53–64.

National Congress of American Indians. (2016). *Tribal Nations and the United States: An introduction*. Retrieved from http://www.ncai.org/tribalnations/introduction/Tribal_Nations_and_the_United_States_An_Introduction-web-.pdf

National Research Council. (1996). *National science education standards.* Washington, DC: National Academy Press.

National Research Council. (2012). *A framework for k-12 science education: Practices, cross-cutting concepts, and core ideas.* Washington, DC: The National Academies Press.

Posner, G. J. (2004). *Analyzing the curriculum* (3rd ed.). New York: McGraw Hill.

Prashad, V. (2012). *The poorer nations: A possible history of the global south.* London/New York: Verso.

Ricoeur, P. (2007). *On translation.* London/New York: Routledge.

Santos, B. (2007). *Another knowledge is possible: Beyond northern epistemologies.* London/New York: Verso.

Santos Jr., R. (2012). *K-12 education program launched,* Rappler. Retrieved from http://www.rappler.com/nation/4298-malacanang-launches-k-to-12-program

Schwab, J. J. (1973). The practical 3: Translation into curriculum. *The School Review, 81*(4), 501–522.

Science Education Institute & University of the Philippines National Institute for Science and Mathematics Education Development. (2011). *Science framework for Philippines basic education.* Manila: SEI-DOST &UP NISMED.

de Sousa Santos, B. (2007). *Another knowledge is possible: Beyond northern epistemologies.* London/New York: Verso.

The Need for Standards. (n.d.). *In next generation science standards: For states, by states.* Retrieved from http://www.nextgenscience.org/need-standards

The World Bank. (2016). *World Databank Home page, The World Bank Group.* Retrieved from http://databank.worldbank.org/data/home.aspx

Tuhiwai Smith, L. (2012). *Decolonizing methodologies: Research and indigenous peoples.* London/New York: Zed Books.

U.S. Department of Education. (2009). *Race to the top program: Executive summary.* Washington, DC: U.S. Department of Education.

USA.gov. (2016). *Learn about life in the United States.* Official Guide to Government Information and Services. Retrieved from https://www.usa.gov/life-in-the-us

Vera Cruz, A. C. (forthcoming). *A framework for cross-cultural curriculum development.*

Vera Cruz, A. C., & Madden, P. E. (forthcoming). *An analysis of the Next Generation Science Standards.*

Verger, A., Altinyelken, H. K., & Novelli, M. (Eds.). (2012). *Global education policy and international development: New agendas, issues and policies.* New York: Bloomsbury.

Wildcat, D. R. (2009). *Red alert! Saving the planet with indigenous knowledge.* Golden: Fulcrum.

Yarrow, T. (2008). Negotiating difference: Discourses of indigenous knowledge and development in Ghana. *PoLAR: Political and Legal Anthropology Review*, *31*(2), 224–242.

Anne Vera Cruz is a multicultural and naturally trilingual local of the Philippines, with an undergraduate degree from the Ateneo de Manila University. Her identity and background in the arts, sciences, education, and business has led her to take an interest in curriculum theory, design, and practice. She is an international doctoral student in Boston College. In the future, she aims to support and create models for schools and organizations in the pursuit of community-based curriculum development.

Paul Madden is a Ph.D., a former secondary mathematics, physics, and debate educator and in-service teacher educator in the United States. His teaching and research focus on addressing the philosophical, pedagogical, and political questions related to the different conceptualizations of teaching and learning science, technology, engineering, and mathematics (STEM) for justice. He is a student in Curriculum and Instruction at Boston College's Lynch School of Education in Chestnut Hill, MA, USA.

Christian Asante is involved in an out-of-school science project designed to get students excited about science. Professionally, he is interested in ethnography, research, and policy with respect to education in Africa and the diaspora. His initial training was in ecology and environmental science at the University of Ghana and the University of Saskatchewan in Canada, respectively. He is a Ph.D. student at Boston College, Massachusetts, in the United States.

High School Teachers' Perceptions Regarding Inquiry-Based Science Curriculum in the United States, Georgia, and Israel

Alia Sheety, Marika Kapanadze, and Fadeel Joubran

INTRODUCTION

The question of how to transform high school science education so that it fosters students' engagement and capacity for scientific discovery has captured international attention. While many educational systems have sought to shift the teaching of science towards more student-centred inquiry-based learning approaches, such efforts have met with limited success. This chapter

A. Sheety (✉)
Cabrini University, Radnor, PA, USA

Walden University, Minneapolis, MN, USA

M. Kapanadze
Ilia State University, Tbilisi, Georgia

F. Joubran
Arab Academic College of Education, Haifa, Israel

Oranim Academic College of Education, Kiryat Tiv'on, Israel

© The Author(s) 2018   59
C. Roofe, C. Bezzina (eds.), *Intercultural Studies of Curriculum*, Intercultural Studies in Education,
https://doi.org/10.1007/978-3-319-60897-6_4

explores high school science teachers' perceptions regarding current practices of an inquiry-based science curriculum (IBSC) and teachers' challenges and needs in implementing such a curriculum in three different countries: Georgia (situated on the dividing line between Europe and Asia), Israel (Asia), and the United States (North America). This will make it possible to identify instructional barriers to implementation that might be hampering more widespread adoption of these educational methods.

This qualitative research study presents multiple case studies—one from each country—in order to better understand high school science teachers' perceptions of the IBSC, current practices, challenges, and needs. Teachers are the facilitators and mediators between the written curriculum and their students; thus, their beliefs, interpretations, and perceptions are of utmost importance in understanding how inquiry-based curricula are implemented in each of the countries. The chapter addresses the educational system in each of the above countries so as to provide the necessary context for understanding the research results in light of each country's political, cultural, and economical situation. It also presents a definition of curriculum and a short literature review on the inquiry-based curriculum, particularly as it is implemented in science education. The final section of the chapter presents a comparison of the research study findings from each of the three countries, conclusions, limitations, and suggestions for further research.

THE EDUCATIONAL SYSTEMS IN THE THREE TARGETED COUNTRIES

The Educational System in Georgia

The educational system in Georgia consists of the following categories: kindergarten, (ages 3–5), elementary school (grades 1–6), secondary school (grades 7–9), and upper secondary school (high school) (grades 10–12). Public schools are free of charge at all educational levels (MES). Private schools demand payment of tuition. Some private schools have their own curricula and issue their own certificates, which differ from national ones. Due to recent legislation, students graduating from private schools that issue their own certificates are now eligible to apply for admission to Georgian state universities.

The general educational system aims at developing citizens as free individuals who are equipped with the essential intellectual and physical skills and capacities and nurturing civil awareness based on democratic and liberal values. The general educational system:

promotes national interests and traditions; enables students to preserve and protect the natural environment, as well as make efficient use of technology; develops the students' personal, family and social life and promotes the formation of independent decision-making skills; enables students to continue to develop their abilities and interests throughout their life; promotes general communication skills; fosters among students mutual respect and understanding, tolerance and respect for law. (WDE 2010/2011)

Curriculum and Reforms

Curricular reforms undertaken in science education in 2004 (WDE 2010/2011) emphasized inquiry-based and student-centred approaches (Kapanadze et al. 2010; Slovinsky 2012). Inquiry-based learning was identified as the preferred method suggested for science curricula (The Portal of National Curriculum, NCP). Physics, chemistry, and biology are taught as separate disciplines from the 8th through the 12th grade. All three science subjects are compulsory for all 10th- and 11th-grade high school students. Each subject is allocated between 2 and 3 hours per week (NCP). By the end of the 11th or 12th grade, all students must pass a computer-adaptive test (CAT) in all three science subjects in order to obtain a high school certificate (NAEC).

Location of the Research Study

Interviews were conducted in Georgia's capital city, Tbilisi, which contains a total of 267 schools, of which 55% are public and 45% private. Georgian is the primary teaching language. Only 11% of the public schools teach in Russian, Armenian, or Azerbaijanian. Less than 3% of the private schools teach using foreign languages (mostly English) or have an English department. Interviews were conducted only at Georgian-speaking schools—two of them were carried out with public school teachers, while teachers from one private school were interviewed.

The Educational System in Israel

The educational system in Israel consists of the following categories: kindergarten (ages 3–6), elementary school (grades 1–6), secondary school (grades 7–9), and upper secondary school (high school) (grades 10–12). According to the Ministry of Education's website, primary and secondary education in Israel are divided into four distinct and separate school systems—secular Jewish, religious Jewish, Arab, and ultra-orthodox. In Israel 80% of the schools are public schools operated by local authorities or the Israeli government. Public schools are free of charge for all educational levels. The remainder (20%) are private schools. In most of the private schools, parents are required to pay for their children's education. Five international schools follow the curricular and certification standards of their designated countries (the United States, France, and England). They are not required to follow Israeli national standards.

Israel's educational system aims at providing well-prepared graduates capable of succeeding in a rapidly changing global village, actively and meaningfully participating in the labour force, and contributing to Israel's economy. Graduates are meant to forge an Israeli society based on love of one's fellows, unity and mutual responsibility, social justice, building up and defending the Israeli homeland, charity-giving, and peace. For the past 4 years, the Ministry of Education has been guided by a strategic plan from which quantifiable and measurable objectives may be derived, and that sets clear goals for the ministry as a whole. Among these goals are: intensifying educating towards values, improving pupils' attainment levels, achieving an optimal school climate, reducing scholastic disparities, raising teaching quality and enhancing teachers' status in society, strengthening vocational education, and adapting the educational system to twenty-first-century requirements (MED(a) 2013).

Curriculum and Reforms

High schools in Israel prepare students for Israeli matriculation exams (named "Bagrut"). These exams cover various academic disciplines, which are studied in units of one to five on an ascending scale of difficulty. In order to graduate from high school, students must complete at least 21 units. Each unit is equal to a total of one weekly hour over 3 years (from 10th to 12th grade).

In September 2014, a new reform was implemented in the educational system in Israel entitled "Israel advances one stage" that involves several changes regarding teaching, learning, and evaluation. The main change is designated as "meaningful learning" MED(b). It is characterized by being active, constructive, and authentic and involving cooperative learning. Thirty percent of the final grades for the various disciplines is assessed by teachers, whereas the remaining 70% is obtained through national matriculation exams.

As a result of this reform, the science curriculum (for physics, chemistry, and biology) has been modified and inquiry-based learning has become the primary recommended method.

Location of the Research Study

Interviews were conducted in the city of Haifa, which contains a total of 131 schools, 61% of which are public and 39% private. Thirteen percent of the 131 schools serve Arab students where Arabic is the primary teaching language and 87% are Jewish schools where Hebrew is the primary teaching language. There are no international schools in Haifa. Interviews were conducted with teachers from five schools—three public (two Jewish, one Arab) and two private (Jewish).

The Educational System in the United States

Although moving towards centralization in the past few years, the educational system in the United States is mostly run by each of the states independently. There is no national curriculum, but there are recommended standards and national tests. In this study, data were collected in the city of Philadelphia, located in the Commonwealth of Pennsylvania.

The Educational System in the Commonwealth of Pennsylvania

Pennsylvania's educational system consists of the following categories: kindergarten (ages 5–6), elementary school (grades 1–5), middle school (grades 6–8), and high school (grades 9–12). There are three main types of K-12 schools: public, independent public charter, and private. The public schools adhere to district policies and regulations (including the district curriculum) and are tuition-free. While independent public charter schools have more autonomy, they are still expected to adhere to many of the school district's regulations. Private schools are autonomously developed and may create their own curriculum, as long as they adhere to Pennsylvania Department of Education requirements for high school graduates. In the past few years, K-12 public and private schools have emerged (PDE).

The mission of the United States Department of Education (USDE) is "to promote student achievement and preparation for global competitiveness by fostering educational excellence and ensuring equal access" (USDE). The mission statement of the Pennsylvania Department of

Education reads: "to academically prepare children and adults to succeed as productive citizens. The department seeks to ensure that the technical support, resources and opportunities are in place for all students, whether children or adults, to receive a high quality education" (PDE).

Curriculum and Reforms

No national science curriculum exists in the United States. The 1996 National Science Education Standards (NSES) initiative focused strongly on inquiry and stated that students must (1) know that inquiry is the major process used by scientists and (2) be given the opportunity to engage in inquiry (NRC, 1996). Although earlier National Science Education Standards were not unique in endorsing such a view, the prominence they gave it renewed the discourse regarding inquiry (Shope and McComas 2015). A recent initiative entitled "The Next Generation Science Standards" (NGSS) developed new K-12 science standards to provide the opportunity to improve science education and students' achievements. The NGSS recommended that states develop their own science curriculum in accordance with the standards. According to the NGSS website, the goal for developing the NGSS was "to create a set of research-based, up-to-date K-12 science standards. These standards give local educators the flexibility to design classroom learning experiences that stimulate students' interests in science and prepares them for college, careers, and citizenship" (NGSS).

High school graduation requirements in the Commonwealth of Pennsylvania include the completion of 120 hours of instruction in 21 credit units from grades 9 through 12. Students are required to take three credits in science consisting of 120 clock hours per year. Currently, Pennsylvania has revised its high school diploma requirements, and the state is in process of implementing a new set of benchmarks for graduates that will go into effect in 2017. The revised requirements do not reflect direct changes in the number of science education hours, but do stipulate a state biology exam.

Location of the Research Study

Interviews were conducted in Philadelphia. The School District of Philadelphia (SDP) is the eighth largest school district in the United States according to enrolment. The School District serves a racially and ethnically diverse community. Of the 218 schools enrolling a total of 134,538 students, the majority (51%) are Black Americans. Forty-three percent are public schools, 41% are private, and 16% are independent public charter schools. Although English is the official language used in all schools, due to the large diversity among learners, many receive support with English since it is their second or even third language. The Philadelphia school district website provides all necessary information and presents official forms in several languages, a strong indication of the diverse population served by its schools.

Interviews for the study were conducted with teachers from three public schools, two private schools, and one public independent charter school.

LITERATURE REVIEW

Curriculum

In order to study the IBSC, it is first necessary to define the term "curriculum". Traditionally, Tyler (1957) defines curriculum as "all the learning experiences planned and directed by the school to attain its educational goals" (p. 79). On the practical side, Ebert et al. (2013) define curriculum as "the means and materials with which students will interact for the purpose of achieving identified educational outcomes". Furthermore, they state that "the curriculum is only that part of the plan that *directly affects* students. Anything in the plan that does not reach the students constitutes an educational wish but not a curriculum" (p. 2). Determining what students learn might sound straightforward; still, it could be viewed from several aspects, such as content, skills, books, dispositions, and habits (ASCD 2016). Lalor (2016) recommends that in order to clarify what students learn, we need to review various layers of the curriculum, such as suggested by Martin-Kniep (1999):

- the formal curriculum that describes what students need to know, are able to do, and value;
- the operational curriculum which translates the formal curriculum into a plan for instruction;
- the taught curriculum, or what is delivered in the classroom;
- the assessed curriculum, or what is evaluated through formal measures; and
- the learned curriculum, or what students walk away understanding as a result of their learning experiences (Lalor 2016).

During the past few years, with the integration of technology into education, various trends are shaping the curriculum. For example, the idea of K-12 education being tailored to students' own interests is becoming more widespread. This has led to developing various inquiry-based activities in which the learner is placed at the centre of the learning process. More important are changes in the manner in which curriculum and learning are viewed. Instead of learning *from* others, that is, teachers, we learn *with* others, that is, peers, leveraging collective wisdom and allowing students to be held accountable for their learning. With knowledge available at their fingertips, twenty-first-century learners need not only the ability to understand knowledge, but the ability to apply critical thinking when consuming knowledge in order to co-create and produce new knowledge (Miller 2016; Trilling and Fadel 2009).

The Inquiry-Based Curriculum

There has been an ongoing effort over the past 30 years to effect a transition in the curriculum from the more traditional view of a content- or teacher-centred approach to a more modern student-centred one. Already in the early 1900s, Dewey (1916) suggested that we learn better by doing. Freire (1970) went a step further and urged teachers to shift from what he called "banking" strategies, where students are passive learners and teachers own the knowledge and deposit it into students' minds, to creating learning experiences and opportunities that engage students as active learners. With the shift towards the student-centred curriculum (Cullen et al. 2012; Doyle 2011; Jones 2007; Weimer 2002), students engage in experiential learning through instructional strategies that include problem-based, project-based, and inquiry-based learning.

Common characteristics of such active learning strategies include less student attention to teacher instruction and more space for students to experience and take an active role in the learning process. Such approaches are constructivist, enabling students to assume greater ownership of learning and to collaborate with others in order to scaffold it.

What, then, is the inquiry-based curriculum (IBC)? According to Anderson (2002), it enables students to develop knowledge and understanding by going through a scientific process of inquiry. This process includes hypothesizing, measuring, and manipulating variables so as to create new or better understand existing knowledge. Day et al. (2004) posit an interactive model of inquiry in which students go through a process of asking, investigating, creating, discussing, and reflecting. Sheety and Rademacher (2015) modify the model (ibid.) by adding reflection to each of the stages of the process (Fig. 1) in order to allow intentional, metacognitive development of higher-order thinking.

The transition to IBC requires a shift in the role of teachers, learners, and textbooks. As Blessinger and Carfora (2015) note, "...with the movement to IBC comes the development of a new mindset about the purpose and nature of teaching and learning" (p. 6). In other words, adopting IBC goes far beyond redesigning a curriculum. It involves adopting a different mindset and attitude regarding the roles of those involved in the learning process (teacher, student, curriculum). It is driven by asking questions and sparking curiosity. Most importantly, it is process-oriented versus the traditional view of performance outcome/orientation. Students learn from the process of inquiry, not only from the outcomes of the topics that they researched.

The Inquiry-Based Science Curriculum

Current science education reforms are emphasizing the importance of inquiry experiences for young learners. This means that teachers must be equipped with the knowledge, skills, and mindset required to mentor their students through authentic investigations (Windschitl 2003). According

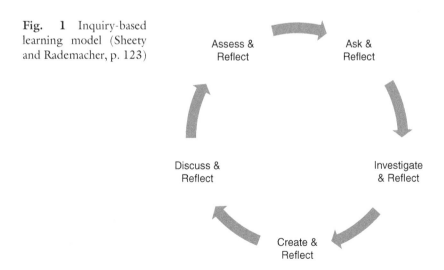

Fig. 1 Inquiry-based learning model (Sheety and Rademacher, p. 123)

Assess & Reflect

Ask & Reflect

Discuss & Reflect

Investigate & Reflect

Create & Reflect

to Shope and McComas (2015), it has been proposed that science curriculum-guided inquiry can help science instructors fulfil two functions: supplying learners with information and, more importantly, helping learners shape and reshape personal understanding. Therefore, it is hoped that by engaging students in inquiry- and research-based processes, they will become active learners constructing their own knowledge. Through inquiry, scientists gather information and propose hypothetical predictions, descriptions, and explanations, all the while accessing and building on their prior experiences and understanding (Shope and McComas 2015). IBSC emphasizes knowledge construction and encourages students to learn science through doing rather than by memorizing facts and theories. It also aims at motivating students to try to discover a solution to an actual problem, the resolution of which demands of them to apply the ideas they have learned (Edelson 2001; Singer et al. 2000). Opportunities to engage students in inquiry should improve science achievement while also improving attitudes towards science. Such improved science achievement and attitudes might ultimately result in increased representation in science careers (Kanter and Konstantopoulos 2010).

METHODOLOGY

Research Questions

To be able to better understand not only what exists in the curriculum but also how it is perceived and implemented by teachers and if they need any support with implementing inquiry-based science curricula, three research questions were posed:

1. How do high school teachers perceive the inquiry-based science curriculum?
2. How do high school teachers implement an inquiry-based science curriculum in their classrooms (current practices)?
3. What support would teachers require in order for them to implement an inquiry-based science curriculum?

Methods

In order to ensure some consistency, the authors of the study interacted on a regular basis using Skype. The online meetings were more frequent at the beginning and towards the end of the study. During those meetings, the authors discussed the best method of addressing the research questions and decided to conduct three case studies, one in each country. The challenge was to ensure consistency concerning the sample and the research process.

Prior to initiating the data collection process, the researchers in the United States and Georgia secured approval of the Internal Review Board (IRB) through their institutions. Once IRB approval was granted, the sample recruitment began. The researcher in Israel did not have IRB in place at the time the data collection started. The three researchers made it clear to the teachers who agreed to take part in the study that they could withdraw from the study at any time and that the data collected would remain confidential. No names or identifying information were used at any point in the study. In addition, all interview transcripts were coded without including any identifying information.

Sample

The study population consisted of a convenience sample of 15 high school science teachers from an urban area in each of the countries included in the study. For consistency, potential participants in the study needed to meet the following criteria: they were currently teaching in an urban high school in at least one discipline: biology, chemistry, and/or physics. The participants were chosen based on availability and willingness to take part in the study. Table 1 provides additional descriptive information about the sample.

The average number of years of teaching experience in Georgia was higher than in Israel or the United States due to the low wage earned

Table 1 General description of the sample

Criteria	Georgia	Israel	United States
Experience			
Average years of teaching	22	15	8.5
	(7–37)	(3–25)	(3–38)
Gender			
Female	100%	60%	67%
Male		40%	33%
Teaching certificate	100%	93%	100%
Teaching as a second career	7%	20%	73%

by teachers, causing the younger generation to choose other professions, such as law or medicine. The same factor could explain the fact that 100% of the teachers in the Georgian sample were female. In the United States, the majority of teachers (73%) have pursued teaching as a second career.

Data Collection

To ensure that the three researchers emphasized the same issues and addressed the research questions from the same perspectives, it was decided to employ a semi-structured interview. The interview questions were developed and discussed thoroughly by the three researchers. The next step was to conduct a small pilot study by interviewing two teachers using the questions. As a result of the pilot, minor changes were made in the order of the interview questions and a few additional follow-up questions were added for clarification. The interviews were conducted in a location convenient for the interviewee. Interviews in each of the countries were transcribed and manually coded by the researchers.

RESULTS

In this section, we present the major findings pertaining to the case studies in the three different countries. The findings are presented according to themes based on responses to the three main research questions. Each of the teachers interviewed was assigned a number to maintain confidentiality. It is important to keep in mind that this is a qualitative study with a small sample with the goal of better understanding the issues from various cultural viewpoints, rather than generalizing from the findings.

Perceptions and Characteristics of Inquiry in the Science Curriculum

Teachers presented different perceptions about the inquiry-based science curricula (IBSC) in all three countries. Our findings indicate that teachers believed the main characteristic of the inquiry-based curriculum to be that students are in the centre of the process and that the learning process supports the development of cognitive skills and scientific literacy. Teachers described students as being more engaged when the learning process was based on inquiry. For example, Teacher 4 from Israel stated: "IBSC teaches the student a lot of skills: hypothesizing, planning, arguing, problem solving". American teachers echoed the same idea. Teacher 4 from Georgia claimed that "I like this document [curriculum]. For me, what is given in the curriculum is very important; Modern teaching methods – I have to use them during my classes. Students have no interest in lecture-type lessons any more...". Teacher 14 from the United States also commented that "with inquiry it's got to be a lot more student-driven, your lessons and demonstrations should be more geared toward arousing the natural curiosity of the student".

Some of the science teachers in Philadelphia, Pennsylvania (the USA), defined inquiry as a guided discovery method that involved higher-level thinking. Teacher 3 from Philadelphia, for example, defined inquiry as "... where you give the students a goal hoping that they will find the actual way in a structural guided way. But you don't want to give them the answers. You want them to list the answers on their own as they go through the process of scientific inquiry". In Georgia and in Israel, teachers had different views and definitions of inquiry, mostly connected with laboratory work: "I don't understand how anyone can implement IBSC outside the school lab. I think that IBSC must include experiments" (Teacher 15, Israel). Another teacher noted, "I understand inquiry as laboratory work" (Teacher 5, Georgia). One of the teachers in Israel said: "In my opinion, a guided experiment is not IBSC, it is like preparing a cake in the kitchen with a recipe" (Teacher 2, Israel).

Most of the teachers in Israel and in Georgia liked their national curricula and expressed their satisfaction with the document. "For me, the curriculum is my supervisor and my compass" (Teacher 2, Israel). "The objectives are presented very clearly and for me it is very easy to work with this curriculum" (Teacher 2, Georgia). Teachers in Pennsylvania provided various responses; some appreciated the curriculum in that "we currently have a very detailed curriculum, both electronic and hard copies in all five science disciplines, biology, chemistry, physics, physical science, and environmental science, including standards, content, teaching strategies, worksheets, PowerPoint presentation, quizzes, test banks, videos and planning schedule time-line" (Teacher 5, Philadelphia, the USA). Others, especially biology teachers, thought that the curriculum did not provide much freedom for teachers: "...there was a time where I would be told you need to teach x. y. & z. It was up to me to write the curriculum. This is not possible anymore. You don't get a chance and time to be creative" (Teacher 4, Philadelphia, the USA). Private school teachers in the United States do not follow the district curricula and the teachers have to develop their own. Those teachers seem to enjoy the freedom to develop and control their own curriculum. A private school teacher included in the study commented, "I feel trusted, I have much more autonomy over the curriculum" (Teacher 6, Philadelphia, the USA). Another stated: "We structure our curriculum and we put a lot of thought into developing it. There is a lot of discussion about it. I do look at the state standards to inform my curriculum, even though I'm not required to do so. I am constantly changing and improving it" (Teacher 9, Philadelphia, the USA).

Some of the teachers from Israel and Georgia claimed that science curricula need improvement. In some cases, the teachers require more clarification about how to conduct the inquiry or how to teach gifted students. One teacher explained, "There are given objectives in curricula. There is one direction – inquiry, but it needs more clarification – how the students should develop inquiry skills isn't presented clearly in this document" (Teacher 14, Georgia). A teacher from Israel indicated that "the curriculum is good for the average student, but it's not suitable for gifted ones" (Teacher 7, Israel). In Philadelphia, four of the public school teachers (1, 3, 4, and 5) estimated that 30–35% of the science curriculum is inquiry-based. But all of them also emphasized that this does not mean that teachers implement aspects of inquiry in their classrooms.

There was a gap among teachers' opinions about the physics curricula. The Georgian teachers did not speak favourably about it; they thought that the contents of physics curricula and those of other science subjects were overloaded, so it was impossible to cover all the material during the lessons. They did not see links between the subjects. Georgian Teacher 6 observed "the content of the physics curricula is mathematically based. In Soviet times we learned major concepts in mathematics, and applied them later to physics. Now I have to explain all the concepts during my lessons. I don't have enough time for that" (Teacher 6, Georgia). Interestingly, physics teachers in the United States also complained about the relationship between math and physics: "Two years ago I had to teach trigonometry before I could teach physics. I had to alter the curriculum to make students see the math through physics instead of seeing physics through math" (Teacher 1, Philadelphia, the USA). Fortunately, physics is not a state-tested subject in Pennsylvania, so teachers feel more autonomy in deciding on content and pace. "The district provides a detailed curriculum. I don't use that. I'm never able to get as far as the curriculum timeline.

I prepare my students for college so I teach forces and motion which is easy to do with labs; once I get to electricity, I don't have equipment" explained Teacher 1, Philadelphia, the United States. Unlike Georgian and American physics teachers, Israeli teachers liked their physics curriculum and its content: "The content in the physics curriculum gives the student a very strong base in mechanics and electricity. Therefore, it adequately prepares them for higher education in the fields of engineering and science" (Teacher 13, Israel).

The majority of biology teachers in Philadelphia expressed dissatisfaction with the biology curriculum for being overloaded with material and very restrictive. Teachers find it hard to align their teaching practices with the timetable listed in the curriculum. They always feel that they are falling behind in preparing students for the state test, named "Keystone". This is a situation that teachers in private schools in the state do not need to face, at least not yet.

Most of the American teachers discussed student inquiry and engagement. Such a learning process raised students' curiosity and interest. One of the interviewed teachers claimed: "I try to have a mix of different things. I do try to give the students plenty of opportunities to practice and take things into their hands. Students work independently, in groups, conduct many small labs" (Teacher 6, Philadelphia, the USA). Another teacher said, "It is more student-centred, much hands-on activities, problem-solving and project-based learning where students are engaged in the learning process" (Teacher 8, Philadelphia, the USA). Georgian and Israeli teachers did not discuss students' engagement during their interviews.

Current Practices and Implementations of Inquiry-Based Science Curricula

The teachers interviewed in Georgia, Israel, and the United States all employ various methods of teaching, even if it is not inquiry-based. Varying teaching methods makes the learning process more interesting for students. Responding to the question concerning implementation of inquiry, teachers from the three countries claimed that they incorporate lab work, discussions, lecture demonstrations, questions and answer sessions, and projects. Teacher 4 from Israel expressed this feeling: "When I see my students 'live' the project, I feel happy and forget about all the difficulties" (Teacher 4, Israel).

In Israel and the United States, students review and work with papers published in scientific journals. The teachers interviewed in Georgia did not mention this option, since there are no scientific journals in the Georgian language.

As an example of inquiry, the teachers interviewed in all of the countries characterized the way they carried out experimental work. First, they presented the content to the class and afterwards they studied it through an experiment. One of the teachers in Georgia stated:

> To understand better what acceleration means, I did this experiment with my students. First, they studied all the equations of the movement. Afterwards, students prepared the equipment for acceleration measurement by themselves with a protractor and a ball hanging from a thread. One of the students' fathers helped us by driving his car and allowing students and myself, [the teacher] to conduct measurements. Of course, they couldn't get exact results from the calculations, but almost all of the students understood what acceleration is. (Teacher 6, Georgia)

The same notion was expressed in the United States "When teaching rotation and motion you really need that inquiry phase to help students engage and process the information. Otherwise they will forget about it soon after we complete the unit" (Teacher 14, Philadelphia, the USA).

During their interviews, American teachers stressed the importance of hands-on activities and open inquiry: "When you give the students a goal or a question, you do not want to give them the answer with the hope that they will figure out the process and provide the answer on their own" (Teacher 4, Philadelphia, the USA). This issue was not mentioned by the Georgian and Israeli teachers.

Assessment was raised as an issue in all three countries. Teachers in Georgia and Israel stressed the importance of assessment in inquiry-based learning. Georgian teachers viewed assessment as the most difficult part of the inquiry process, for which they mostly used formative assessment. Israeli teachers used a combination of formative and summative assessment tools. In the United States, the issue of assessment was raised with different perspectives. One was that it was more challenging to assess inquiry-based learning since it was more about the process rather than the outcome. The second issue that a few teachers raised was the challenge resulting from assessing inquiry-based learning. For example, three of the teachers who taught in private high schools in Pennsylvania stressed the importance of teaching students to learn from their failures, especially in science. One teacher commented, "It is a challenge when you have competitive students and parents who want high grades" (Teacher 3, Philadelphia, the USA). Another teacher indicated the challenge of preparing a grading rubric for formal assessment of inquiry-based learning. Several examples provided by teachers in Pennsylvania about how they assessed inquiry involved asking students to reflect on what they had done by starting the next class with a question related to the inquiry activity that students had completed in the previous lesson (Teachers 3, 5, 6, 7, and 12, Philadelphia, the USA).

Georgian and Israeli teachers had a different understanding concerning indicators of proper assessment of student inquiry skills. Georgian teachers stressed students' performance of inquiry skills, but Israeli teachers emphasized assessment tools. It was noted that "if the students are able to discuss the ideas on their own and reach decisions without my help; if the students are able to observe, classify, assess, analyse and model; if the students have developed the skills to reach a final decision, then I know that learning has taken place" (Teachers 8, 14, and 15, Georgia). Similarly, "For me, interviewing is the best assessment tool, but you should be a good interviewer. There is no one tool that can be considered the best for IBL assessment; it is integration between formative assessment and interview or any other integration" (Teachers 4 and 12, Israel).

Challenges and Support Implementing an IBSC

To be able to share the support required by teachers in order to implement an inquiry curriculum, we asked teachers to enumerate the challenges they face in implementing IBSC or obstacles that prevent them from implementing IBSC.

Science teachers in Georgia, Israel, and the United States described many challenges impacting the implementation of an IBSC. All interviewed teachers, regardless of country or school type (public or private), stressed that time is a big challenge during implementation of such a curriculum. A Georgian teacher said, "Sometimes my students are conducting the inquiry, but afterwards we have no time to discuss their results; I try to write down those questions and discuss them during the next lessons, but the motivation isn't the same; or we don't even have time in the next lesson" (Teacher 2, Georgia). Again it was "time and time and time. Even without IBL we don't have enough time to prepare for the 'Bagrut' exam" (Teacher 15, Israel). The lack of time is the reason why some of the teachers seldom use inquiry. Furthermore, "sometimes we start with the questions during the lessons, but as we don't have enough time, we continue work on it in the clubs [after-school activities]" (Teacher 1, Georgia). All teachers discussed time in relationship to the official state final exams. Time is spent preparing students for the exams; this leaves little time for implementing inquiry. In Georgia and Israel, teachers of all three subjects complained about this issue. In the United States, only biology teachers mentioned this as a problem, because biology is the only science subject that students are tested on by the state.

American teachers raised other challenges related to time, which involved preparation time and bilingual classes. Teachers 13 and 14 teach in a school where Spanish is the native language of more than 50% of the students. The teachers conduct classes in both Spanish and English, which requires additional time.

All teachers interviewed in these countries mentioned class size. An Israeli teacher said, "I can't implement IBSC for 30 students, not even for 20 students. It demands huge amounts of time to follow and assess them" (Teacher 2, Israel). Likewise, "I'd like to acquire knowledge about how to conduct inquiry with 30–35 students" (Teacher 14, Georgia). Regarding smaller classes, "If we have small groups of students, then we should get better quality" (Teacher 4, Georgia). In the United States, the class size also arose as a safety issue: "The Science Teachers' Association states the safe number of students in the lab to be 16 to one. I have 30 students, with no lab assistant" (Teacher 2, Philadelphia, the USA).

Two main issues raised fell under the heading of budget and equipment. The first was the lack of lab personnel to support science teachers in preparing and implementing inquiry activities. Both the Georgian and American teachers stressed the importance of the assistant during the lessons. Israeli teachers did not complain about this, since there are official positions there for lab technicians. Interviewees recalled: "I need an assistant to help me prepare for the experiments. Some students need practical help, some students need support during the experiments, and I am alone with 35 students" (Teacher 3, Georgia). And "[we have] no lab person in our school and we need to do everything by ourselves, set up the lab, clean, etc." (Teacher 2, Philadelphia, the USA). Other teachers echoed the notion and some claimed that they engaged students in the preparation and cleaning-up process any time they had a lab experiment.

The Georgian and American science teachers also discussed the importance of equipment for inquiry-based learning. In some Georgian and US schools, they either did not have equipment or what they did have was very outdated and unsuited for use during the lessons. Teachers in public and charter schools in the United States stated that they bought materials privately, enabling them to conduct inquiry activities: "Every time I see candles on sale, I buy a few. I bought glasses a few years ago and I still use them. I had to buy all the needed materials out of my own pocket if I wanted to implement inquiry when teaching gas loss" (Teacher 3, Philadelphia, the USA). The situation with equipment is much better in Israel.

Georgian teachers generally stressed collaboration among science teachers in conducting integrated lessons. American teachers discussed both collaboration among high school science teachers and colleges in the area and collaboration among more inexperienced teachers in IBL, or support in content knowledge from the better teachers. "I was lucky the teachers I worked with were phenomenal and it really prepared me to be able to conduct inquiry. I think what you need is an exemplar, somebody who does it well and who is willing to talk with you about it" (Teacher 10, Philadelphia, the USA). "To collaborate with colleagues is very pleasant for me. For example, if I teach the topic 'proteins', I prepare the lesson together with the chemistry teacher. We exchange our ideas and experiences. Or we studied some ecological topics and performed water analysis from the Mtkvari River with the chemistry teacher" (Teacher 3, Georgia). In addition, American teachers emphasized collaboration with higher education and pharmaceutical companies.

Teachers from Georgia and Israel stressed the importance of professional development (PD) in the field of IBS education. They expressed the same sentiment: "We need professional development courses in IBSE" (Teacher 8, Georgia). In the United States, teachers stressed the need for support in providing communal preparation time for science teachers so that they could collaborate in developing inquiry activities for their science classes. The reason American teachers did not stress the need for PD courses could be that they were required to take a specific number of such courses in order to maintain their science discipline teaching certificate. One teacher pointed out the lack of connection between taking a PD course and implementation in classroom and preferred having a learning community within her school:

> The Philadelphia school district actually had an inquiry-based PD because we had a grant for inquiry-based science and history. I believe that all you need is an exemplar, someone who's implemented inquiry and who could inspire and work with you. I prefer the support of my colleagues over having a PD, I love it when the coordinator comes to my classroom and then provides ideas of how I could have done things differently. (Teacher 1, Philadelphia, the USA)

There is no lack of PD offerings in the United States, since Philadelphia hosts many higher education institutions who offer Science PDs that could be of benefit to teachers. Teachers 5, 6, 7, 10, 12, 13, and 15 in Philadelphia agreed upon the need to create an in-school learning community to enable teachers to support one another.

Preparing the environment is essential, or as Teacher 5 from Philadelphia, the United States, put it, "groundwork needs to be laid in order for inquiry-based learning to be successful" (Teacher 5, Philadelphia, the USA). The stakeholders involved in the learning need to be prepared for the shift in teaching, learning, assessment and the roles of those involved in it. "Students are used to being told something and then giving it back as an answer. It is important that students know that it is okay to be creative and come up with interesting and unusual answers, that it is okay to be wrong and reflect on this, and that it is okay to think outside the box" (Teacher 5, Philadelphia, the USA). Another challenge related to students' absences was raised mostly by public school teachers in Philadelphia. This creates inconsistency for teachers and makes it more challenging to make up an inquiry class.

Georgian teachers were the only ones who discussed the issue of teachers' salary in their country. Some of them have little motivation to stay at school after the lessons or to work at home, as their salaries are very low. One teacher said, "Teachers can find time to prepare some experiments for the lesson, but we also need support from the Georgian government; our salaries are very low. I have never included inquiry in my teaching practice" (Teacher 12, Georgia).

All teachers interviewed from Georgia, Israel, and the United States emphasized that support from the administration is crucial for the implementation of inquiry-based curricula.

DISCUSSION

Similarities and differences among the three countries were found in the three aspects that were studied: perception, implementation, and challenges and support. However, there were also differences, even within the same country. For example, in Pennsylvania, the United States, differences were noted among teachers who were required to prepare for a state exam (biology) and those who were not (physics and chemistry). Differences were also apparent among teachers who worked in private school and public and charter schools, especially with regard to budget and support issues. In Georgia some of the interviewed teachers have not engaged in inquiry-based teaching because they do not know how to implement it. Not all participant teachers use curricula during their lesson planning. Some use a teacher's guide and consider it more helpful than the curriculum. In Israel, some teachers engage in inquiry-based teaching, despite the difficulties; others have never engaged in inquiry-based teaching because it is not required and they do not perceive that they are well-prepared to implement it. Different opinions were expressed regarding the types of experiments that reflect inquiry-based learning. Some teachers claim that guided experimentation *does not constitute* inquiry-based learning, but open experimentation *does*. For others, every experiment can reflect some components of inquiry-based learning.

The political-cultural situation of each of the countries provided an important context for the issues raised in them. For example, the low salaries in Georgia, the transition from a communist country to an independent one, and the need to restructure and improve the educational system may have contributed to perspectives expressed by teachers there. The lack of science research articles available in the Georgian language eliminates the possibility of using these as sources for teaching science literacy. In the United States (Pennsylvania), significant ethnic diversity raised issues such as how to teach inquiry in a classroom comprised largely of students for whom English is a second language. The economic situation is also well reflected in the public school system in Philadelphia (the USA) as a result of the 2008 economic crisis. Having a majority of teachers who practice teaching as their second career supports a culture of collaboration with outside agencies such as higher education and industry and allows teachers to feel more comfortable when implementing inquiry.

A key difference that could have an effect on students' learning and teachers' planning of science classes is the minimum of science studies required in order to graduate from high school. The main assumption in Georgia is that each student must learn each of the science subjects throughout his/her high school years. In Israel, according to the most recent reform, the minimum requirement is that each student learns at least one science subject for 3 hours per week in the 10th grade. The assumption in Pennsylvania is that each student should graduate from high school having completed a total of at least five weekly hours of science each year for 3 years, with the option of choosing from various approved scientific disciplines.

CONCLUSIONS

This study aimed at better understanding how IBSC is perceived by high school science teachers in three different countries, especially given the increased international interest in innovations in the science curriculum. It emerges clearly from our study that science teachers are aware that IBL supports the development of cognitive skills and scientific thinking. We believe that there is a gap between teachers' desire and capacity to effectively implement IBSC. Common barriers to implementation cited among teachers from the three countries included insufficient time, the pressure of official exams, and overly large classes. Other country-specific reasons included low salaries, a lack of materials in the Georgian language, or highly diverse classrooms in the United States, where teachers must accommodate students whose second or third language is English. In order to effect changes in the curriculum and create more opportunities to implement IBSC, it is our opinion that all obstacles preventing teachers from effectively implementing IBSC should be taken into consideration. Potential interventions could include the professional development of IBL assessment tools.

Further research on this topic is needed, including an in-depth comparison of the actual curricula in each of the countries, a comparison of teachers' preparation, studying each science discipline separately in order to better understand the effect of the specific science discipline's content on how teachers perceive inquiry, and finally designing a quantitative or mixed-method study so as to allow the incorporation of a larger sample.

REFERENCES

Anderson, R. D. (2002). Reforming science teaching: What research says about inquiry? *Journal of Science Teacher Education, 13*(1), 1–12.
ASCD. (2016). Association for Supervision and Curriculum Development. http://www.ascd.org/Default.asp

Blessinger, P., & Carfora, J. (2015). Innovative approaches in teaching and learning: An introduction to inquiry-based learning for multidisciplinary programs. In P. Blessinger & J. Carfora (Eds.), *Inquiry-based learning for multidisciplinary programs* (1st ed., pp. 3–22). Bingley: Emerald Group Publishing.

Cullen, R., Harris, M., & Hill, R. (2012). *The learner-centered curriculum*. San Francisco: Jossey-Bass.

Day, J., Foley, L., Groeneweg, R., & Mast, C. (2004). *Enhancing the classroom learning experience with web lecture*. Georgia Institute of Technology, GVU Technical Report, pp. 1–11.

Dewey, J. (1916). *Democracy and education*. New York: Macmillan.

Doyle, T. (2011). *Learner centered teaching, putting the research on learning into practice*. Sterling: Stylus Publishing, LLC.

Ebert, E. S., II, Ebert, C., & Bentley, M. L. (2013). *The educator's field guide*. Thousand Oaks: Corwin.

Edelson, D. C. (2001). Learning-for-use: A framework for the design of technology-supported inquiry activities. *Journal of Research in Science Teaching, 38*(3), 355–385.

Freire, P. (1970). *The pedagogy of the oppressed*. New York: The Continuum Publishing Company.

Jones, L. (2007). *The student centered classroom*. New York: Cambridge University Press.

Kanter, D. E., & Konstantopoulos, S. (2010). *The impact of a project-based science curriculum on minority student achievement, attitudes, and careers: The effects of teacher content and pedagogical content knowledge and inquiry-based practices*. Retrieved November 20, 2016, from http://onlinelibrary.wiley.com/doi/10.1002/sce.20391/full

Kapanadze, M., Janashia, S., & Eilks, I. (2010). From science education in the soviet time, via national reform initiatives, towards an international network to support inquiry-based science education – The case of Georgia and the project SALiS. In I. Eilks & B. Ralle (Eds.), *Contemporary science education* (pp. 237–242). Aachen: Shaker.

Lalor, A. (2016). *Ensuring high-quality curriculum: How to design, revise, or adopt curriculum aligned to student success*. Published by The Association for Supervision & Curriculum (ASCD).

Martin-Kniep, G. (1999). *Capturing the wisdom of practice: Professional portfolio for educators*. Published by The Association for Supervision & Curriculum (ASCD) Development.

MED(a) – Ministry of Education of Israel. (2013). Retrieved November 20, 2016, from http://meyda.education.gov.il/files/minhalcalcala/facts.pdf

MED(b) – Ministry of Education of Israel. Retrieved November 20, 2016., from http://cms.education.gov.il/EducationCMS/Units/LemidaMashmautit/mashmautit/HagdaraMashmautit.htm

MES – Ministry of Education and Science of Georgia. Retrieved November 16, 2016., from http://www.mes.gov.ge/?lang=eng

Miller, S. (2016). Implementations of the 4Cs of 21st century learning skills within the blended coaching model. A doctoral dissertation completed at Brandon University. ProQuest Dissertations Publishing. 10119299.

National Research Council (NRC). (1996). *National science edcuation standards 1996*. Washington, DC: National Academy Press. Retrieved from: http://www.nap.edu/catalog/4962.html

NAEC – National Assessment and Examinations Centre. Retrieved September 15, 2016., from http://www.naec.ge/#/en/index

NCP – The Portal of National Curriculum. Retrieved September 15, 2016., from http://ncp.ge/en/home

NGSS – Next Generation Science Standards. Retrieved October 22, 2016., from http://www.nextgenscience.org

NSES – National Science Education Standards. Retrieved October 10, 2016., from http://www.csun.edu/science/ref/curriculum/reforms/nses/

PDE – Pennsylvania Department of Education. http://www.education.pa.gov/Pages/default.aspx#tab-1

SDP – School District of Philadelphia. http://www.philasd.org/about/

Sheety, A., & Rademacher, N. (2015). Inquiry-based learning as foundational pedagogical tool for critical examination of social justice in theory and practice. In P. Blessinger & J. Carfora (Eds.), *Inquiry-based learning for multidisciplinary programs* (1st ed., pp. 119–137). Bingley: Emerald, Pages.

Shope, F., & McComas, W. (2015, October 13). *Modeling scientific inquiry to guide students in the practices of science: The ED3U teaching model of conceptual change in action*. In Inquiry-Based Learning for Science, Technology, Engineering, and Math (STEM) Programs: A Conceptual and Practical Resource for Educators, pp. 217–240. Permanent link to this document: 10.1108/S2055-36412015000004013. Retrieved April 26, 2016, At: 08:16 (PT).

Singer, J., Marx, R. W., Krajcik, J. S., & Chambers, J. C. (2000). Constructing extended inquiry projects: Curriculum materials for science education reform. *Educational Psychologist, 35*(3), 165–178.

Slovinsky, E. (2012, August). *SALiS and educational policy in Georgia*. Proceedings of the student active learning in science final conference, Tbilisi.

Trilling, B., & Fadel, C. (2009). *21st century skills; learning for life in our times*. San Francisco: Jossey-Bass, A Wiley Imprint.

Tyler, R. (1957). *The curriculum then and now*. Proceedings of the 1956 invitational conference on testing problems. Princeton: Educational Testing Service.

USDE – United States Department of Education. *Overview mission*. Retrieved October 16, 2016., from http://www2.ed.gov/about/overview/mission/mission.html

WDE – World Data on Education, VII ED. (2010/2011). Retrieved September 15, 2016., from http://www.ibe.unesco.org/fileadmin/user_upload/ Publications/WDE/2010/pdf-versions/Georgia.pdf
Weimer, M. (2002). *Learner centered teaching.* San Francisco: Jossey-Bass.
Windschitl, M. (2003). Inquiry projects in science teacher education: What can investigative experiences reveal about teacher thinking and eventual classroom practice? *Science Education, 87*(1), 112–143.

Alia Sheety is an associate professor at the Department of Educational Policy and Leadership at Cabrini University, the United States. She holds a PhD in Curriculum and Instruction from Arizona State University. Her research involves studying restorative pedagogy, metacognition, student-centred curricula, inquiry-based learning, professional learning groups, and the transition to online learning. Her primary areas of teaching are critical analysis of research, curriculum development, instruction, and assessment. Sheety is an author of various publications and has presented nationally and internationally on inquiry-based learning, adult learner preferences of learning, metacognition, and the transition to online learning.

Marika Kapanadze is an associate professor in science education. She holds a PhD in physics from the Institute of Protein Research, Pushchino, Moscow. She is engaged in development, implementation, and evaluation of student-centred curricula and new curricular materials in science. Her research interests are teacher professional development, science curriculum development, and investigation of science teachers' attitudes. Kapanadze is the head of Science Education Research Centre SALiS at Ilia State University, Georgia. She develops courses in inquiry-based learning in physics for pre- and in-service teachers. She is an author of methodological books in science education in Georgia and many scientific publications.

Fadeel Joubran received his PhD in physics education from Technion—Israel Institute of Technology in 2012. His thesis title was "Contribution of Haptic Feedback to Learning of Motor-Cognitive Skills in a Virtual Environment". For the last 25 years, he has taught physics in high schools. He began teaching in educational academic colleges since 2007. He is interested in inquiry-based learning, simulation in physics, and argumentation in physics teaching. Joubran is involved in the implementation of ERASMUS+ project ARTIST & Co at Arab College for Education—Haifa.

Music as a Platform for Intercultural Understanding: Early Childhood Curriculum and a Growing Neoliberal Imperative

Aleksandra Acker and Berenice Nyland

INTRODUCTION

In a lecture on social change and intercultural understanding, Professor Bartleet from Griffith University (2016) discussed the role of music:

> For every major social movement, social change and social upheaval throughout history, music has been present, sometimes driving change, other times resisting change, other times documenting and commenting on that change.

Bartleet started researching the role of music as a tool of reconciliation in Australia. She recalls how, as a young child, in apartheid South Africa:

> music was used as a vehicle for protest and self-determination, a way of subversively spreading an anti-colonial agenda, and a way of healing the past but also imagining a different future. (2016)

A. Acker (✉) • B. Nyland
School of Education, RMIT University, Melbourne, Australia

© The Author(s) 2018
C. Roofe, C. Bezzina (eds.), *Intercultural Studies of Curriculum*, Intercultural Studies in Education,
https://doi.org/10.1007/978-3-319-60897-6_5

85

It is not difficult to find the presence of music in most groups in our communities. Human societies have traditions of passing on their stories. Music, especially song, has been a powerful narrative strategy for the sharing of history across generations. Music can be experienced as culture, as language, as emotion, as communication, as performance, as religion, as self-expression and as a discipline in which to gain mastery. Music is linked to well-being (MacDonald et al. 2012) and infant development (Trainor and Heinmuller 1998) and plays an important role in human society and culture. Music transcends global and linguistic barriers to form new communities of consumers (Garfias 2004). This chapter focuses on the early childhood years and describes research that has examined young children's music experiences in education settings as an illustration of the value of music both within and across cultures. The aim is to argue for a child's right to music as part of an education to nurture awareness of self and others in a medium that has universal, cultural, historical, contextual and political importance. For this research children's musical learning has been documented using *Learning Stories* (Carr 2001).

We discuss the role of music in early development, especially in relation to interpersonal and intercultural understanding. Literature on the relationship between a neoliberal educational agenda and the arts is presented. To support the argument that music is intrinsically and extrinsically valuable, empirical data in the form of observations are presented to indicate the wealth of everyday interactions when music becomes a shared experience. The observations have been recorded as *Learning Stories* (Nyland and Ferris 2009), which is a socio-cultural approach to interpreting everyday experiences within a particular social context. Concluding discussion is concerned with the inherent and growing inequalities contained in a neoliberal educational agenda that privileges competition, economic growth, human investment, outcomes and accountability above a more humanitarian approach (Gibson et al. 2015; Sims and Wanganayake 2015). Within this context, the quality of education and the accompanying question of the role of the arts, in this case music, is highlighted.

THE CONTEXT: PRESCHOOL IN THREE COUNTRIES

Human capital theory (Heckman 2011) is one of the strong narratives running through government attitudes towards the importance of preschool education in the three countries featured in this research. In Australia, this has led to a national curriculum (DEEWR 2010), teacher standards and regulations, all aspects of the audited society (May 2002). There is universal access for 4-year-olds and there are a variety of qualifications for educators. Teachers must have a 4-year bachelor degree to be eligible to become a teacher. The national curriculum is non-prescriptive and process oriented. Although there are suggestions for the use of the arts, including music, in the document (DEEWR 2010), there is no necessity to apply these suggestions to programme delivery. There is an emphasis on literacy and numeracy and 'Standard Australian English' (p. 41).

Preschool attendance in Serbia is still relatively low, especially for vulnerable children (UNICEF 2012). As in the other two countries, preschool is seen to have educational and economic benefits and at present the immediate workforce support role is given priority. Investing in preschool is important and the brain research is referred to in terms of advantages, particularly for language development. There is a national curriculum with an emphasis on areas of development and child-centred practices. Given the extended age range, 3–7 years, there is an academic component. Teacher training for early childhood educators consists of 4 years at a university with a significant part of the degree directed towards the arts, including music. Group activities are most common.

China shares the Australian and Serbian interest in the notion of investing in children for improved economic growth and a quality workforce (Zhu 2015). Since the 1978 opening-up of the economy, several reforms have been enacted with implications for curriculum content, quality of staff and management of centres. Early childhood education policy represents a mix of educational perspectives represented by European and American ideas, traditional Chinese approaches and recent historical changes which have brought in an era of reform that is reflected across the globe. China is working towards universal access for 3 years of preschool, a goal achieved in many urban areas. Curriculum guidelines include a focus on child-initiated activity and play and list specific content areas. Teacher training is largely at degree level but many practitioners are not in possession of a first degree. Piano skills are compulsory in many early childhood teaching degrees.

These brief comments on the education systems in the three countries involved with this research indicate differing attitudes to the arts, but all share the global concern about quality control as expressed through documents like curriculum guidelines and teacher standards. Human capital theory and the work of Heckman (2011) are cited in policy documents for all three countries. We have emphasised this commonality as it supports the argument we have expressed about the neoliberal education agenda where arts do not necessarily flourish.

LITERATURE REVIEW

> Music helps children understand other people and their cultures and gives increased opportunities for social and emotional development. Music also provides a means for the aesthetic enrichment and growth of every child. (Bayless and Ramsey 1991, p. vii)

The quote above is taken from a well-known text *Music: A way of life for the young child*. This text is a mainstream representation of the attitude to music in the early childhood field until the twenty-first century. Music was seen as an important part of life, increasingly so in the life of infants (Trevarthen 2008). Music was recognised as part of the range of early childhood activities offered under the label 'expressive activities' and was considered an expression of culture and history that supports development, physical, social, emotional and cognitive. Children had a right to music, and although music is often used for instrumental reasons (Geist et al. 2012), these should not be allowed to be privileged over the enjoyment of music per se (Bayless and Ramsey 1991).

The idea of music being linked to child culture has always been strong. Marsh (2010) explored theories of children's musical knowledge, creativity and oral transmission. Data was drawn from playgrounds in Australia, Norway, the UK, the USA and Korea. Detailed are the children's own musical practices as they share versions of musical play they bring from their own experiences outside the school. The musicality observed of the games children experienced in the outdoor playground was greater than the music Marsh (2010) observed in classrooms. Many of the games Marsh (2010) recorded in the different countries shared provenance. In one Australian setting, the children from many language backgrounds found they had songs and games in common. By sharing their clapping and singing games, the children were able to celebrate their own culture. While many researchers still take a multicultural approach to the cultures children bring with them, Barrett (2003) explored how children construct their own musical meanings in the world they encounter. She used children's popular culture to research questions of musical choice, agency and curriculum decisions.

As well as cultural significance, music has long had a role in issues of social justice (Allsup and Shieh 2012; Benedict et al. 2015). Byrd and Levy (2013) have described how music was actively integrated into their teaching as a method for students to learn about social justice. In early childhood, there are many examples of music being introduced into education settings as deliberate interventions against disadvantage. One example is the Australian project, *The Song Room* (Vaugn et al. 2011), a national not-for-profit organisation that provides music programmes to schools and professional development for teachers and assists in building musical partnerships with families. Research projects have targeted education settings where there is no music agenda, poor performance at national tests, settings that serve high numbers of newly arrived families and isolated indigenous communities. Results from these projects report better grades, higher levels of social/emotional well-being observed through engagement with the curriculum and for the most 'at-risk' group higher rates of attendance.

Music is an important part of early childhood education significant for its role in assisting in cultural sharing and helping children maintain engagement in the social institutions of early childhood, preschools and the early years of primary schools. Against this background, there is an argument that present educational ideology has had a negative influence on the presence of arts in education. This has been manifested through lack of training for generalist teachers (Nyland and Ferris 2007), curriculum documents and testing regimes that privilege literacy and numeracy and growing inequality as the wealthier private education providers, a large and growing group in Australia (Connell 2009), can continue to support the presence of 'luxury' subjects, like music, in their programmes. In Australia, a neoliberal approach to education at all levels is now supported by both major political parties.

Although there is some debate about the term neoliberalism in some disciplines (e.g. Braithewaite 2005) in Australian early childhood education circles, there is acceptance by many scholars that present relationships and practices in early childhood settings are dominated by human capital theory that constructs children as units of investment (Gibson et al. 2015) and therefore the presumption that the role of the educator is that of an investment broker. Sims and Wanganayake (2015) take up this theme in a discussion of early childhood educators and the requirement for compliance in practice. They perceive a process of de-professionalisation and a workforce less able to be reflective of local needs or work collaboratively.

The first national curriculum, *Belonging, Being and Becoming: The Early Years Learning Framework* (EYLF) (DEEWR 2009), is outcome based, and although The Music Council of Australia put in a submission requesting an outcome that included music as having a proven record that it benefits children in 'gaining confidence through music-making and more showing music's contribution to a sense of personal and community identity' (deVries and Letts 2011, p. 5), this was not accepted. The outcomes in the EYLF are 'process' outcomes, meaning the inclusion of music, or many other content areas, to achieve these outcomes is optional. In a climate where international competitiveness has become a measure of educational success for the state (Tucker 2012), an introduction to the arts has disappeared from most early childhood teaching programmes, resulting in the situation that an informed presence of music in many educational settings has become serendipitous.

In the research presented here, we report on three observed music events in three contexts. These are analysed using the method of *Learning Stories* (Carr and Lee 2009) with emphasis on the learning that took place (St John 2016; Vygotsky 1978). We argue that children have a right to experience opportunities for literacies like music. That for many educational settings the fact that music is no longer a part of the curriculum is a sign of growing inequality. The music observations recorded here are examples of the rich learning and social exchange children can share when music is a valued part of the curriculum.

The Research

The research described in this chapter had a focus on young children's musical competence and the potential of music for the child's social and emotional development. The role of music in promoting an awareness of the value of diversity was of specific interest. The approach taken in this research uses a socio-cultural contextual view of children and their learning and assumes that learning occurs on a social level of engagement with others and is appropriated by children as protagonists in their own learning (Vygotsky 1978). Music is viewed as a language. Relationships, context, aesthetics and personal interest are an important foundation for children's learning dispositions which are recorded in a *Learning Story* as: *taking an interest, being involved, expressing an idea or a feeling, persisting with difficulty, taking responsibility* (Carr 2001, p. 149).

The Settings

There are three settings where the observations of music events took place. We have chosen diverse settings deliberately to support the idea that music is a valuable part of childhood and is a language where children can be imaginative, expressive, creative, knowledgeable, share meanings and culture in myriad ways across contexts.

The first observation was recorded in an Australian parent-run child-care centre for children 6 weeks of age to 6 years. It was on the outer edge of a large city and the children attending the centre came from a variety of socio-economic groups, and there was a representation of newly arrived families who did not share the dominant language. The second observation took place in a kindergarten in Belgrade, Serbia. The third centre was a public kindergarten in Beijing and the group observed were the 3-year-old children. These observations were collected across several studies focussing on young children and music. Ethics approval for the observations was gained from the RMIT University (Melbourne, Australia) research committee.

The Participants

The main protagonist in the first observation was a child named Halina (all children have been given pseudonyms). Halina was from Hungary and was finding her way in the Australian setting. The second *Learning Story* is about Kasija and was set in Belgrade. Kasija attends kindergarten and participates in a music group where the children are being introduced to songs in languages from around the world. The third story involves a 3-year-old group who attend a Chinese public kindergarten in Beijing. This was an example of music being used for a different purpose, that is, the learning of English as second language.

Method

Data for this research took the form of direct observation, video recordings and field notes. The observations have been recorded and analysed using a *Learning Story* format (Carr and Lee 2009). Representative observations were chosen for each context/country. In the Australian setting, music or other predictable formats are often found to be successful strategies for the inclusion of children new to the culture and language. In Serbia, the idea of performance is one that is common and children frequently prepare for concerts. In China music, singing especially, is often used for the introduction of concepts and English language programmes focused on songs are popular.

Data Analysis

Learning Stories were used to record and analyse our observations for this research. *Learning Stories*, or *Learning Narratives*, were initially developed for the early childhood context and were designed as a socio-cultural tool to support New Zealand's bicultural/bilingual curriculum framework, Te Whariki (NZMOE 1996). The concept was derived from Bruner's notion of narrative to record and analyse children's emerging stories about their own learning (Bruner 1975).

Learning Stories have three main sections. The first section is the context and the story which may be recorded as a written anecdote, a photographic sequence or even as a transcript of a conversation (see example *Learning Story* template below). The second element is the analysis of the story itself which explores the story and identifies what learning dispositions the protagonists brought to the particular situation. The strength of this approach to analysis is that it is contextual and therefore includes all actors who have participated in the event (Rinaldi 2006). The third element of the *Learning Story* is interpreting the event in relation to the context and the learner's responses, as determined by dispositions displayed, to plan for the future, based on the learning that was visible and the potential for learning. *Learning Stories* often have multiple perspectives as they can include many voices. *Learning Stories* can identify learning situations that promote an environment that is socially supportive and aesthetically stimulating, where children are guided by others and have choice of movement, use of time and appropriate materials. In the following vignettes, children display their ability to actively engage with musical concepts. For this chapter, we have provided a full example for the first *Learning Story* and the other two are truncated. In the truncated *Learning Stories*, the vignette is presented, the learning dispositions are briefly summarised and the findings, 'what learning was visible' section, are described. Finally, we identify the potential behind these situations.

The Learning Stories
The Learning Story Template adopted for this research.

Learning story narrative
Context and observation recorded—here
Learning dispositions
Taking an interest, being involved, persisting with difficulty, expressing an idea or a feeling, taking responsibility
  Taking an interest
  Finding an interest here—a topic, an activity, a role. Recognising the familiar, enjoying the unfamiliar, coping with change
    Being involved
  Paying attention for a sustained period, feeling safe, trusting others. Being playful with others and/or materials
    Persisting with difficulty
  Setting and choosing difficult tasks. Using a range of strategies to solve problems when 'stuck'
    Expressing an idea or a feeling
  In a range of ways, e.g. oral language, gesture, music, art, writing, etc.
    Taking responsibility
  Responding to others, to stories, and imagined events, ensuring that things are fair, self-evaluating, helping others, contributing to programme
Short-term review
  What learning do I think went on here? (main points of 'learning story')
What next?
  How might we encourage this interest/ability/strategy/disposition to be:
  more complex
  appear in different ways

Adapted from Carr (2001, p. 149)

Learning Story 1: Halina in an Australian Centre
Context: Halina was a girl who had recently arrived in Australia with her parents and had been enrolled in a local child care centre. According to her parents, she had a good command of her mother tongue (Polish) but no previous exposure to the English language. Halina was described as a dynamic learner, capable of switching from being an active observer and a discrete non-verbal communicator, to more a vocal, expressive and confident child. She was a sharp-eyed girl, able to utilise visual information, looking at others for non-verbal cues. She laughed when one of the researchers tried to talk to her in Polish. The following observation documents Halina was participating in a music session at the centre on her second day of preschool. She sat near the preschool teacher joining in the

actions. This was her first indication of wanting to be part of the group and showing social initiative in being aware of the parts of the activity she could actively participate in.

The Narrative About Halina

The children were playing a circle game, *Hey, hey, what's your name?* This game involves children suggesting actions and inviting each other to take part, sometimes in pairs and sometimes with the whole group. Halina tried to follow by watching the others but miscued as she did not understand the basic instruction of inviting partners into the game. For example, when two children had a turn to dance, Halina jumped up and joined them, clapping to their movement throughout the chant. When the whole group stood in a circle, clapping to the beat of the chant, Halina hopped in the middle. The children were accepting of Halina's novice status by a friendly tolerance to her misunderstanding of the rules of the game. Realising the conventions of remaining in the circle, Halina moved back. By the end of the session, she was able to use and understand the phrase 'My turn'.

Learning Story analysis (these categories are taken from the template developed by Carr [2001]).

Taking an Interest

Finding an interest here—a topic, an activity, a role. Recognising the familiar, enjoying the unfamiliar, coping with change

There was a shared interest in the form of the music game. Most of the group were familiar with the format of the game and they were tolerant of the one child who was not. Halina engaged in the music and coped with change by showing the confidence to join in and learn the rules by doing so.

Being Involved

Paying attention for a sustained period, feeling safe, trusting others. Being playful with others and/or materials

The involvement of the players suggested all felt safe and the situation was viewed as basically playful and therefore not knowing the rules was not of great import. Halina felt safe and trusting in the group as she joined in with enthusiasm and was not deterred by miscuing more than once.

Persisting with Difficulty

Setting and choosing difficult tasks. Using a range of strategies to solve problems when 'stuck'

The children in the group accepted that Halina was not familiar with the game and were prepared to continue playing, thereby showing her the rules. Halina was eager to join, not daunted by not knowing the rules and the disadvantage she was under in not understanding and being able to communicate in the language. Yet, she persisted with confidence.

Expressing an Idea or a Feeling
In a range of ways, e.g. oral language, gesture, music, art, writing etc.
The children were playing a formulaic game and therefore there was little room for creative self-expression. However, the social environment was positive. The group were accepting of the stranger and the stranger was willing to accept their welcome and become part of the game.

Taking Responsibility
Responding to others, to stories, and to imagined events, ensuring that things are fair, self-evaluating, helping others, contributing to programme
All displayed levels of responsibility. Halina was responsible for her own learning as she became involved but also observed the others closely so her involvement became more accomplished. The children in the group playing the game were exhibiting an ability to be fair and help another by not emphasising Halina's 'mistakes'.

Findings
What learning was visible?
Halina's enthusiasm and the need to be part of the group as well as her strong interest and disposition to engage with the music enabled her to become competent at the music game and gain two words in English because of the contextual nature of the learning activities (Acker 2008) and the social acceptance of the group (Acker 2006). Play situations where actions and responses can be learnt through observation within the context are considered an optimal environment for preschool children to learn languages (Clarke 2009). The children gained another member of the group in a social atmosphere that was inclusive.

In this case the activity that Halina participated in was able to scaffold her understanding of the game template and make her gain two new words in English and the lived experience, and helped her to begin to establish a sense of self and belonging within this group. The group comprised participants who contributed to the experience, and this can lead to a sense of interdependence (Rinaldi 2006) and create an enabling social environment for future musical engagement.

Learning Story 2: Kasija in a Serbian Centre
Context
Kasija's teacher reports that she is a child who enjoys physical activities and takes risks. Kasija's interests include roller-blading, swimming, drawing and singing. She goes to kindergarten 5 days a week and, with her sister and older friends, looks after stray cats and dogs in the neighbourhood. She articulates a love of music and has been observed dancing in a variety of dancing styles. She says 'I feel nice when I listen to music; music creates love. I like playing the guitar ('Air guitar!')'. Her parents believe that she has learnt the dance vocabulary from her older sister and concerts she has been taken to. Kasija's teacher says she joins in the songs, in a variety of languages, that the children have been learning in the kindergarten and she sings reasonably accurately. She makes up her own words to fit melodies that she likes. Kasija is 6 years old, and the children in this programme are used to being taught songs in groups and performing for parents and the local church. They are preparing a concert called 'Travelling around the world'. The inspiration behind this planned concert was a nearby refugee camp of Syrian asylum seekers. The children were aware and anxious about this camp in their midst.

The Narrative About Kasija and Friends
Morning, after breakfast. The children had a music group session where they had been practicing an African (Ghanaian) song which they were preparing for an upcoming music festival. After this session, the children then engaged in spontaneous play in their respective learning centres prepared by their teachers before a trip to a nearby park. Kasija went to the visual arts area, sat down at a table and proceeded to draw a picture on A3 paper while humming a tune—it is clearly recognisable as the African song the children have been preparing as one of the main themes from their concert repertoire. Her friend Kaja approaches, 'Have you seen this?', presenting a book with a face of an African girl with plaits on the cover. The book was the picture story *Handa's Surprise* (Browne 1995). Kasija starts singing the African chant from the concert.

Tue tue, barima tue tue
Tue tue, barima tue tue
Abofra ba ama dawa dawa
Tue tue
Abofra ba ama dawa dawa

Tue tue
Barima tue tue
Barima tue tue
Barima tue tue

Kaja leaves and comes back immediately holding a hand drum that she took from the music corner. Kasija repeats the song while Kaja accompanies her. They repeat the song, and Kasija says, 'now, we've been to Afffffffffffffffffffffffrrrrrrricaaaaaa!' She sounds out the single sounds with most emphasis on the 'f', 'r' and 'a'. Both girls laugh. Kasija starts singing a French song. Kasija takes another piece of paper and starts drawing a parasol for the French girl in the song for when she goes to Africa because 'it is hot there', she explains to Kaja.

Learning Dispositions
There was interest in the songs for the concert as the two children displayed familiarity with melody and words. Kasija spontaneously instigated the engagement and readily accepted her friend's suggestions to extend the activity. There was shared interest, ideas were played with and these children took responsibility for their own learning through self-chosen actions.

Findings
What Learning Was Visible?
This learning situation that provided the foundation for the vignette was a formal one. The information the children received in the formal singing session provided affordances (Needham 2007) and a scaffold (Leont'ev 1994) for the event observed. The children were learning songs for a performance and were practicing so they would know the words and sing accurately. The knowledge of the Ghanaian song was an affordance for these children to play with ideas from their own general knowledge and associations with the content. They associated Africa with drums and heat and liked the word itself as evidenced by Kasija's sound play with the word 'Africa'. The book *Handa's Surprise* is a favourite for early-years classrooms and is considered a valuable resource in teaching about diversity. The presence of the book may have given Kaja an entry into Kasija's activities and it is indicative of the teacher's approach to teaching about different countries. A broad sweep approach and the children could not know that Africa is a vast continent and that Kenya and Ghana are as diverse as France and

Serbia. That they could move the French girl to Africa with her parasol is a nice touch suggesting an ability to move images around mentally as well as Kasija visualising their shared ideas in her drawing.

Learning Story 3: A Gift of a Song

Context: This vignette was recorded as a photo story in a public kindergarten in Beijing. Australian academics were visiting a number of Chinese kindergartens and spending a day in each recording observations across the day. This observation has been included here as it represented a commonly observed use of music in the Chinese programmes. Visitors to the kindergarten had been taken to the 3-year-old room to observe the indoor programme. The room was well equipped and had learning spaces for a number of different activities set up around. There was a book corner, home corner with dress-ups and a child-sized kitchen, a drawing corner, a block corner and two tables with manipulative materials. These latter two were set up Montessori style with a book case next to each table and the different materials set out on trays. A child would choose a tray and bring it to the table, call a teacher over when they had finished constructing with the material and then could return the tray and choose another one or move onto another activity. There was a whiteboard at the front of the room with an open space in front and a piano off to the side and against the wall. When the teacher played, the children would sing and dance behind her.

The Narrative of the Chinese Class

During a visit to a kindergarten in Beijing, we were led into the room of a group of 3-year-old children who had just completed their morning English lesson. The teacher explained they had finished, but as a gift to the visitors, the children would sing a song from the lesson. She went back to the computer near the whiteboard and put on the English DVD she had been using. As the music and song started, she called the children to attention by putting her hands together and started to model actions and singing. Most of the children joined in enthusiastically. The singing was a good-natured yell, actions were expansive, and the children were interested in the reaction of the visitors to their performance. The teacher signalled the end of the song as she had started, by bringing her hands together.

One boy, in an orange jacket, was interested in the visitors, watched us carefully at the beginning and then turned and concentrated as the teacher went through the performance. At the end, he turned and looked straight at us to see what our reaction to the song performance was.

Learning Dispositions

The children were interested in having visitors in their room, and from the noise and expansive actions, they were very familiar with this material. The child in the orange jacket displayed sustained attention and he seemed to take the task seriously as he did not turn to the visitors throughout the song but turned around as soon as it was finished. The material was familiar, and as the video supplied all cues, the children indicated their willingness to help the teacher through their loud voices and large arm movements. From the material being presented, there was little opportunity for individual responsibility to be shown, and the song itself had a didactic purpose, body parts, actions and numbers which gave limited opportunities for exploration. The children's interest was in the visitors; they were willing to perform when asked by their teacher.

Findings

What Learning Was Visible?

The children were cooperative in that they were willing to repeat a song just sung as part of their 'English lesson' at the behest of their teacher. The singing was a raucous yelling with no attempt to make it a musical experience. The song had a mnemonic purpose only. The presence of the visitors acted as a scaffold for the children to repeat the song with gusto. The interest, expressed through gaze direction and body language (Laevers 2005), suggested this was more of a social interaction than a musical one.

Discussion and Implications

In this final section of the chapter, we return to the two parts of the argument we are presenting. One is the role of music as a valuable human experience that can promote interpersonal and intrapersonal relationships. Shared experiences through music can enhance well-being for individuals and the group, and early childhood is an important time to encounter relationships and understandings with others that can lead to lifelong attitudes towards diversity and difference. We comment on the potential of the observations presented in terms of what knowledge of people and things these young children could display. Implications emerge from this discussion when we return to the notion that neoliberal education policy is threatening the arts in education to the extent that the arts and especially music have become a luxury and another measure of disadvantage and growing inequality.

The three observations, in terms of children's growing understanding of the world and others, a precursor to the idea of the 'golden rule', contained rich affordances. For Halina, an atmosphere of acceptance gave her room to take risks and to learn from and with others. In this case the affordance was the social environment that had been created in the centre, perhaps because of the diversity of families using the service and the scaffold of the formulaic music game. For the two Serbian children, there was a more homogenous setting, and the exploration of the world was being done through performing songs in other languages. Music gave an affordance for exploration as evidenced by the singing, the drums and transferring a French child in another song into an African setting. More of a formal primary school project, initiated by the teacher to assist the children in confronting their anxieties, the children's extension of their music session into the 'free' play time was an indication of the depth of their interest. The Chinese children were engaged in singing in English for a didactic purpose but were able to turn this into a social event.

Learning Stories provided a tool for exploring the meaning of learning in a broad sense. Alfayez (2008) refers to *Learning Stories* as a 'storied approach' and suggests why this is such an inclusive method of recording, assessing and sharing experience: 'it is the logic of the familiar, together with the emotional demand of storytelling, which helps attract children and families ' (p. 21).

CONCLUSION

As stated in the introduction, the aim of this chapter was to argue for a child's right to music as part of an education to grow awareness of self and others in a medium that has universal, cultural, historical, contextual and political importance. We have provided examples of music and its value in three contexts whilst focusing on the question: What happens to the stories we tell under a neoliberal agenda? The predominant neoliberal theory that impacts early childhood education is that of human capital development. Gibson et al. (2015) argue that through such an approach, children become units of investment and the investment is aimed at the future workforce required for a knowledge economy in an ever-increasing competitive environment. Benchmarking of national and international testing has become a measure of our education systems. Yelland (2010) says that the consequence of adopting such a narrow economic approach is of growing concern. She states: 'Poverty and inequality are marginalised and children are often regarded as creatures to be manipulated' (p. 61). Individual success becomes the measure and the idea of the benevolent state no longer exists. This situation creates a 'push-down' curriculum that has implications for disadvantaged populations who are most vulnerable to changing policies and political agendas. Strauss (2016) wrote in *The Washington Post:*

> Soon many of our nation's young children will be starting school for the first time. What they will likely find is something dramatically different from what their parents experienced at their age. Kindergartens and pre-K class-rooms have changed. There is less play, less art and music, less child choice, more teacher-led instruction, worksheets, and testing than a generation ago. Studies tell us that these changes, although pervasive, are most evident in schools serving high percentages of low-income children of color.

The music observations reported on in this chapter all occurred in cen-tres where a diverse population of families had access. Such learning and experience should be the right of all children, and the presence of the arts in the early childhood curriculum should be promoted as a strategy to build social harmony. Allsup and Shieh (2012) highlight the idea that the value of music is such that music teachers even have a special responsibility:

> At the heart of teaching others is the moral imperative to care. Social justice education begins with adopting a disposition to perceive and then act against indecencies and injustices. ... Music educators must embrace this social con-tract by "going public" or "coming out" ... into larger and more inter-twined social, artistic, and political domains. (p. 47)

REFERENCES

Acker, A. (2006). Understanding diversity through music and song. *Victorian Journal of Music Education, 1,* 45–52.

Acker, A. (2008). Making the multicultural learning environment flourish. *Australian Journal of Early Childhood, 33*(1), 9–16.

Alfayez, S. (2008). *Learning stories – Practice driving theory: How university staff introduce a new assessment approach for early childhood.* Unpublished master's thesis, School of Education, RMIT University.

Allsup, R. E., & Shieh, E. (2012). Social justice and music education: The call for a public pedagogy. *Music Educators Journal, 98*(4), 47–51.

Barrett, M. S. (2003). Meme engineers: Children as producers of musical culture. *International Journal of Early Years Education, 11*(3), 195–212.

Bartleet, B. (2016, June 7). *Music can change the world.* Public lecture, Griffith University. https://www.youtube.com/watch?v=tyZ2dWs8HFc

Bayless, K., & Ramsey, M. (1991). *Music: A way of life for the young child.* New York: Merrill.

Benedict, C., Schmidt, P., Spruce, G., & Woodford, P. (2015). *The Oxford handbook of social justice in music education.* Oxford: Oxford University Press.

Braithewaite, J. (2005). *Neoliberalism or regulatory capitalism.* https://www.anu.edu.au/fellows/jbraithwaite/_documents/Articles/Neoliberalism_Regulatory_2005.pdf

Browne, E. (1995). *Handa's surprise.* London: Walker Books.

Bruner, J. S. (1975). The ontogenesis of speech acts. *Journal of Child Language, 2,* 1–40.

Byrd, D., & Levy, D. (2013). Exploring social justice through music. *Observer, 26*(4). http://www.psychologicalscience.org/observer/exploring-social-justice-through-music#.WIlG-lN96Uk

Carr, M. (2001). *Assessment in early childhood: Learning stories.* London: Paul Chapman Publishing.

Carr, M., & Lee, W. (2009). *Learning stories: Constructing learner identities in early childhood.* Singapore: Sage. http://www.vcaa.vic.edu.au/documents/earlyyears/eyaddlangresource.pdf

Clarke, P. (2009). *Supporting children learning English as a second language in the early years (birth to six years).* Melbourne: Victorian Curriculum and Assessment Authority 2009. http://www.fletchermontessori.com.au/uploads/supporting_children_english_2nd_language.pdf

Connell, R. (2009). Good teachers on dangerous ground: Towards a new view of teacher quality and professionalism. *Critical Studies in Education, 50*(3), 213–229.

De Vries, P., & Letts, R. (2011). *Productivity commission. Inquiry into the education and training workforce: Early childhood development.* Submission by the Music Council of Australia. http://www.pc.gov.au/inquiries/completed/education-workforce-early-childhood/submissions/sub051.pdf

DEEWR. (2009). *Belonging, being, becoming: The early years learning framework.* Canberra: Australian Government, Department of Education Employment and Workplace Relations, Commonwealth of Australia.

DEEWR. (2010). *Being, belonging, becoming: The early years learning framework.* Canberra: Commonwealth of Australia.

Garfias, R. (2004). Music the cultural context. National Museum of Ethnology: Senri Ethnological Report 47.

Geist, K., Geist, E. A., & Kuznik, K. (2012). The patterns of music: Young children learning mathematics through beat, rhythm, and melody. *Young Children, 67*(1), 74–79.

Gibson, M., McArdle, F., & Hatcher, C. (2015). Governing child care in neoliberal times: Discursive constructions of children as economic units and early childhood educators as investment brokers. *Global Studies of Childhood, 5*(3), 322–332.

Heckman, J. (2011). The economics of inequality: The value of early childhood education. *American Educator, 31*, 31–47.

Laevers, F. (2005). The curriculum as means to raise the quality of ECE. Implications for policy. *European Early Childhood Education Research Journal, 13*(1), 17–30.

Leont'ev, A. (1994). The development of voluntary attention in the child. In R. Van der Veer & J. Valsiner (Eds.), *The Vygotsky reader* (pp. 289–313). Oxford: Blackwell Publishers.

MacDonald, R., Kreutz, G., & Mitchell, L. (Eds.). (2012). *Health and wellbeing.* Oxford: Oxford University Press.

Marsh, K. (2010). *The musical playground: Global traditions and change in children's songs and games.* Sydney: Oxford University Press.

May, H. (2002). Aotearoa-New Zealand: An overview of history, policy and curriculum. *McGill Journal of Education, 37*(1), 19–36.

Needham, M. (2007, September 1–3). *Affordances: Crossing the border from personal perceptual schemas to socially medicated learning dispositions.* Proceeding of the European Early Childhood Education Research Association (EECERA) conference, Prague.

Nyland, B., & Ferris, J. (2007). Early childhood music: An Australian experience. In K. Smithrim & R. Uptitis (Eds.), *Listen to their voices: Research and practice in early childhood music education, Biennial series "Research to practice"* (Vol. 3, pp. 182–195). Letts: Canadian Music Educators' Association.

Nyland, B., & Ferris, J. (2009). Researching children's musical learning experiences within a learning story framework. *New Zealand Research in Early Childhood Education, 12*, 81–95.

NZMOE. (1996). *Te Whariki: He Whariki matauranga: Early childhood curriculum.* Wellington: Learning Media.

Rinaldi, C. (2006). *In dialogue with Reggio Emilia: Listening, researching and learning.* New York: Routledge.

Sims, M., & Wanganayake, M. (2015). The performance of compliance in early childhood: Neoliberalism and nice ladies. *Global Studies of Childhood, 5*(3), 333–345.

St. John, P. (2016, July). Discovering musical identity: A meta-analysis of scaffolded efforts and musical engagement among young music makers. In C. Lum & A. Niland (Eds.), *Young children's musical identities: Global perspectives.* Proceedings of the Early Childhood Music Education Commission, Ede.

Strauss, V. (2016, August 23). *The Washington Post.*

Trainor, L., & Heinmuller, B. (1998). The development of evaluative responses to music: Infants prefer to listen to consonance over dissonance. *Infant Behaviour and Development, 21*(1), 77–88.

Trevarthen, C. (2008). The musical art of infant conversation: Narrating in the time of sympathetic experience, without rational interpretation, before words. *Musicae Scientiae, 12*(1), 15–46.

Tucker, M. (Ed.). (2012). *Surpassing Shanghai: An agenda for American education built on the world's leading systems.* Cambridge, MA: Harvard Education Press.

UNICEF (United Nations International Children's Fund). (2012). Investing in early childhood education in Serbia. https://www.unicef.org/serbia/Booklet_Investing_in_Early_Childhood_Education_in_Serbia_FINAL.pdf

Vaugn, T., Harris, J., & Caldwell, B. (2011). *Bridging the gap in school achievement through the arts: Summary report.* The Song Room. http://www.songroom.org.au/wp-content/uploads/2013/06/Bridging-the-Gap-in-School-Achievement-through-the-Arts.pdf

Vygotsky, L. S. (1978). *Mind in society.* Cambridge, MA: Cambridge University Press.

Yelland, N. (Ed.). (2010). *Contemporary perspectives on early childhood education.* London: McGraw Hill, Open University Press.

Zhu, J. (2015). Early childhood education and relative policies in China. *International Journal of Child Care and Educational Policy.* doi:10.1007/2288-6729-3-1-51.

Aleksandra Acker is a musician, a lecturer and a researcher, specialising in Music Education in Early Childhood at RMIT University, Melbourne, Australia. She has presented and published on her research in international and national forums. Aleksandra is presently the early childhood representative on the Australian Music Education Council and has strong interest in child rights.

Berenice Nyland is an adjunct professor with RMIT University, Melbourne, Australia. Human rights, early language and the literacies of childhood, especially music, have been her long-time research interests. She has published nationally and internationally and has been involved in comparative studies in Europe and China with children and practitioners for over a decade.

Transformative Teacher Leadership in the Dominican Republic, Jamaica and the United States: Potentiality and Possibility in Curriculum Making and School Reform Efforts

Eleanor Blair

INTRODUCTION

Of all the civil rights for which the world has struggled and fought for 5,000 years, the right to learn is undoubtedly the most fundamental... The freedom to learn... has been bought by bitter sacrifice. And whatever we may think of the curtailment of other civil rights, we should fight to the last ditch to keep open the right to learn, the right to have examined in our schools not only what we believe, but what we do not believe; not only what our leaders say, but what the leaders of other groups and nations, and the leaders of other centuries have said. We must insist upon this to give our children the fairness of a start which will equip them with such an array of facts and such an attitude toward truth that they can have a real chance to

E. Blair (✉)
Western Carolina University, Cullowhee, NC, USA

© The Author(s) 2018
C. Roofe, C. Bezzina (eds.), *Intercultural Studies of Curriculum*, Intercultural Studies in Education,
https://doi.org/10.1007/978-3-319-60897-6_6

judge what the world is and what its greater minds have thought it might be. (Du Bois 1970, pp. 230–231)

I begin this chapter with a quote from W.E.B. Du Bois because nothing that I have to say is important without the acknowledgement that learning and access to knowledge is a fundamental right that belongs to all people; this is what curriculum is all about and this should be the moral and ethical underpinning of all curriculum theory, policy and practice. Regardless of whether you are Dominican, Jamaican or an American, the freedom to learn is at the root of all of our battles over schools, and ultimately, the control of the curriculum is both a political and social act that has far-reaching ramifications for struggles over power, status and authority. Although Du Bois wrote these words many years ago, his sentiments are just as applicable today. Cross-cultural studies of teaching and learning in different countries highlight the role of schools as public places where ideological choices are made regarding the process and product of knowledge workers and their clients. In its broadest sense, curriculum is about teaching and learning and preparing children to take their rightful places in global economies that no longer adhere to the strict borders that designate and separate one country from another. We live in a world where our shared futures are more important than our individual destinies. We live in a world where we must be interdependent; the problems of one become the problems of all. As such, teaching and learning are politicized acts that challenge us to not only own our values and beliefs, but fight for them if necessary. It is not sufficient to simply define learner outcomes in the staid language of the bureaucrats who attempt to pretend that knowledge and learning are not value-laden, but rather the outcomes of a positivistic guided vision of pedagogy. Reyes-Guerra and Bogotch (2011) describe this work in the following:

> Curriculum theory and inquiry is, in its essence a study of a nation's culture through the needs of its learners. It begins and continues as the practice of democratic values. As such, the legitimacy of educational leadership as a profession is not in raising test scores but rather in ministering to meet the needs of its citizenry. (p. 150)

It can be argued that ideology, passion and aesthetics have shaped the design of curricula and schools throughout history and that these forces have also impacted education and schooling in the countries that we are discussing. Each of these systems has been moulded and shaped by the various forces of modernity, immigration, urbanization and industrialization, as well as the political, social and cultural forces that schools are continually responding to in their efforts to meet both the needs of society and government. And as such, schools naturally reflect current ideological orientations along with the various fads and trends that regularly circulate throughout the education literature. Curriculum work in each of the three countries addressed in this chapter is the foundation for the delivery of the most relevant knowledge, skills and experiences, but teachers are the most important actors in this drama. Charlotte Danielson (2006) refers to these individuals as teacher leaders who possess:

> That set of skills demonstrated by teachers who continue to teach students but also have an influence that extends beyond their own classrooms to others within their own school and elsewhere. It entails mobilizing and energizing others with the goal of improving the school's performance of its critical responsibilities related to teaching and learning. (p. 12)

In this equation, the powerful impact of teachers rising to the surface as leaders with transformative visions regarding how, what and why we teach establishes a symbiotic connection between teacher leaders and school efficacy as an important component of curriculum narratives.

Teaching and learning in the Dominican Republic, Jamaica and the United States are very different phenomena, and yet, the differences and similarities highlight the important role of curriculum in the progress and development of schools throughout the world. The significance of place cannot be ignored in a study that examines the intersection of teacher leadership and curriculum making in three countries; the context adds another layer of richness to the narratives that emerge from these comparisons. Historically, American public schools have never been true to democratic ideals of equity and access; however, seemingly there was the steady progress of reforms that seemed to continually redefine the potential of public schools to respond to changing societal needs and demands. More recent critiques of the schools challenge these conclusions and document the lack of success seen in schools that serve poor and often diverse students from both urban and rural environments (Giroux 2012; Kozol 2012; McLaren 2015). Similarly, contemporary Jamaican and Dominican schools also function within a broader democratic ideology and yet, suffer from the limitations of large bureaucracies that often subjugate broader public needs and purposes to the political and economic agendas of a few.

Teaching, learning and leading in twenty-first-century schools in both the Caribbean and in the United States require the adoption of transformative practices that have the intent of redefining the parameters of educational leadership in contested public spheres to include a commitment to critical thought and social justice as key components of curriculum development.

Cross-Cultural Comparisons of Teachers' Work

At the core of any discussion of schools and curriculum is the essential role played by teachers. In this chapter, the thread that holds it all together is the link between curriculum and teachers acting as transformative leaders to guide our visions of what twenty-first-century school reform efforts should look like; a teacher-created vision that becomes a bottom-up rather than top-down restructuring of the organization of school hierarchies and the redesign of teaching and learning spaces. Regardless of the culture, teaching is hard work; it is even harder in schools that are under-resourced and over-crowded. And yet, dedicated and passionate people still choose teaching as a profession despite the knowledge that their work will be full of challenges and few rewards. At the end of most days, there is only the reminder that they work in low-status jobs with little of the status and autonomy granted to other professionals. Today, in the Dominican Republic, Jamaica and the United States, we see increasing efforts to support and perpetuate the emergence of teachers who are highly qualified and well-educated, and yet, their participation in educational decision-making is extremely limited. The inherent contradictions between changes in the educational level of teachers and the lack of change in the professional status of teachers are seldom noted by those in decision-making positions; however, it is important to this discussion. Better educated and more highly qualified teachers will demand a different kind of profession; they will not be happy with the status quo. In each of these countries, there are public expressions of dissatisfaction with the process and product of public education, and yet, efforts to address aspects of the teaching profession that act as impediments to teacher efficacy are often seen as frivolous amendments to already beleaguered educational institutions. Things like higher pay, participation in curricular decision-making and mediated entry into the profession with subsequent opportunities for teacher leadership are not the focus of discussions regarding the reforming of public educational spaces. Better educated, highly qualified teachers are increasingly frustrated by the antiquated hierarchical educational bureaucracies that continue to limit teachers to semi-professional roles. Teacher roles and responsibilities, like test scores, are viewed as potential tools of reform and not something worthy of dissection, critical analysis and reconceptualization. Teacher attrition in all three countries is high despite improvements in the profession (Evans 1993; Feistritzer 2011; Jennings 2001; Rodgers-Jenkinson and Chapman 1990). Teacher pay has steadily increased, but working conditions have remained stagnant. Typically, school reform efforts that focus on teachers' work identify three key variables that have the potential to improve the profession: first, increasing the educational requirements for entry into the profession; second, improved salaries and working conditions; and third, encouragement of collaboration and shared decision-making among major stakeholders, internal and external to the school community (Goldstein 2015; Green 2015). These attempts to recognize the various levels of skill, education and expertise of teachers are prerequisite to real changes in the work of teachers, but unfortunately, these changes seldom have as their goal the creation of opportunities for teachers to assume important leadership roles, both formal and informal, beyond the classroom. Typically, leadership roles for teachers involve the assumption of administrative duties. Roles that challenge traditional notions of school leadership and provide opportunities for teacher leaders to find meaningful and sustainable opportunities to participate in curriculum planning that connects theory to practice are limited or nonexistent. Ignoring opportunities to incorporate teachers working in traditional teacher roles into the leadership and decision-making activities of schools ignores an important resource that has the potential to positively impact schools without requiring the allocation of additional monetary resources. Again, the role of teachers acting as leaders is an essential one that is key to curriculum planning and school improvement across various cultural contexts.

TRANSFORMATIVE TEACHER LEADERS

Henry Giroux (1988) first introduced the idea of the teacher as intellectual, but he expanded that notion to argue that the teacher must be a transformative intellectual "if students are to become active, critical individuals" (p. 127). He went on to suggest that "central to the category of transformative intellectual is the necessity of making the pedagogical more political and the political more pedagogical" (p. 127). As such, it is imperative that curriculum work engages teachers acting as transformative intellectuals in "the struggle to overcome economic, political and social injustices, and to further humanize themselves as part of the struggle" (Giroux 1988, p. 127). Within this framework, the notion of transformative teacher leadership imbued with an ideological commitment to social justice emerges as a key feature of the teacher leader acting as an intellectual in twenty-first-century schools.

Teacher leadership, an important element of most successful school improvement efforts, depends upon the idea that "teachers who are leaders lead within and beyond the classroom, identify with and contribute to a community of teacher learners and leaders, and influence others toward improved educational practice" (Katzenmeyer and Moller 2009, p. 6). Katzenmeyer and Moller go on to describe the power of teacher leadership as a "sleeping giant" with the potential to transform both the profession of teaching and the nature of school reform in schools. As such, discussions of curriculum and school reform demand that we consider the potential impact of transformative teacher leadership within a larger framework that encompasses curriculum theory and practice, a discussion that is almost nonexistent in the literature, although individuals like Anderson (2009), Freire (1968) and Giroux (2012) have laid the groundwork for these discussions within a critical ideological framework. A vision of transformative leaders must be conceptualized as a piece of a larger theoretical and ideological vision if it is to ultimately have the potential to transform the public schools and, subsequently, demonstrate the intersection of curriculum making and teachers acting in transformative leadership roles. This chapter provides a multicultural framework that envisions teacher leaders transcending previously narrow definitions of their work and participating in the creation of a dream—a dream for a profession that possesses the status, power and influence to lead us into the twenty-first century and create schools that are responsive to the needs of all constituencies. As previously noted, schools in the three countries under study aspire to these aims and purposes, but at this time, the outcomes are disappointing and there is much work to be done. In the United States, movements to privatize schools and disenfranchise the public agenda for education are thriving. Likewise, challenges to public education are also prevalent in the Caribbean schools of both Jamaica and the Dominican Republic where a legacy of failed school reform efforts has instilled a lack of confidence in the ability of both government agencies and teachers to promote lasting, sustainable change in schools and the students they serve. Comparing Caribbean schools with those in the United States documents both the similarities and differences between countries struggling to overcome intransigent attitudes about change that begin at the curriculum planning level. Freire's (1968, 2000, 2013) ideas clarify the need to construct a leadership narrative that focuses on a view of transformative teacher leadership as "interventionist activism" that is imbued with hope and a commitment to advocacy that has the potential to change "frontline" curricular decision-making in public schools. Utilizing descriptive research and data from scholars working in the Dominican Republic, Jamaica and the United States, this chapter "paints" a comparative picture of contemporary schools in these countries and considers the challenges faced by transformative teacher leaders working in twenty-first-century schools where the curriculum lacks relevance and often reflects the needs of another time, another place. As a consequence of long traditions of oppressive practices that grant authority only to those in formal administrative roles, teachers' work typically consists of efforts to follow the rules and enforce the policies and practices that have been "handed down" to them. The outcomes of this process, according to Freire (1968), are teachers who are less likely to:

> Develop the critical consciousness which would result from their intervention in the world as transformers of the world. The more completely they accept the passive role imposed on them, the more they tend simply to adapt to the world as it is and to the fragmented view of reality deposited in them. (p. 73)

The realization that teachers function in roles more similar to those of students than leaders highlights the difficulties that they encounter in their pursuit of full professional status and the obstacles they face in their attempts to successfully advocate on behalf of parents and students from families and communities where the public schools continue to fail to provide suitable environments for teaching and learning all children. As such, inherent to this discussion is a reconsideration of the roles of teachers with an emphasis upon understanding the kinds of questions that must guide the development of a critical consciousness that is prerequisite to new roles and responsibilities and, ultimately, the creation of schools that directly challenge the oppressive forces that create obstacles to the ethical and courageous pursuit of schools that address the needs of ALL students in meaningful, substantive ways.

WHAT'S CURRICULUM GOT TO DO WITH IT?

This chapter examines the potential role of transformative teacher leadership in curriculum development in three countries. Curriculum planning and development as it is broadly defined is a fundamental part of efforts to create twenty-first-century schools in a new image that reflects a more global interconnected world where diversity and differences are the norm and accountability for academic excellence among all children is prerequisite for the successful social, political and economic growth and development of a nation. Examining schools in countries as different as the Dominican Republic, Jamaica and the United States brings to the surface of the discussion the most salient (and often contested) facets of public educational spaces where access to knowledge is limited for those lacking political and economic power. It is important to begin this discussion by highlighting the depth and breadth of curricular issues and the role it plays in shaping specific learning outcomes.

William Pinar (2004) argues that curriculum theory and development is a "complicated conversation" (p. 185). Reyes-Guerra and Bogotch (2011) suggest that it is important for us to understand the difference between how "curriculum theorists conceptualize their field from how we in educational leadership write about our roles and our preparation programs" (p. 143). They want us to understand that "curriculum makes leadership stronger ....and educational leadership can potentially make curriculum theory stronger" (p. 143). Their arguments depend upon on an element of interdependency in these relationships and rely on ideas that are central to the notion that discussions about curriculum theory, policy and practice benefit from being considered within the framework of teacher leadership that is transformative.

According to Walker and Soltis (1997), curriculum "refers not only to the official list of courses offered by the school-we call that the 'official curriculum'-but also to the purposes, content, activities, and organization of the educational program actually created in schools by teachers, students, and administrators" (p. 1). Curriculum, broadly defined, includes everything we do in schools and impacts the lives of teachers and students. Ralph W. Tyler (1949) defined curriculum planning as needing to include a consideration of the following questions:

1. What educational purposes should the school seek to attain?
2. What educational experiences can be provided that are likely to attain these purposes?

3. How can these educational experiences be effectively organized?
4. How can we determine whether these purposes are being attained? (p. x)

Unfortunately, most discussions of curriculum focus on what is being taught and tested. Too often, tested knowledge becomes the official programme of study and that is a clear example of "getting the cart in front of the horse." Tyler's questions are elegant in their simplicity, and yet, they highlight what curriculum planning should look like. The answers to these questions are less important than the kinds of discussions they produce; discussions that under ideal circumstances regularly occur among major stakeholders committed to creating school communities that promote and support social justice. Unfortunately, this is seldom the case. Larger, philosophical issues that are prerequisite to quality curriculum planning; issues related to questions regarding the relationship between what, why and how we teach are ignored; even bigger issues related to social justice, equity and advocacy; and issues that are, perhaps, more important to school outcomes are seldom included in these discussions. Regardless of whether we are talking about schools in the Dominican Republic, Jamaica or the United States, how we define the problem ultimately determines the solution. If we don't spend the requisite time understanding what we believe and value in teaching and learning and thinking deeply about defining and understanding the issues, we will never come up with solutions that are relevant and sustainable.

Curriculum planning and development are critically important to school reform efforts, and in less advantaged nations, the curriculum is too often managed by centralized bureaucracies that allow little room for the voices of diverse stakeholders with an interest in the decision-making and learning outcomes. Teachers stepping out of their traditional, semi-professional roles and participating in curriculum planning are essential to meaningful school reform in all schools. Cross-cultural comparisons of the schools and the nature of teachers' work in different countries provide a different perspective on how we unpack the curriculum and systematically begin to answer each of the questions posed by Ralph W. Tyler. Teacher leadership that is transformative has the potential to affect not only the curriculum but the lives and work of all teachers and students.

TEACHER AND LEARNING IN THREE COUNTRIES: "BEGIN WITH THE END IN MIND"

Examining the status of education in three very diverse countries is not an easy task. Both the Dominican Republic and Jamaica can be viewed as developing countries seeking to take their places in an increasingly inter-dependent global world where economic gains frequently follow wide-spread social reforms. Oddly enough, the United States, a country once seen as a leader in universal access to education, is now seen as a nation struggling to reconcile issues of equity and justice with the mediocre educational opportunities and outcomes among poor children from diverse backgrounds. Stephen Covey's (2013) idea of "beginning with the end in mind" is relevant when we talk about schools and attempt to visualize a future that would benefit all major stakeholders: children, families, communities, teachers and so on. We must articulate a vision of where we want to go prior to establishing the road that will get us there. The differences between the three countries being discussed in this essay are immense, and yet, each one, in its own way, acknowledges the importance of education and schooling to a viable participation in a twenty-first-century global economy. While entire essays...even books...could be written about education and schools and teachers in the Dominican Republic, Jamaica and the United States, this chapter is an attempt to focus on both the problems and the progress of schools in three disparate nations and then focus on the potentially momentous role that teachers could play in revamping these systems in ways that are transformative for both the teaching profession and the schools that are the recipients of these efforts. As long as large numbers of children in the Dominican Republic, Jamaica and the United States are ill-prepared to meet twenty-first-century demands in the areas of literacy, numeracy and technology, these countries will see their forward movement into the next century slowed by their educational failures. As the numbers of children challenging the success of these systems grows, economic and social stability will also be at risk. In the sections that follow, I attempt to provide short vignettes that describe the status of schools in the three countries under discussion.

Schooling in the Dominican Republic

The United States doesn't have a monopoly on notions regarding the importance of educational equality and access; education and schooling is equally valued, but often unattainable to the general population of the Dominican

Republic, and again, the problems are complex and the solutions not easily discerned. The Dominican Republic is a sovereign country that occupies the eastern two-thirds of the island of Hispaniola; the western one-third of the island is occupied by the nation of Haiti. A Spanish-speaking nation, it currently has a population of approximately 10 million people. Schools are seen as important to the success of their nation, but the problems afflicting their system of public education are large, varied and, most times, seemingly insurmountable. Francisco Chapman's 1987 dissertation, *Illiteracy and Educational Development in the Dominican Republic: An Historical Approach*, examined the historical roots of the Dominican's ongoing crisis in education. Chapman explored the tensions between the cultural diversity that exists in the country and the steady migration of Dominicans to the United States as important dimensions of life in the Dominican. While schooling is compulsory in the Dominican Republic, compared to other Latin American and Caribbean nations, the word "worst" is most often used to describe the Dominican schools, both past and present.

Since 2008, the country has been attempting to implement its third Ten-Year Education Plan. "The United Nations Educational, Scientific and Cultural Organization (UNESCO) and the World Forum, international organizations that assess the quality of education, released information in 2010 ranking the Dominican Republic's primary education as the worst of the Central American and Caribbean region" ("Education is the most critical issue facing the Dominican Republic," n.d., n.p.). In a piece titled, "Dominican Republic Revamps Failing Education System," Manning (2014) describes the schools in the Dominican Republic as some of the worst in the world:

> In the Caribbean nation of nearly 10 million people, the education system ranks among the worst in the world. Test scores in urban areas are as low as in rural areas. Poor students can't escape the failing public education system, making it difficult for them to break out of poverty.
> Like its neighbors, the Dominican Republic struggles with overcrowded classrooms in shoddy facilities. There's a high dropout rate, an outdated curriculum, overage students who fail classes and have to repeat grades, among other problems. But perhaps the most worrying issue is poorly trained teachers. (n.p.)

Other reports confirm the problems described in the previous passage:

> Many people understand that the public education system in the Dominican Republic leaves much to be desired, but comparing it to that of the United

States helps one to understand the depth of the problem. The net enrollment rate for primary schooling in the Dominican Republic is 90%, which is
only 4% lower than in the U.S. However, the dropout rate for students in
primary education is 25.2%, which is more than triple the 6.9% dropout rate
in the U.S. Another sobering statistic shows that the net enrollment rate for
secondary education in the U.S. is 88%, whereas it is only 40% in the
Dominican Republic.

These unfavorable public education statistics are reflective of the poor
quality of education that the children receive. Students in public schools in
the Dominican Republic do not receive enough individual attention at
school due to the high student-to-teacher ratio; 25 or more students to 1
classroom teacher in primary education. In United States primary education
there are around 13 students to 1 classroom teacher. This discrepancy has
devastating effects on a child's ability to learn as they are not able to receive
extra support while learning difficult lessons and certainly contributes to
students dropping out of school early or failing. ("Education in the
Dominican Republic," n.d., n.p.)

To its credit, Manning (2014) notes that "the Dominican Republic is the
first country in the Caribbean to undertake a major education overhaul. In
2012, voters convinced all presidential candidates to promise—if elected—
to double the education budget. Now President Danilo Medina is staking
his reputation on education reform. The country will spend 4 percent of
its GDP—almost 2 billion euros in 2014" (n.p.). Will it work? Some are
optimistic, others not so much.

The quality of education has been and continues to be an unresolved problem in the Dominican Republic. The Dominican Republic is ranked 140 out
of 142 countries in Latin America, making the country close to the worst in
education. Under a law created in 1997, the Dominican government must
spend at least 4% of their GDP on education, but the DR has never even
appropriated 2%. As a result, schools often do not have the proper funding
to give adequate resources and time to their students. In fact, most students
only have a half day of school. (Creed 2012, n.p.)

Acknowledgement of these problems has led political leaders in the
Dominican Republic to initiate widespread reforms in several key areas:
curriculum, funding for construction of schools, lower teacher-student
ratios, increased teacher pay and longer school days. The articulation of
these changes is a first step; however, the next step will be in the implementation and sustainability of these proposals. Deep cultural changes are

necessary if families are to embrace these initiatives and support attempts to change both the process and product of public education. Manning (2014) documents that "about 40 percent of boys and girls leave school before eighth grade. Even those who get through high school and complete 12 years of school start college at a sixth-grade reading level, according to a Dominican university study" (n.p.). As such, change is imperative for the future survival of schools in the Dominican Republic; however, the future of the country is also tightly wrapped up in these changes.

While there is little research that examines the roles of teachers in this country, it is apparent that teachers are ill-prepared to meet the needs of twenty-first-century students. Despite the changes that have been implemented, "maybe one of the striking issues in the Dominican Republic is that, despite the investment and advances in teacher training and certification, students had the lowest scores in the regional test SERCE, which examined reading and math skills in 3rd and 6th grades of primary education" (OREALC/UNESCO 2008, cited in Guzmán et al. 2013, p. 10).

It has been noted by the Ministry of Higher Education, Science and Technology (MESCyT) that there are five priorities related to initial teacher training: (a) strengthen programs though hiring full time teacher educators, promoting online teacher networks and implementing standards; (b) upgrade the profile of candidates who wish to enter teacher programs; (c) promote internationalization of teacher training; (d) implement accreditation of teacher training programs and (e) stimulate teachers' involvement in research within the classroom. (PREAL/CIEDHUMANO 2012; cited in Guzmán et al. 2013, p. 10)

Furthermore, Guzmán et al. (2013) have cited numerous statistics documenting that the Dominican Republic faces many complex and interrelated challenges in relation to teacher training (see PREAL/EDUCA 2010; PREAL/CIEDHUMANO 2012):

(a)Data from 2010 indicate that only 1.2% of the 1,868 teacher educators hold a doctorate degree. (b) Although there might be a concern about requiring higher formal education to teachers (for example, a graduate degree), previous training and certification at the licenciatura level has not so far produced good results on student learning as it is shown in national tests14 (see PNUD 2008). In addition, this is reinforced by low scores of Dominican children in international tests (OREAL/UNESCO 2008). (c) There is a test (Prueba de Orientación y Medición Académica—POMA) to enter higher education; its results, however, aren't used for admission of applicants to education programs, including teacher training. (d) Pedagogical issues are emphasized in initial teacher training but content of the disciplines and teaching practice are rather weak. (e) Although in-service teacher training is scarcely evaluated, studies available show it has low impact on teacher performance and, hence, on student learning. (f) Although some teachers received training supported by ICT, this resource is not available for many schools. (g) Performance standards for teachers and principals were established in 2009 but a definition is needed about how those standards will be implemented and measured. At some point, it would be advisable to link standards to teacher pre- and in-service training. (p. 11)

Clearly needed in the Dominican Republic is an upgrading of the teaching profession and the creation of informal and formal opportunities for teachers that encourage collaborative leadership roles in the schools as an important aspect of emerging teacher leadership. While the status of teacher leadership in the Dominican Republic today is quite low, it is encouraging that there are official recommendations that recognize teachers as a primary part of school reform efforts. Increasingly, one sees calls for the involvement of highly qualified teachers in professional development efforts and the dissemination of research in classrooms noted in the literature on Dominican education.

Schooling in Jamaica

Jamaica is the largest English-speaking island in the Caribbean. It is the fourth largest island in the area with a population of 2.8 million people. A former British colony, Jamaica achieved full independence in 1962. Jamaicans are nothing, if not optimistic. Their perspective is captured by the motto, "Out of Many One People" or the popular notion of "One love, one heart, one Jamaica"; these sound bites echo across the island in music and advertisements for various all-inclusive resorts and tourist attractions. However, these messages often obscure a view of Jamaica as a complex country where race, economics and social justice issues regularly emerge in frequently contentious discussions regarding the progress and product of the island as an independent country, but more specifically, in the establishment of appropriate aims and purposes for public education.

Jamaica is an interesting case study for many reasons; however, the Jamaican identity is one place to begin a quest to understand Jamaica. Kirk Meighoo (1999) explores the complexity of Jamaican identity and compares it to the popular local cuisine epitomized by curry goat:

Despite being Jamaica's second largest ethnic group, Indians have yet to be referred to as a meaningful or "real" Jamaican community in the same way that the Black, Brown, White, Chinese, or Syrian/Lebanese communities are. Indeed, Indo-Jamaicans largely exist in a situation where non-Indians? who greatly outnumber them? barely (and often only insultingly) recognize their existence. On the other hand, Indians do blend in quite naturally and inconspicuously in the Jamaican mélange.... "Jamaicanness" must move from an obscuring, assimilative and reluctant plurality to a plurality that is celebratory, open and revealing. I propose that the present-day place of curry goat in Jamaican identity symbolize the direction for this future transformation. As curry goat is quite easily and readily seen as both Jamaican and Indian, so too must Jamaican identity itself be seen. (p. 43)

Jamaican identity is important because the legacy of the years spent as a British colony (1655–1962) has led to an ongoing struggle to establish what is really Jamaican and what is simply the inheritance of the British occupation. Nowhere is this battle more clearly fought than in the attempts to build an educational system that is truly Jamaican and not simply a shoddy remaking of the system created for them by the British. Language is the site for many of the most obvious struggles over identity issues related to the chasm between British and Jamaican cultural norms. While most Jamaicans clearly speak a Jamaican Standard English (JSE) that reflects the British influence, in reality, a large percentage of Jamaican are bilingual, and in private circles and in the deep country, Patois is spoken. Patois is the preferred language of many Jamaicans; a creole blended English that until recently was treated as inferior to JSE. While controversy still swirls around discussions of Patois as a legitimate language, the school, as an instrument of political power and a purveyor of official knowledge, still prefers JSE as the language of instruction, and in many schools, punitive actions result for any student caught speaking Patois. This issue is just one of many that serves to separate Jamaicans and create a class-based system that separates and stigmatizes certain sectors of society.

In Jamaica, free, universal education is encouraged across the island in schools run by the Ministry of Education, Youth and Information. Nevertheless, all-age schools serving children in the lower grades are often over-crowded and under-resourced with dramatic differences occurring between schools in urban areas and those in the deep country. The low academic performance of students at primary and secondary levels is well-documented. An article in *The Daily Gleaner* (2011), Jamaica's leading newspaper, noted that "the stark fact of the matter is that most of the nation's schools are failing schools. If one takes the bare minimum standard of 50 per cent of students meeting basic minimum performance requirements, many schools are failing. If one ups this to a far more reasonable 75 per cent, the vast majority of primary and secondary schools are failing" ("Education Performance and Failing Schools," 2011, n.p.). The essay concludes that "Jamaica has one of the worse performing education system in CARICOM (Caribbean Community and Common Market), despite all the money thrown at it" (n.p.). In 2004, the Taskforce on Educational Reform Final Report, *Jamaica, A Transformed Education System*, described the situation in the following way: "The education system caters to approximately 800,000 students in public and private institutions at the early childhood, primary, secondary and tertiary levels. Over 22,000 teachers are employed in 1,000 public institutions. Only 20% of teachers are trained university graduates" (p. 9). Unfortunately, they concluded that

> the system's performance is well below acceptable standards, manifested in low student performance. Data from the Ministry of Education Youth and Culture, reveal that in 2003, less than one-third of the children entering grade 1 were ready for the primary level, some 30% of primary school leavers were illiterate, and only about 20% of secondary graduates had the requisite qualification for meaningful employment and/or entry to most secondary programmes. (p. 47)

A more recent discussion of education in Jamaica described the status of education in the following essay, "Fix Our Broke and Broken Education System" (2016); they state unequivocally that "it is clear to us that Jamaica's education system fails to address the needs of our workforce" (n.p.). The essay argues that schools have been waylaid by a government focus on debt and crime and that the education system is misaligned to the needs of Jamaican students. They advocate for innovation that recognizes the uniqueness of each student and moves toward examining the best educational practices of other nations. In conclusion, they promote the following vision for Jamaican schools:

- Remodel existing, under utilised schools and infrastructure to create special regional institutes that cater to the interests and competences of individual students for example high schools for: the visual and performing arts, more specialised institutions for physical education and sports, development and technologies, and entrepreneurship, agriculture, like the so far successful remodelling of Trench Town High School into a polytechnic college.

- Develop a streamlined process for the monitoring and assessment of overall progress of students through the development of personal learning plans (PLPs) and separate students based on areas of interest and regional location rather than the traditional versus non-traditional institutions that currently exist.
- Base classroom instructions on what was gathered in these PLPs and ensure there are various academic intervention programmes in these specialised schools.
- If the issue is that we cannot afford too much reform then we must recognise sustainability issues as an immediate priority. If we have limited capital spending and the rest of the budget is dedicated to paying overhead costs including electricity, then an immediate priority is to dedicate capital spending of one or two years to eliminate unnecessary costs and become as energy- and food-sufficient as possible. ("Fix Our Broke and Broken Education System," 2014, n.p.)

Following these recommendations are more recent articles in *The Daily Gleaner* advocating for teachers as the key to these reform measures. In the essay, "Target Teacher Training—Education Needs Top Quality for Transformation" (2016), they cite recent research noting the need "for a fresh, new template for training teachers" (n.p.). This work emerged "from a group of education thinkers who acknowledge that raising teacher quality is a key factor in student achievement" (n.p.). Furthermore, in this essay, they advocate for teachers and issue the following demands:

> Better-qualified and committed teachers, effective management and accountability, robust school boards and greater parental and community involvement in education.... Various reforms have been undertaken in the name of education over many years, including revamped curriculum, shift system and free education, but the conclusion of Fourth Floor participants was that they all fall short of the impact of having a good teacher in the classroom. ("Target Teacher Training—Education Needs Top Quality for Transformation," 2016, n.p.)

The system is as equally broken as schools in the Dominican Republic; however, the differences have to do with the conflicts that arise because of national identity issues. Jamaicans struggle with the intersection between identity and cultural norms. To the outsider, it seems that they are still working their way towards complete independence from the British influence and that creates myriad issues that must be addressed in the reforming of an educational system that is unique to Jamaicans.

While there is widespread recognition and acceptance of the link between social mobility and education, the discrepancies that exist between the various social classes exacerbate the chasm between low- and high-performing schools. Add to that the low status of teachers and one has created a context for the steady decline in the numbers of those choosing to teach and attrition among those who became teachers. Hyacinth Evans (1993), a notable Jamaican scholar and writer, laments the reasons that teaching as a career has become less than desirable, "harsh conditions and at times the absence of equipment and resources, especially in the all-age and primary schools, have reduced the attractiveness and the status of teaching. Above all, however, teachers' salaries have not kept pace with the rapidly rising cost of living. All these factors have operated to make teaching a less automatic choice than it was twenty or thirty years ago" (p. 229). As such, the teaching profession in Jamaica is fraught with difficulties, and yet, there are committed teachers willing to pursue their work with commitment and passion. The Ministry of Education, Youth and Information has continued to press forward with reforms that require all teachers to be licensed at the baccalaureate level, increase teacher salaries and address issues related to the elimination of shift schools and general funding of the public schools and, finally, curriculum review and revision at all levels. In the end, the Taskforce on Educational Reform Final Report, *Jamaica, A Transformed Education System* (2004), describes strategies of "achieving the vision through transformation.... If the nation continues to travel along the 'current path', it will not achieve the shared vision. What is required, is to get on the 'transformation path'. The difference between the 'current path' and the 'transformation path' is the transformation gap, which we must close" (p. 65). They affirm the *National Shared Vision for Education in Jamaica* that includes the following:

> Each learner will maximise his/her potential in an enriching, learner-centred education environment with maximum use of learning technologies supported by committed, qualified, competent, effective and professional educators and staff. The education system will be equitable and accessible with full attendance to Grade 11. Accountability, transparency and performance are the hallmarks of a system that is excellent, self-sustaining and resourced

and welcomes full stakeholder participation. The system produces full literacy and numeracy, a globally competitive, quality workforce and a disciplined, culturally aware and ethical Jamaican citizenry. (p. 11)

In line with these recommendations, it seems that there is a place for a more in-depth examination of the roles that teacher leaders could play in this vision of transformation. While many of the reports on Jamaican education consider the role of administrative leaders, there is an absence of any discussion of the role of teacher leaders is school reform. It is interesting that a country can advocate for higher levels of teacher preparation and an upgrading of the professional status of teachers and yet ignore the potential power of these teachers in new roles, both informal and formal, that allow teachers to assume leadership in the schools and participate as major actors directing efforts to reform the schools. It can be argued that that one piece of the future Jamaican educational tapestry might be the most cost-effective mechanism for real and sustainable change. Perhaps, of all the recommendations for school reform that might be suggested, this one thing could be the most controversial. Teachers acting as leaders, in a profession dominated by women, would challenge the status quo and usurp preconceived notions regarding the work of teachers.

Schooling in the United States

Writing about education and schooling in the United States should be an easy task, but it's not. There are no easy summaries regarding the status of schools. Schools are expensive and controversial, and yet, a free, publicly funded education that is available to all students is a fundamental cornerstone of the most basic democratic ideals. And while there are many entirely reasonable debates regarding the veracity of the promises made under the guise of democratic ideals, public schools are still important. For many children and their families, public schools offer a promise of equal access and social justice that is not found in many countries. Public schools and the state-mandated curriculum are hotly debated topics throughout the country; however, the fierceness of these arguments only highlights the importance of the institution and the knowledge that it serves up to children on a daily basis. In contrast to the Dominican Republic and Jamaica, there is no centralized organization for schools, schools are controlled by the states and interventions from the federal government occur through specialized programmes, constitutional issues, laws, grants and other initiatives through the US Department of Education.

Despite efforts to extend the privatization of schools through charter schools and school vouchers, public education in the United States currently serves approximately:

> 50.4 million public school students entering prekindergarten through grade 12 in fall 2016, White students will account for 24.6 million. The remaining 25.9 million will be composed of 7.8 million Black students, 13.3 million Hispanic students, 2.7 million Asian/Pacific Islander students, 0.5 million American Indian/Alaska Native students, and 1.5 million students of two or more races. The percentage of students enrolled in public schools who are White is projected to continue to decline through at least fall 2025, as the enrollments of Hispanic students and Asian/Pacific Islander students increase. (National Center for Educational Statistics 2016, n.p.)

In the United States, the public schools enrol 90% of all school age children leaving 10% to private or home-based education (Jennings 2013, n.p.). These statistics are powerful; the demographics of the public schools are changing, and yet, data consistently show that the schools are not successfully responding to the needs of twenty-first-century students.

Important to any discussion of public schools and twenty-first-century students in the United States is a consideration of two basic questions: First, how much do we spend on education, and second, what is the relationship between funding and educational outcomes. In response to these questions, Lips et al. (2008) make the following key points:

1. American spending on public K–12 education continues at an all-time high and is still rising, reaching $9,266 per pupil in 2004–2005. Total real spending per student (including all levels of government funding) has increased by 23.5 percent over the past decade and 49 percent over the past 20 years.
2. Federal spending on elementary and secondary education has also increased dramatically. Since 1985, real federal spending on K–12 education has increased by 138 percent.
3. Continuous spending increases have not corresponded with equal improvement in American educational performance. Long-term NAEP reading scale scores and high school graduation rates show that the performance of American students has not improved dramatically in recent decades even though education spending has soared.

4. Instead of simply increasing funding for public education, federal and state policymakers should implement education reforms, such as parental choice in education, designed to improve resource allocation and boost student performance. (n.p.)

Their conclusions from this data were that "taxpayers have invested considerable resources in the nation's public schools. However, ever-increasing funding of Education has not led to similarly improved student performance. Instead of simply increasing funding for public Education, federal and state policymakers should implement Education reforms designed to improve resource allocation and boost student performance" (Lips et al. 2008, n.p.) According to Hanushek (2004):

> One possibility is that the impact of resources is complicated—involving interactions with various inputs that are not observed or are not understood. The simplest notion is that teacher quality interacts with resources to determine outcomes. In the illustrative calculations, teacher quality essentially determines the efficiency with which resources are converted into student achievement. In this, we see that resource estimates are biased and also tend to be statistically insignificant. (p. 170)

Of course, these conclusions address some of the controversy that plagues schools in the United States; school reform that promotes school choice is often another moniker for the privatization of public schools. And while school choice among public schools could potentially yield more viable public institutions, choices that drain public schools of both resources and students are not satisfactory. Public schools require a constituency of major stakeholders who are diverse in educational and economic circumstance and who provide a rich context for "fixing" what is wrong with the schools invested with the job of serving all students. However, the focus of this chapter is on teachers, and once again, the potential of teacher leaders to change the schools is largely ignored in the general literature.

Teachers in the United States today are better educated than ever before:

> More than half of public school teachers hold at least a Master's degree. In the overall teaching force, there has been a slight shift in highest degree held. In 2005, a master's degree in education was the highest degree held by nearly half of the teaching force (47 percent); an additional 10 percent held a Master's degree in a field other than education. In 2011, the

proportion of the teaching force holding masters' degrees in education as their highest degree was 43 percent; 12 percent held Master's degrees. (Feistritzer 2011, p. x)

As such, "More than two decades of research findings are unequivocal about the connection between teacher quality and student learning" (The Center for Public Education 2005, n.p.). Good teachers with both experience and education make a difference in the overall achievement of students in their classes and could potentially take that knowledge and experience and apply it through key leadership roles in school improvement efforts. Again, similar to the situation in Jamaica, teachers with increasingly higher levels of education quite naturally expect new roles in the schools and changes in the tasks and responsibilities associated with their work, they are better qualified and more expert; therefore, they should receive the accoutrements of increased professional status and responsibilities. However, that is not happening and the myriad reasons for that general resistance to change are complicated and mired in a tradition steeped in sexist views of teachers and static notions of power and authority. Touting the important role of teachers in school improvement efforts, *What Matters Most: Teaching for America's Future* (1996), the report of the National Commission on Teaching and America's Future, identified three simple (and basic) premises in its blueprint for reforming the nation's schools. They are:

- What teachers know and can do is the most important influence on what students learn.
- Recruiting, preparing and retaining good teachers is the central strategy for improving our schools.
- School reform cannot succeed unless it focuses on creating the conditions under which teachers can teach and teach well. (p. 10)

Hanushek's (2004) work is encouraging in that he focuses upon the relationship between teacher leaders and decisions regarding the use of resources. Throwing more money at the schools is not a solution for what ails schools, but using that money in constructive ways to promote thoughtful solutions is a powerful idea that can be fuelled by tapping into the vast resources represented by highly trained and experienced teacher leaders working on the front line of public schools.

TRANSFORMATIVE TEACHER LEADERSHIP AND CURRICULUM MAKING

Ideas about teacher leadership took shape within the school improvement movement very quickly. Silva et al. (2000) discussed the evolution of teacher leadership in terms of three waves: (1) teachers as managers committed to increasing the efficacy of education organizations, (2)teachers as instructional specialists and (3) teachers as the primary directors of school culture. Now is the time for the emergence of a fourth wave. Teacher leadership for the twenty-first century must move beyond a consideration of teacher roles and relationships as subordinate to the work of other leaders within school organizations and consider the possibilities for a transformation of these relationships within the context of the teacher leadership movement, a transformation based on a different understanding of teachers' work that puts the needs and interests of teachers at the forefront of a revolution to transform schools and classrooms. Teachers must open themselves to questions concerning the meaning of their own individual existence and how answering the "call" to teach did not help them find sufficient meaning to their work as teachers. Placing this discussion within the context of Freire's (1968, 2000, 2013) work causes us to begin to look at teaching through a different lens that moves beyond a mere consideration of teaching and learning and instead focuses on key questions that seek to define the theoretical and ideological framework that governs how we think about models for understanding the roles and relationships of all leaders within educational organizations and has implications for how these leaders work together. Freire (1968) was unequivocal in his belief that leadership is defined by an ideological commitment to the principles of liberation and a disdain for actions and mandates that seek to control and oppress. Questioning and challenging the sources of oppression and creating spaces for negotiation and debate are the tasks of transformative leaders; to do anything less reflects a lack of courage and vision. Thus, the ideas in this chapter form the basis for an advocacy leadership situated within research that posits a theoretical and ideological framework for defining a fourth wave of teacher leadership that places this leadership within a framework of critical theory and examines the relationships between major stakeholders working in varying capacities within educational settings.

Teacher leadership has the potential to change not only how we think about the teaching profession generally but more specifically teacher leadership, by necessity, should be the cornerstone of all school reform in the Dominican Republic, Jamaica and the United States. Each of these countries struggles with issues related to resource allocation and a reconceptualization of curriculum making that should address the unique social and economic problems that afflict the schools in these countries. Each of these countries is simultaneously confronting issues related to the transformative changes occurring in the education and training of teachers, shifts that demand changes in the ways that we view teachers' roles and responsibilities in schools and classrooms. Thinking about curriculum making and asking the kinds of questions suggested by Tyler's (1949) work require that we start curriculum planning as a group process that involves the participation of various stakeholders representing diverse interests. Lambert (2005) suggests that there is a constructivist element to learning and leading that encompasses four dimensions of collaborative action:

1. Evoking our beliefs, assumptions, and perceptions.
2. Inquiring into practice in order to discover new information and data.
3. Constructing meaning or making sense of the discrepancies or tensions between what we believe and think and the new information that we have discovered is essential.
4. Acting collectively in community comes as a result of learning and deciding about what will be planned, created, or done differently. (p. 96)

In this way, teacher leaders have the opportunity to explore the various dimensions of the curriculum within a context that addresses the interface between curriculum making and the dynamic and fluid issues that impact our conceptions of teaching and learning within larger frameworks that are both ideological and practical.

Adding a transformative dimension to discussions of teacher leadership is a natural consequence of thinking about teacher leadership as having a strong ideological component. Henry Giroux (1988) had a vision of teachers acting as transformative intellectuals in classrooms, schools and communities. He saw teachers as intellectuals as having the potential to visualize the schools we need for the students we serve. Well-educated, thoughtful teachers acting as intellectuals and activists have the capacity to exercise radical manoeuvres to implement school reforms that address the myriad problems affecting the schools where they work. As previously stated, Giroux believed that "central to the category of transformative intellectual is the necessity of making the pedagogical more political and the political more pedagogical" (p. 127). In a similar vein, Cochran-Smith (1991) conceptualized the notion of "teaching against the grain." She described this skill in the following way:

> Teaching against the grain stems from, but also generates, critical perspectives on the macro-level relationships of power, labor, and ideology-relationships that are perhaps best examined at the university, where sustained and systematic study is possible. But teaching against the grain is also deeply embedded in the culture and history of teaching at individual schools and in the biographies of particular teachers and their individual or collaborative efforts to alter curricula, raise questions about common practices, and resist inappropriate decisions. These relationships can only be explored in schools in the company of experienced teachers who are themselves engaged in complex situation-specific, and sometimes losing struggles to work against the grain. (p. 280)

Teacher leadership that is transformative requires a commitment to not only "teaching against the grain" but also "leading against the grain." Carolyn Shields (2011) argues that "transformative leadership emphasizes the need for education to focus both on academic excellence and on social transformation" (p. 2). Additionally, she describes transformative educators as leaders who will:

- Acknowledge power and privilege;
- Articulate both individual and collective purposes (public and private good);
- Deconstruct social-cultural knowledge frameworks that generate inequity and reconstruct them in more equitable ways;
- Balance critique and promise;
- Effect deep and equitable change;
- Work towards transformation—liberation, emancipation, democracy, equity, and excellence;—and Demonstrate moral courage and activism. (p. 384)

Curriculum making that revises past narratives and addresses contemporary injustices requires transformative teacher leadership that reflects a commitment to "moral courage and activism" and fosters collaborative activism. Teachers in each of the countries discussed in this chapter have compelling responsibilities to serve as advocates for children and families who lack the power and status to affect meaningful and sustainable changes for themselves. Viewing the curriculum and the tasks associated with curriculum making as part of this larger vision requires a "transformative vision" similar to the one described in the Jamaican *Task Force on Educational Reform Final Report* (2004) where we were asked to consider that "if a nation continues to travel along the 'current path', it will not achieve the shared vision. What is required, is to get on the 'transformation path.' The difference between the 'current path' and the 'transformation path' is the transformation gap, which we must close" (p. 65). Closing the "transformation gap" is a necessary mandate for teacher leaders in the Dominican Republic, Jamaica and the United States.

CONCLUSIONS

There is an idea that I refer to in my work quite often; Spindler and Spindler (1982) urged us to "make the familiar strange and the strange familiar" (p. 15) to understand what is happening in the schools of any culture. In this chapter, we have briefly looked at the problems and issues that affect the schools of three very different countries. Initially, I am certain that most people easily see the similarities between the Dominican Republic and Jamaica; both countries represent developing Caribbean countries facing similar challenges. However, I contend that there is also meaning to be gained from comparing and contrasting the schools of the United States with those of the other two countries. Despite tremendous wealth and access to many first-world resources, schools in the United States are still afflicted by social and economic problems associated with the great divide that exists between those with varying levels of social, cultural and economic capital. In order to "make the familiar strange and the strange familiar," I have presented countries that, at first glance, seem strange and different, and yet, the teachers in each of these countries play key roles in the closing the "transformation gap"; familiarizing one's self with these schools provides lessons for examining the ways in which transformative teacher leadership could function in a variety of scenarios for the betterment of schools as well as improvements in pedagogy and the teaching profession. The possibilities and potentialities for a transformation of the teaching profession and a subsequent transformation of teaching and learning in public spaces are unlimited. Curriculum is the foundation of these change efforts, and transformative teacher leadership is the mechanism for conceptualizing, implementing and sustaining meaningful change while simultaneously changing the very nature of teachers' work. It is only in this way that curriculum theory, policy and practice can interface with transformative teacher leadership to meet the needs of twenty-first-century schools, families and communities in the Dominican Republic, Jamaica and the United States where the development and dissemination of universal education is essential to their progress and success.

REFERENCES

Anderson, G. (2009). *Advocacy leadership: Toward a post-reform agenda in education.* New York: Routledge.

Center for Public Education. (2005). *Teacher quality and student achievement.* Retrieved from http://www.centerforpubliceducation.org/Main-Menu/Staffingstudents/Teacher-quality-and-student-achievement-At-a-glance/Teacher-quality-and-student-achievement-Research-review.html

Chapman, F. (1987, January 1). *Illiteracy and educational development in the Dominican Republic: An historical approach.* Doctoral Dissertations Available from Proquest. Paper AAI8805902.

Cochran-Smith, M. (1991). Learning to teach against the grain. *Harvard Educational Review, 51*(3), 279–310.

Covey, S. (2013). *The 7 habits of highly successful people: Powerful lessons in personal change* (Anniversary ed.). New York: Simon & Schuster.

Creed, J. (2012). *The dilemma of education in the Dominican Republic.* Retrieved from http://study-abroad-blog-santiago-dr-sl.ciee.org/2012/09/the-dilemma-of-education-in-the-dominican-republic.html

Danielson, C. (2006). *Teacher leadership that strengthens professional practice.* Alexandria: Association for Supervision and Curriculum Development (ASCD).

Dominican Republic revamps failing education system (2016). *DW: Made for minds.* Retrieved from http://www.dw.com/en/dominican-republic-revamps-failing-education-system/a-17625149

Du Bois, W. E. B. (1970). The freedom to learn. In P. S. Foner (Ed.), *W.E.B. Du Bois speaks* (pp. 230–231). New York: Pathfinder. (Original work published 1949).

Education in the Dominican Republic. (n.d.). Retrieved from http://www.makariosinternational.org/education-in-the-dr.html

Education is the most critical issue facing the Dominican Republic. (n.d.). Retrieved from http://www.dominicanwatchdog.org/page-Education_is_the_most_critical_issue_facing_the_Dominican_Republic

Education performance and failing schools. (2011, September 11). *The Daily Gleaner.* Retrieved from http://jamaica-gleaner.com/gleaner/20110911/focus/focus1.html

Evans, H. (1993). The choice of teaching as a career. *Social and Economic Studies*, *42*(2/3), 225–242. Retrieved from http://www.jstor.org/stable/27865902

Feistritzer, C. E. (2011). *Profile of American teachers in the U.S. 2011* (pp. v–86). National Center for Education Information. Retrieved from http://www.edweek.org/media/pot2011final-blog.pdf

Fix our broke and broken education system. (2014, January 24). *The Daily Gleaner*. Retrieved from http://jamaica-gleaner.com/article/lead-stories/20160124/fix-our-broke-and-broken-education-system

Freire, P. (1968). *Pedagogy of the oppressed*. New York: Continuum.

Freire, P. (2000). *Pedagogy of freedom: Ethics, democracy and civic courage*. Lanham: Rowman & Littlefield.

Freire, P. (2013). *Education for critical consciousness* (Reprint ed.). New York: Bloomsbury Academic.

Giroux, H. (1988). *Teachers as intellectuals: Toward a critical pedagogy of learning*. Westport: Begin & Garvey.

Giroux, H. (2012). *Education and the crisis of public values: Challenging the assault on teachers, students, & public education*. New York: Peter Lang Publishing, Inc.

Goldstein, D. (2015). *The teacher wars: A history of America's most embattled profession*. New York: Anchor Books.

Green, E. (2015). *Building a better teacher: How teaching works (and how to teach it to everyone)*. New York: W.W. Norton & Company, Inc.

Guzmán, J. L., Castillo, M., Lavarreda, J., & Mejia, R. (2013). *Effective teacher training policies to ensure effective schools: A perspective from Central America and the Dominican Republic*. Partnership for educational revitalization in the Americas (PREAL), The Central American Educational and Cultural Coordination (CECC/SICA), UNESCO—Santiago—Regional Bureau for Education in Latin America and the Caribbean.

Hanushek, E. A. (2004). What if there are no 'best practices'? *Scottish Journal of Political Economy, 51*(2), 156–172.

Jennings, Z. (2001). Teacher education in selected countries in the Commonwealth Caribbean: The ideal of policy versus the reality of practice. *Comparative Education, 37*(1), 107–134. Retrieved from http://www.jstor.org/stable/3099735.

Jennings, J. (2013, May 28). Proportion of students in private schools is 10 percent and declining. *The Huffington Post*. Retrieved from http://www.huffingtonpost.com/jack-jennings/proportion-of-us-students_b_2950948.html

Katzenmeyer, M., & Moller, G. (2009). *Awakening the sleeping giant: Helping teachers develop as leaders* (3rd ed.). Thousand Oakes: Corwin Press.

Kozol, J. (2012). *Savage inequalities: Children in America's schools* (Reprint ed.). New York: Broadway Books.

Lambert, L. (2005). Constructivist leadership. In B. Davis (Ed.), *The essentials of school leadership* (pp. 93–109). London: Paul Chapman Publishing and Corwin Press.

Lips, D., Watkins, S., & Fleming, J. (2008, September 8). *Does spending more on education improve academic achievement?* Retrieved from http://www.heritage.org/research/reports/2008/09/does-spending-more-on-education-improve-academic-achievement

Manning, K. (2014). *Dominican Republic revamps failing education system.* Retrieved from http://dw.com/p/1Bx6b

McLaren, P. (2015). *Pedagogy of insurrection: From resurrection to revolution.* New York: Peter Lang Publishing, Inc.

Meighoo, K. (1999). Curry goat a metaphor for the Indian/Jamaican future. *Social and Economic Studies, 48*(3), 43–59. Retrieved from http://www.jstor.org/stable/27865148

National Center for Education Statistics. (2016). *Fast facts.* Retrieved from http://nces.ed.gov/fastfacts/display.asp?id=372

National Commission on Teaching and America's Future. (1996). *What matters most: Teaching for America's future.* Retrieved from http://nctaf.org/wp-content/uploads/WhatMattersMost.pdf

OREALC/UNESCO. (2008). *Segundo Estudio Regional Comparativo y Explicativo. Los aprendizajes de los estudiantes en América Latina y el Caribe.* Santiago: Author.

Pinar, W. (2004). *What is curriculum theory?* New York: Routledge.

Planning Institute of Jamaica (2010). *Vision 2030: Jamaica national development plan, planning for a secure and prosperous future.* Jamaica: The Herald Limited.

PNUD. (2008). *Desarrollo Humano. Una cuestión de poder. Informe de Desarrollo Humano de la República Dominicana.* Santo Domingo: Author.

PNUD. (2010). *Hacia un Estado para el desarrollo humano. Informe nacional desarrollo humano 2009–2010.* Guatemala: Author.

PNUD. (2012). *¿Un país de oportunidades para la juventud? Informe nacional de desarrollo humano 2011–2012.* Guatemala: Author.

PREAL/CIEDHUMANO. (2012). *Taller sobre políticas docentes.* Unpublished draft, Santo Domingo.

PREAL/EDUCA. (2010). *El reto es la calidad. Informe de progreso educativo de República Dominicana.* Santo Domingo: Author.

Reyes-Guerra, D., & Bogotch, I. E. (2011). Curriculum–inquiry as a transformational educational leadership skill. In C. Shields (Ed.), *Transformative leadership: A reader* (pp. 137–154). New York: Peter Lang Publishing, Inc.

Rodgers-Jenkinson, F., & Chapman, D. W. (1990). Job satisfaction of Jamaican elementary/school teachers. *International Review of Education/Internationale Zeitschrift für Erziehungswissenschaft Revue Internationale de l'Education, 36*(3), 299–313. Retrieved from http://www.jstor.org/stable/3444507.

Shields, C. (Ed.). (2011). *Transformative leadership: A reader.* New York: Peter Lang Publishing, Inc.

Silva, D. Y., Gimbert, B., & Nolan, J. (2000). Sliding the doors: Locking and unlocking possibilities for teacher leadership. *Teachers College Record, 102*(4), 779–804.

Spindler, G., & Spindler, L. (1982). Roger Harker and Schöenhausen: From familiar to strange and back again. In G. Spindler (Ed.), *Doing the ethnography of schooling: Educational anthropology in action* (pp. 20–46). New York: Holt, Rinehart, and Winston.

Target teacher training—Education needs top quality for transformation. (2016, September 7). *The Daily Gleaner.* Retrieved from http://jamaica-gleaner. com/article/lead-stories/20160907/target-teacher-training-education-needs-top-quality-transformation

Taskforce on Educational Reform Final Report. (2004). *Jamaica: A Transformed Education System,* pp. 1–176.

Tyler, R. W. (1949). *Basic principles of curriculum and instruction.* Chicago: University of Chicago Press.

Walker, D. F., & Soltis, J. F. (1997). *Curriculum and aims* (3rd ed.). New York: Teachers College Press.

Eleanor Blair received her Ph.D. from the University of Tennessee, Knoxville. She is an associate professor at Western Carolina University and teaches courses in curriculum, teacher leadership and history/philosophy of education. She is a frequent presenter at regional, national and international conferences and has authored chapters and essays in books and journals.

PART 2

Critical Issues Beyond Pedagogy

1.1 INTRODUCTION

This section starts off with an interesting chapter that helps the reader to appreciate how different societies determine what knowledge is worthy of discussion through its school curricula, thus reflecting the cultural, philosophical and political beliefs the education authorities/policymakers uphold. The purpose of the study undertaken by Varbelow and Gee was to explore the role educational experiences in Vietnam, Mexico and the USA play in how people create life purpose. Through the use of narrative enquiry and adopting Huebner's (1975) perspective that people exist in three relationships simultaneously, the authors focused on what kinds of relationships curriculum encounters nurture—with the world, other and self.

The study allows the reader to think about the curriculum and the purpose of school with an epistemological lens that illuminates how the educational experiences and the contextual factors in which they occur influence a person's beliefs about life purpose. Varbelow and Gee note that the divide between policy and practice is quite evident in the developing world, here represented by Mexico and Vietnam. They note that national goals may call for addressing the social and financial gaps that exist between people living in urban and rural regions, yet the realities prove otherwise.

Varbelow and Gee propose that we should approach curriculum issue not from a macro-or micro-level but from a meso-level in order to reflect the balance between globalization and cultural context. The responses from the study's participants present some interesting insights into apparent differences among the three countries.

The American respondents describe their experiences with teachers as hands-on and their relationships with *others* as one created by coming to terms with one's place in social relations. The authors point out that American encounters with *self* reflect the ideal behind the American dream—that is, that hard work pays off. This may not mean that life presents us with an easy passage, but the encounters in life allow people to persevere, to engage. It is those engagements—varied as they may be—that prepare one to find one's path, to think about oneself in terms of what matters to her/him. Searching for those life-changing epiphanies is very much dependent on how one is supported early on in life to appreciate and work to search for meaning.

The Mexican curriculum encounters portrayed a rather different engagement. Relationships with teachers depended on respect and obedience to those in authority. They spoke of caring and supportive teachers who encouraged them to do well. The importance of the family came out strongly in their responses and was also reinforced by the school and teachers who saw education as a means of giving a good job that helped the financial position of their families. The *self* was perceived as a person responsible for the family and their own development. Thus, encounters with curriculum further an understanding of *self* as part of one's immediate and extended family.

On the other hand, the Vietnamese responses depicted a different scenario. The respondents spoke of their relationship with their teachers as one of absolute acceptance. The focus was on passing examinations which dictated the type of relationship between the teacher and students. The rapport described seemed cold and clinical. If one failed her/his exams, you were deemed a failure. Even though you may succeed in passing exams and graduating with a degree, job opportunities were slim given the state of the country where connections determined whether one got on in life. At the same time, maybe because of this, the respondents spoke of fortitude, of never giving up in spite of the difficulties one encountered in life.

Overall, the findings indicate that whilst in the USA the purpose of school is to enable self-understanding and self-determination, in Mexico the kind of purpose furthered by the curriculum is to better oneself for the sake of the family. In Vietnam however the curriculum is used to transfer knowledge and the purpose of school is the passing of examinations which validates parents' sacrifices and determines a student's worth. Verbelow and Gee argue that these findings reflect a major difference between the two developing countries and the Western one. Whereas in the USA, the "I" is at the centre of things, with communities being based on personal interest which could either be natural strengths or the prospect of financial gains. In contrast, for Mexicans and Vietnamese, the source of energy for life purpose is the community one finds herself/himself in. The individual thrives if the community thrives, for which reason the impetus derives from group needs. In the USA they are born out of individual needs.

As reflected through the views of the respondents, whilst remaining cautious of gross generalizations, we can see that the views of Western countries may be different from non-Western ones. We would argue that a country's education system, even regional or local ones, influence how life purpose is created and actualized by the individual. This is complicated further by both local and global contexts that put pressure—positive and/or negative pressures—as we go through life. The way in which society educates its young reflects what knowledge it considers to be of most worth. It shapes the beliefs and values the curriculum fosters, which influence an individual's self-understanding and how a person places herself/himself in the communities she/he forms part of. Ladson-Billings (2016) argues that curriculum is about the essence of knowledge and therefore primarily an epistemological and metaphysical endeavour.

The chapter encourages the reader as educator to explore the phenomenon called school and how we relate to the curriculum in our daily lives and how this influences the way we relate to students. The question beckons: what is our purpose as educators? What role do we play to allow individuals to engage at the personal, family and community level to create a meaningful existence? The authors argue that "a fundamental notion when thinking about purpose of school has to be the cultivation of critical consciousness necessary for a worldview that goes beyond the truths learned and experienced through the curriculum." The conclusion highlights the importance of the person as explored by David Brooks in his book *The Road to Character*. Brooks notes that we all possess two natures:

> one focuses on external success, that is wealth, fame, status and a great career. The other aims for internal goodness, driven by a spiritual urge not only to do good but to be good – honest, loving and steadfast. The inner self doesn't seek happiness superficially defined; it seeks emotional commitments without counting the cost, and a deeper moral joy. Individuals and

societies thrive when a general balance is struck between these two imperatives. (2015, inside cover)

It is here that the experiences of the six respondents in Varbelow and Gee's study take on added significance. We should not strive to reach so-called Western ideals but appreciate that individuals and societies need to create a culture that helps us connect and follow the humble path to use the journey metaphor coined by Brooks.

The next chapter by Vu explores how ideologies are embedded in the secondary school history textbooks of three countries, the USA, China and Vietnam, through the narratives of World War II. The study employed a combined qualitative method of ideological discourse analysis and narrative discourse analysis and gathered data from textbooks in the three countries. The author argues that history textbooks help us to construct our past, represent our national identity and reinforce certain dynamics of power-knowledge interrelationships. History textbooks, it has been suggested, play a significant role in political socialization and promoting patriotism. However, as Altbach (1991) notes, textbooks play a part in portraying and disseminating certain knowledge particularly of those countries who enjoy access to multinational publishers. Chau notes that whilst various studies have been undertaken on the ideological and political agenda of a country's curriculum, on history education as part of nation-building, others have investigated the ideologies embedded in textbooks as singular countries. However, a multinational perspective is still missing. This contribution tries to address this void.

The study undertaken by Vu through van Dijk's (1995) framework of ideological discourse analysis and Foster and Nicholls' (2005) narrative analysis method sought to provide a multifaceted representation of World War II and examines the ideological agendas of contemporary societies. As Barker (2000) points out, ideology is maps of meaning which purport to be universal truth but are in fact specific understandings historically and intentionally constructed to obscure certain groups' power while restraining that of others. In this manner, education is institutionalized and, through textbooks and other means, aims to mould and regulate thoughts and behaviour. The author argues that the reader should be able to engage with textbooks with an open mind, recognizing them for what they are and represent.

The author contends that history textbooks tend to be embedded with political ideologies, mainly democracy, socialism and Marxism-Leninism.

The three countries shared similar attempts to promote exceptionalism and nationalism through the textbooks they produced. According to Vu textbooks have been granted too much power in deciding what is taught and how knowledge is constructed from a homogenous perspective. As Nicholls (2006) argues, textbook researchers can never attain a neutral position to observe the objects being researched from above; hence they "will always be bound to a location, socially, politically and culturally enmeshed in relations of power and knowledge" (p. 105).

The way forward is to encourage students to explore different perspectives and to engage with different sources rather than be limited by a textbook, hence perspective and ideology. The role of the teacher in this endeavour is far from an easy one as the educator herself/himself is conditioned by the context they form part of. The challenge remains of how to teach for meaning, leading to what Vu describes as the "critical pedagogy of engagement, of learning."

In a similar vein the chapter by Ramírez and Salinas explores a particular theme in science textbooks for speakers of Spanish in Colombia, Mexico and the USA. A microanalysis of these texts reveals a strong market-based neoliberal influence on the textbook used in the USA. At the micro-level, the comparative systemic functional linguistic analysis of these three texts reveals the distinct linguistic organization of the mirror text in relation to the other two. Using Martin and Rose's (2007) systemic functional linguistics (SFL) framework, the authors were able to discern how language structures and macrostructures in each of the reviewed textbooks were organized to describe, report and inform on the subject area chosen for review, namely, "Matter." By using an SFL-informed analytical approach which recognizes that language is structured according to meaning, the authors were able to distinguish and compare the academic language choices in each text across a common genre and purpose both within and beyond the clause.

This chapter helps to bring out that the educational context of the USA is a context that has responded to the global economic and political restructuring in the service of free market imperatives. This is the official recontextualizing field (ORF). ORF is controlled by the state, selected agents and ministries in charge not only of transforming specialist knowledge through the development of syllabi, curricula and assessment regimes but, importantly, responsible for legitimizing through standards and mandates what is to be learned in schools. Its marketization efforts have resulted in the intensification of teachers' work that in turn has led to degeneration of teacher professionalism, where teachers are less trusted as qualified candidates to make value judgments on the best learning paths for students who they know best. This "distrust" was found to be operationalized in the pedagogic recontextualizing field through the textbook contents. As revealed in the analysis, even though the texts share the same topic (matter), the same grade level (3rd grade) and the same register (informational texts), they are indeed very different texts with distinct consequences for students and teachers. The mirror text used in the USA was found to miss important lexical connections between the everyday and the academic register in Spanish and impose an English-dominant syntactical straightjacket on Spanish, nor present in the other two texts. More importantly, explored at the micro-level, the text was found to assume a burdening interactional pattern that foregrounds interpersonal affiliation at the expense the disciplinary knowledge Emergent to Advanced Bilingual (EAB) students require for success in academic settings. Explored at the macro-level, it serves as yet another illustration of the intensification of teacher's work with dire consequences for the education of all students, including EABs.

Findings of this analysis strongly suggest that EABs enrolled in bilingual programmes across the USA may benefit from having access to texts that are originally written in Spanish. Indeed, and as part of Mexico's Free Textbook Distribution Program, the Secretary of Public Education and the Secretary of Foreign Relations (through the Mexican Cultural Center) have begun to provide the state of Colorado in the USA with resource books for 1–6 grades that are used for Mexico's national curriculum, as a resource for binational students. The authors end by stating that policymakers, educators and research must continue to advocate for quality education for all EAB students.

As we have seen throughout this book, understanding curriculum and how this is manifested through its different facets and perspectives is an extremely complicated endeavour. Whilst some of the critique put forward may have presented us with a bleak picture, albeit a real one, we conclude this section by exploring the role of the Arts as an integral part of society and how the Arts, more so in today's world, can help us appreciate the value of life as the thread that can bring people together and challenge the artificial boundaries that we have created even through the very educational institutions that we form part of. The three countries selected for the chapter are Australia, Canada and Malaysia. They were chosen due to

CRITICAL ISSUES BEYOND PEDAGOGY

their similarities in population, English as a language priority, connections to the monarchy and indigenous populations.

For the purpose of the chapter, the secondary arts curriculum documents were examined from Australia, Canada and Malaysia; then cultural differences were considered using Geert Hofstede's Six Dimensions of National Cultures (Hofstede 2016). Hofstede conducted research into cultural structures with an aim to explain how people from different nations think, feel and act. From his research over 40 years and examining 70 countries, he constructed six dimensions in which to better understand different culture. The six dimensions are *Power Distance, Individualism, Masculinity, Uncertainty Avoidance, Long-Term Orientation* and *Indulgence*. Through these lenses, a deeper understanding of "difference" can be gained in order to reveal more insight to how these factors influence educational systems and the Arts, in an increasingly complicated world. Lierse argues that the way the Arts are taught and represented in the school curriculum is a reflection of their aesthetical values and cultural significance. And, as Robinson and Aronica (2009) argue, she feels that the Arts can reveal how society represents current themes and issues such as indigenous cultures, globalization and the environment.

We would argue that the Arts can serve a central and critical role in education and society if teachers are allowed to develop meaningful experiences which are not hindered by the shackles of the neoliberal world we are in. Halpin (2003) argues that "every human society has its own shape, purposes and meanings or culture. Indeed, the making of society – reproducing and transforming it – is centrally to do with looking for and identifying common meanings and directions through active debate and amendment" (p. 120).

Worthy of note is the way each country looks at the Arts from a formal school perspective. In Australia, students are encouraged to follow the Arts but the programme is not compulsory. The country recognizes the central role of education in building a democratic, equitable and just society and the Arts are recognized as an important medium to achieve this goal. Interesting to note that in Canada, in the province Ontario, teachers are expected to model Arts knowledge, skills and strategies across all subject areas and which are connected to their overall lives. Even in Canada the Arts are not compulsory but one can see that there is a focus on indigenous culture so that students gain a better and deeper understanding of the society/communities they form part of. Similarly, in Malaysia the Arts are not compulsory but considered as an important area. In fact a number of art schools specializing in developing the artistic talents of students have opened up.

Through examining Hofstede's Six Dimensions of National Culture in these countries, the chapter presents some insights into what is valued and prioritized by society. Furthermore, they reflect the decisions governments make in relation to education and the arts. These values are sometimes overtly expressed, but more often than not, these cultural assumptions are ingrained into the nation's psyche. Understanding cultural values for each country is complex and multidimensional. The scores for Australia and Canada were similar in Power Distance, Uncertainty Avoidance and Indulgence displaying that the power relationship in schools was relatively equal, can deal with some change and enjoyed the nice things in life. Australia scored highly in Individualism and Masculinity but low in Long-Term Orientation. How this would apply to an arts programme is that schools would value achievement of individuals and would be competitive, but would hold onto traditions. Schools would value the arts, especially when the programmes were successful. Canada is similar to Australia but is a more Feminine society and scored higher in Long-Term Orientation. Arts programmes in schools would be more adaptable to change and the school community, more cooperative. Malaysia in contrast scored the highest in Power Distance showing a set hierarchy between students and staff but more collective than being competitive. An arts programme would be managed by the school leaders and there would be a collective culture within the classroom rather than promoting select individuals. The arts programmes in schools would be influenced by the cultural values of the nation and manifested in their curriculum documents.

Such a study takes us back to the observation made by Halpin—that society's reproduce themselves. What is critical is whether, in this case, through the Arts one can transform society to achieve the laudable goal of building a democratic, equitable and just society or whether it only helps to perpetuate the existing differences.

Altogether the four chapters in this section provide the reader with interesting insights into the critical role the curriculum plays in a society. The authors have shown how ideologies and purposes are manifested through textbooks, programmes and the teachers who implement them reiterating the need for the awakening of the learners' critical consciousness in deciphering truths.

REFERENCES

Altbach, P. G. (1991). Textbooks: The international dimension. In M. W. Apple & L. K. Christian-Smith (Eds.), *The politics of the textbook* (pp. 242–258). New York: Routledge.

Barker, C. (2000). *Cultural studies: Theory and practice.* London: Sage.

Brooks, D. (2015). *The road to character.* New York: Allen Lane.

Foster, S., & Nicholls, J. (2005). America in World War II: An analysis of history textbooks from England, Japan, Sweden, and the United States. *Journal of Curriculum and Supervision, 20*(3), 214–233.

Halpin, D. (2003). *Hope and education – The role of the utopian imagination.* London: RoutledgeFalmer.

Hofstede, G. (2016). National culture. Retrieved from https://www.geerthofstede.com/national-culture.html

Huebner, D. (1975). Poetry and power: The politics of curricular development. In V. Hillis (Ed.) (1999), *The lure of the transcendent: Collected essays by Dwayne E. Huebner* (pp. 231–240). Mahwah: Lawrence Erlbaum Associates.

Ladson-Billings, G. (2016). And then there is this thing called the curriculum: Organization, imagination, and mind. *Educational Researcher, 45*(2), 100–104. doi:10.3102/0013189x16639042.

Martin, J. R., & Rose, D. (2007). *Working with discourse: Meaning beyond the clause* (2nd ed.). New York: Continuum.

Nicholls, J. (2006). Beyond the national and the transnational: Perspectives of WWII in U.S.A., Italian, Swedish, Japanese, and English school history textbooks. In S. J. Foster & K. A. Crawford (Eds.), *What shall we tell the children? International perspectives on school history textbooks* (pp. 89–112). Charlotte: Information Age Publishing.

Robinson, K., & Aronica, L. (2009). *The element: How finding your passion changes everything.* London: Penguin.

Van Dijk, T. A. (1995). Discourse analysis as ideology analysis. In C. Schäffner & A. L. Wenden (Eds.), *Language and peace.* Amsterdam: Harwood.

The Curriculum in Praxis: How Purpose of School is Actualized in Vietnam, Mexico, and the USA

Sonja Varbelow and Donna Gee

INTRODUCTION

What is the purpose of school, and what role does culture play in how that purpose is actualized? How this question is approached reflects how society thinks about what knowledge is of most worth, which ultimately reflects cultural, philosophical, and political ideas about life purpose (Huebner 1975/1999; Kincheloe 2008). This study explores how curriculum influences the way people create life purpose in Vietnam, Mexico, and the USA. The theoretical framework is narrativity; the data analysis framework is narrative inquiry. The findings point to how curriculum reflects cultural and political beliefs about life purpose and how each country uses its education system as an instrument to further evolve truths. These findings allow educators to think about curriculum and the purpose of school

S. Varbelow (✉) • D. Gee
Angelo State University, San Angelo, TX, USA

© The Author(s) 2018   145
C. Roofe, C. Bezzina (eds.), *Intercultural Studies of Curriculum*, Intercultural Studies in Education,
https://doi.org/10.1007/978-3-319-60897-6_7

with an epistemological lens that illuminates how educational experiences and the contextual factors in which they occur influence a person's beliefs about life purpose. For the parameters of this study, we define *life purpose* as the impetus for individual decision-making processes.

We begin this chapter by delineating fundamental features of each country's education system followed by a review of the pertinent literature. We then outline the methodology for this study before representing the findings. We conclude this chapter with a discussion of what the findings contribute to fundamental questions about the purpose of school and what knowledge is of most worth.

THE EDUCATION SYSTEMS OF THE USA, MEXICO, AND VIETNAM

In this section, we provide an overview of the basic characteristics of the education systems of each country. Table 1 compares the three systems.

The Education System of the USA

Education in the USA is compulsory for kindergarten through 12th grade. Elementary school starts with kindergarten at the age of five and continues through 5th grade. Students then move on to middle school, which typically comprises grades 6–8. High school consists of 9th–12th grade (U.S. Network for Education Information 2008). Students take standardized tests starting in 3rd grade. Since the curriculum is designed by each state, the tests are based on state-mandated requirements and promotion and retention measures differ among the states. Generally a failing student must attend remedial courses. Failure in grades 5 and 8

Table 1 Comparison of the education system in Vietnam, Mexico, and the USA

Characteristic	Vietnam	Mexico	USA
Compulsory schooling	Primary and middle school only	X	X
Free public schooling	–	X	X
School choice (private, charter, etc.)	Dependent on financial means	X	X
High-stakes testing	X	–	X
College-oriented	X	–	X
National curriculum	X	X	–

usually results in automatic retention. A high school diploma is obtained with passing scores for the five End Of Course Exams that are administered in biology, algebra, history, and twice in English (U.S. Department of Education 2016). From elementary through high school, children are oriented toward college.

The Education System of Mexico

Education in Mexico is compulsory from preschool through 12th grade (Amanti 2013). Primary education comprises grades 1–6. Students then enter lower secondary for grades 7–9. Upper secondary consists of grades 10–12, although a few states identify grade 11 as completion of upper secondary (Magaziner and Monroy 2016). Compulsory education laws require students to remain in school until all grade levels are completed (Amanti 2013). However, Puryear et al. (2012) reported that almost half of all students at the secondary level drop out and do not graduate. Students from low socioeconomic families have a higher dropout rate than children of higher socioeconomic status (Amanti 2013; Puryear et al. 2012). The high school curriculum includes mathematics, natural and social sciences, and language and communication with courses usually including "biology, chemistry, physics, a foreign language, arts, and technology" (Magaziner and Monroy 2016, n. p.).

The Education System of Vietnam

Vietnamese children attend elementary school for grades 1–5 and middle school for grades 6–9. The new Education Law, passed in 2006, states that "learning is the right and obligation of every citizen" and that families have the responsibility to help members between the ages of 6 and 14 to obtain "universalized education" (United Nations Educational, Scientific, and Cultural Organization 2010/2011, n.p.). Although attendance is officially compulsory, no repercussions are in place for parents who do not send their children to school. Article 10 of same law requires the State to ensure social equity in education; however, particularly in poor rural areas, children forsake regular education to help provide food for their families. Officially, attendance for grades 1–9 is free, but the government permits the collection of tuition fees (World Bank Group 2016), which change monthly.

Primary education enables children to achieve basic literacy in writing, reading, mathematics, physical and moral education, art, and science as it pertains to personal health and hygiene (Hằng et al. 2015). In middle school, history and geography are added. At the end of 9th grade, students take a comprehensive exam whose results determine whether they can continue on to high school. The test results also determine if students can attend the high school of their first or second choice or whether they have to go to the neighborhood school, which limits their chances of education beyond 12th grade.

High school streams students into three tracks: basic, natural sciences, and social sciences (World Bank Group 2016). For three years, students prepare intensely for a high-stakes comprehensive exam, which they must pass to obtain their high school diploma. The scores simultaneously determine whether they can move on to higher education, which requires an almost perfect score.

Review of the Literature

Curriculum Theory as a Concept for Understanding Purpose of School in the USA

The US education system is driven by its official political goal, which is to prepare students for global competitiveness (U.S. Department of Education 2016). For the past three decades, schools have implemented a one-size-fits-all curriculum to get every high school graduate ready for college. While this might be an arduous and worthy goal, it is not working because only 75% of all high school students graduate and yet fewer enroll in college (Barton and Coley 2011).

Further, a society's needs go beyond getting high school students ready for college or career. It takes other skills to do well in life and additional skills to seek a profession, get employed, and hold a job. Ravitch (2016) voiced her fears regarding a minimalist curriculum, which trains, not educates, a generation of children who lack the cognitive and social skills to think for themselves and to make decisions. As long as a nation's primary goal for education is to outdo other countries on international tests, such as the PISA,[1] or in the global economy, this goal cannot be achieved because this is a shortcut approach that belies the fact that education is a process and not a result. Educating a nation means to educate individual people in ways that enable them to share their constructed knowledge for the good of their communities, small and large (Kincheloe 2008). In order for that to be possible, the reward and punishment system that has become the foundation of evaluation must be changed to one that allows teachers, schools, and districts to use evaluation methods honestly in order to analyze strengths and needs.

Curriculum Theory as a Concept for Understanding Purpose of School in Mexico

The Mexican education system is regulated by both the federal government, through the Secretaría de Educación Pública (SEP), and by the individual states (Magaziner and Monroy 2016). It has been the object of several reforms within the last two decades such as teacher education and professional development, curricular reforms, and increased compulsory schooling.

Further, the government has revised teacher evaluations to include promotions based on increased student achievement (Levinson 2014). Levinson (2014) indicated, "It is no coincidence that the proposed Mexican assessment regime bears a striking resemblance to the high-stakes testing inaugurated by No Child Left Behind in the United States. These are truly global trends" (51). The idea of raising student achievement is an important goal, but contextual factors, such as socioeconomic status, play a role in school achievement as pupils from high socioeconomic status tend to have much higher levels of academic success than their less wealthy counterparts, particularly indigenous students or those in rural locations (Amanti 2013; Puryear et al. 2012).

With regard to content, abovementioned SEP controls textbooks and the curriculum (Amanti 2013; Santibañez et al. 2005). Mexico employs a national curriculum that all schools must follow. Textbooks used at the primary level are published and distributed by the government. Secondary schools receive a list of approved textbooks from which they must select. Regardless of the control over the curriculum and required textbooks, scores have lagged on international exams, such as the PISA, with Mexico ranking in the bottom third of all countries (Levinson 2014; Puryear et al. 2012).

Curriculum Theory as a Concept for Understanding Purpose of School in Vietnam

The official goal of the Vietnamese education system is to develop "human resources for the industrialization and modernization of the country" (United Nations Educational, Scientific, and Cultural Organization

2010/2011, p. 10). The purpose of education is to form the socialist Vietnamese personality (United Nations Educational, Scientific, and Cultural Organization 2010/2011). Vietnam has a national curriculum, which was fundamentally restructured between 1997 and 2007 with focus on the renovation of teaching methodology, new textbooks, and English language learning.

While the new curriculum is designed to enable citizens to help their country progress, there is a fundamental discrepancy between theory and praxis. Most notably, the inequality of access to English language learning in rural areas widens the social and financial gap between urban and rural populations. Rural teachers are alone in their efforts, marginalized, and poorly trained. They do not have support from colleagues, administrators, parents, or the community because English is not used or even remotely present in the communities' lives (Chinh et al. 2014). Parents cannot help children with homework and have more pressing needs than supporting their children's English language learning. In urban areas, on the other hand, children encounter English in daily life, e.g., in the form of billboards and TV commercials while students in rural areas lack the social capital to even understand concepts like "museum" and "standing in line" (Chinh et al. 2014). Rural students are often considered less intelligent when, in fact, they have as much potential as their urban peers but lack their opportunities. As a result, by the time they meet their urban counterparts in middle or high school, they are already behind and feel inferior. The notion to make English mandatory in the third grade is an arduous and important goal, but it is executed in ways that further social injustice.

Despite basic cultural differences between Vietnam and the USA, it appears that the Vietnamese education system looks toward the USA as a model. For example, the National Institute for Education Management in Vietnam (NIEM) (National Institute of Education Management 2016) organized a conference in Hanoi to explore how the USA evaluates teacher effectiveness, which is based on students' test scores. And yet, research has shown that connecting students' test scores to teacher evaluation improves neither learning nor teaching (Darling-Hammond et al. 2012; Ravitch 2016).

The way in which a society educates its young reflects what knowledge it considers to be of most worth. It shapes the beliefs and values the curriculum fosters, which influence an individual's self-understanding and, eventually, how a person places her/himself in the communities of which s/he is a part. The undeniable influence of the USA points to the importance of economic power over other values, which bears the danger of clashing with culture and traditions in non-Western countries. Curriculum is about the essence of knowledge and therefore primarily an epistemological and metaphysical endeavor (Ladson-Billings 2016). It is not useful to approach curricular questions from the macro level of globalization nor from the micro level that reduces curriculum theory to practical know-how questions and people to human resources. In order to change education in ways that further a person's, and thereby a society's, becoming, all approaches have to meet at some meso level that resembles the balance between globalization and cultural context.

METHODOLOGY

The methodology employed to gather, analyze, and represent data was narrative inquiry. Narrative inquiry is based on the idea that people make meaning of experiences by thinking of them as stories. This study was conducted with six participants over a period of four months. Data was collected through structured and conversational interviews and memoirs. Data was collected in English, which all participants spoke fluently. The research sites for this project varied. Interviews were conducted face-to-face and via Skype within the country of residence, which for both researchers and participants was the USA. Part of the data collection and analysis processes were numerous member checks to assure trustworthiness and academic rigor (Glesne 2011). This research project was approved by the Internal Review Board to which the researchers report in order to ensure that all ethical requirements for social research were followed.

Participant Selection

In an attempt to explore how educational experiences influence a person's life purpose, we started our data collection with two participants in their late 60s. At this age, a person has lived a great part of his life and therefore has the unique ability to reflect on his life's choices retrospectively, which is an important aspect of exploring life purpose. Thomas and Julio[2] went to school in the USA during the 1960s at which time the US education system was similar to present-day education in Mexico and Vietnam as shown in Fig. 1.

Julio and Thomas' kindergarten through 12th grade experiences were characterized by social and academic challenges, respectively. Thomas

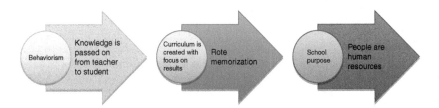

Fig. 1 Basic characteristics of the education systems of the USA, Mexico, and Vietnam at the time pertinent to the six participants

grew up as a White male in a middle class family, which means that education was a priority and a college degree always the goal. As a result, his dyslexia and dyscalculia, which were undiagnosed in the 1950s, had a major influence on his early educational experiences. By contrast, Julio, who is academically gifted, grew up as a Hispanic in a Mexican-American border town as the son of an auto parts sales clerk and a housewife. According to tradition, he was expected to end education with a high school diploma and get a job. Education for social mobility was not considered. Today Julio is a biologist and currently teaches at a private university in Texas. Thomas is an internationally renowned visual artist and teaches at a university in the Northern USA.

Our Mexican participants included a female in her late 30s and another who just celebrated her 50th birthday. At this time in life, purpose tends to be actively actualized rather than retrospectively reflected upon. Zoraida[3] completed grade 12 and two years of college, whereas Maria completed the required compulsory education, which at that time, ended with 9th grade. Zoraida's and Maria's parents encouraged and supported their education even though their families struggled financially. Both grew up in Mexico but currently live and are employed in the USA.

Finally, in order to understand something about the processes by which the lived curriculum influences how a person elects purpose for him/herself, we invited two Vietnamese students in their early 20s to participate in this study. Lý and Heidi[4] moved from Vietnam to the USA two and five years ago, respectively, and are currently taking classes for their bachelor's degree at different Texas universities. Heidi's father comes from a family who was too poor to support an education and dropped out in 6th grade. Her mother finished school, which, in the 1980s, ended with the 9th grade. Both parents made education for their children a priority. Similarly, Lý's mom dropped out after 6th grade while her father completed school.

Lý was raised with the notion that education is a means for upward social mobility. For example, her mother taught her how to write before Lý started school.

Glesne (2011) referred to this form of participant selection as purposeful selection. Patton (2002) explained that purposeful sampling allows the researcher to study a phenomenon in depth because s/he can "learn a great deal about issues of central importance to the purpose of research" (Patton 2002, p. 230). Of central importance to the purpose of this study is how people's educational experiences influence the way they create purpose for themselves. The different generations of participants offer diverse angles from which to illuminate this process, which helps to explore it in depth.

Data Collection, Analysis, and Representation

Primary data was collected in the form of conversational, semi-structured, structured, and member-check interviews; as well as written pieces such as memoirs, electronic mail, and text messages. Secondary data consisted of the researchers' reflections, analytic memos, and peer reviews.

The data analysis framework for this study is paradigmatic cognition, which uses stories as data that are analyzed through an inductive process. Polkinghorne (1995) stated that this approach to narrative analysis brings order to experiences by understanding how they are similar and form patterns (Polkinghorne 1995). We represent the data in the form of analytical narratives that contain in vivo quotes.[5] The findings were member-checked to assure accuracy, trustworthiness, and academic rigor.

Limitations

This study is limited by the number and choice of participants. While the six participants completed public school education, all three countries have a noteworthy number of children who drop out of school and whose approach to life purpose remains unexplored in this study. Another limitation consists in the researchers' subjectivity, which is grounded in our own experiences and beliefs and consequently influences how we make meaning of and represent the co-constructed truths that are the findings of this study. Hence, these findings cannot immediately be transferred to people other than those whose truths they represent. It will take the reader's interpretations to make them transferable. This means the findings of any

154   S. VARBELOW AND D. GEE

study are rather individual truths whose purpose is to serve as a source of criticism and imagination (Huebner 1979/1999). Individual analysis is needed to better understand how educational experiences and contextual factors influence a person's beliefs and life purpose.

FINDINGS

The purpose of this study was to explore how the lived curriculum influences an individual's life purpose. In order to answer these questions, we analyzed the data with focus on what kinds of relationships curriculum encounters nurture. People exist in three relationships simultaneously—with self, other, and world (Huebner 1975). The tables below summarize our findings regarding the nature of those relationships by country. In the classroom, *World* consists of the relationship between student and teacher and student and content; *Other* consists of student with student relationships; *Self* is how curriculum encounters are experienced and interpreted (Tables 2, 3, and 4).

The Role of US American Curriculum Encounters in Creating Life Purpose

When Thomas was asked how he felt about school, his immediate reply was: "I can't think of anything I liked about school." He noted the best teachers were those who left him alone to figure things out, perhaps

Table 2 The role of US American curriculum encounters in creating life purpose

Relationship	Curriculum encounters	Nature of the relationship	Influence on how life purpose is created
World	Student–teacher	Trust in authority	The world is there to help me
	Student–content	Need for immediate relevance	How can I fit in based on my talents and interests?
Other	Student–student	Competitive ethics Role of social status	What is my place in my social relations?
Self	With self	Trust in the system: hard work pays off Not standing out in socially detrimental ways	What matters to me, and how can I engage in those matters?

Table 3 The role of Mexican curriculum encounters in creating life purpose

Relationship	Curriculum encounters	Nature of the relationship	Influence on how life purpose is created
World	Student–teacher	Respect for authority Parenting-like	The teacher will help me I am helped if I am obedient
	Student–content	Interested Trusting in the teacher-parent	I am liked if I do well
Other	Student–student	Family oriented Socializing	Family is priority Contribute to the family's survival
Self	With self	Responsible for helping family	How does what I do matter and contribute to my family?

Table 4 The role of Vietnamese curriculum encounters in creating life purpose

Relationship	Curriculum encounters	Nature of the relationship	Influence on how life purpose is created
World	Student–teacher Student–content	Respect for age and wisdom Non-questioning	I am worthy if I am academically successful The teacher is wise
Other	Student–student	Helping each other Blending in rather than standing out	How can I help my communities (extended family, friends)?
Self	With self	Fortitude—life is hard and you cannot give up High work ethic Return the sacrifice	How can I matter, and what do I need to do?

trusting in their guidance while he was finding his ways. Julio replied to the same question: "I loved school! I LOVED SCHOOL!" He reflected an inherent trust in his teachers when he explained: "They took it upon themselves that they knew what we had to know to be successful later on in life." Based on Thomas' and Julio's narratives, it appears that students' relationships with *World* are characterized by their trust in the authority figure Teacher, which leads to a purpose creation based on the premises that the world is there to help you. When we talked about content, Julio, academically gifted, remembered mischievously, "I did my assignments ...uh ...

I didn't pay attention to a lot of teachers because I was … I had the book from class, and I was reading my own science fiction books." For Thomas, relevant learning was mainly hands-on experiences. He remembered, "We built Indian villages and all kinds of other stuff, and TVs, and made bows and arrows, you know, and sort of tomahawks …. It was enjoyable to do these things, and it wasn't a matter of analyzing." In terms of students' relation with content, there seems to be a need for relevance, the absence of which leads to reluctance. Julio and Thomas narrated their early educational experiences in a way where their meaning-making is focused on how they fit into their world in terms of interests and talents.

When asked about their relationships with other children, both Julio and Thomas experienced competitive ethics and the importance of one's social status. For example, Thomas explained, "[N]o matter how much I studied or whatever, I never could get a hundred on a spelling test…. and so part of it was intimidation and, you know, a sense of feeling of being put on the spot." Julio remembered,

> I was kind of a loner. Except in elementary … But when I got to high school, some of the athletes recognized that I was able to do stuff … with words … and so I would do homework for one of the big football players. And he would protect me from everybody else. I was a scrawny little kid, and so that was how we traded power. I had the power with words, and he had the power like being physical.

These insights suggest that in relationships with *Other*, purpose is created by coming to terms with one's place in social relations.

US American curriculum encounters with *Self* reflect the general idea of the American dream: hard work pays off, which indicates a basic trust in the system. So Thomas suffered through school and college because getting a college degree was what his parents and teachers told him a successful person does even though he was not academically successful. He explained that it was his experiences in his first drawing class that made things fall into place for him. Continuing his education paid off for him because his MFA degree allows him to teach art in higher education. He pointed out that the importance of this opportunity lies in the fact that he can enable those who are differently abled to find their ways.

Julio, on the other hand, despite being academically gifted, followed his father's request to earn money and took a job as a car parts sales clerk after graduating from high school. He later enrolled in a community college and joined the environmental club. He recalled the experience as follows: "It was like OH MY GOD! This is where I got to go! This is where I could do the stuff that I dreamed about! I said, 'The hell with the cars and that stuff.'" This turned out to be a life-changing epiphany for him as he continued his education to earn his PhD in biology. Thomas' and Julio's reflections indicate US American curriculum encounters afford the individual to think about himself in terms of what matters to him and how he can engage in these matters.

The Role of Mexican Curriculum Encounters in Creating Life Purpose

When asked to describe her teachers, Maria indicated, "They get mad only with the kids that don't pay attention or do their homework. If you do your homework, you're good." It appears that students were deserving of the teachers' attention through obedience. When asked what were typical things teachers would say to her or to other students, Zoraida recalled being told, "You are a good student. And you are strong in what you want to do." In answering that same question, Maria reflected that teachers encouraged students to "always be good. And they push us and encourage us to study" as well as "Be careful with who [you] talk ... stay away from bad people." When asked what experience she remembered the most, Maria explained, "When he says 'Maria is the only one that got a 100,' I'm like "Yay!"" In this context, students seek their teachers' appreciation. Such encouragement and recognition reinforces students' sense of worth. Classes often have 40–50 students, thus the acknowledgment of their individual achievement was a positive experience. Zoraida and Maria stated several times that they liked their teachers and school. Such comments support the caring relationship to which Zoraida and Maria allude. Students trust teachers to acknowledge their self-worth when they master content, which appears to also influence students' interest in and enjoyment of school. Thus, it appears students' relationship with *World* with respect to Teacher is characterized by respect for authority and a parenting-like quality.

When asked what were typical things other students would say to her, Maria indicated she did not remember anything specific but discussed how she cried when she graduated as she realized she would not see her classmates on a regular basis. She shared that she continues to communicate with some of those friends. Both Zoraida and Maria recalled school as a place to socialize with friends. Zoraida emphasized the strong focus on family. Children live at home until they complete school and start working full time or get married. Thus, they tend to live at home while attending college. This dependence on and the strong tie to family is a common occurrence. Thus, the relationship of the student with the *Other* is characterized through socialization and a focus on the family.

When asked if there was anything that teachers would do to make her feel good about being in school, Maria noted, "They always tell us how to do the right thing and study. If we want to have a better job or something..." This indicates teachers emphasized how school assisted in their development. When asked to describe the schools, Zoraida indicated that attending school is also linked to family responsibility in that there is an expectation that children will help in taking care of the family. She gave the example of how it is common for children who graduate from college to assist their siblings, through financial and other means, to attend and complete college. Maria added that her school set up a type of savings account that students could contribute to throughout the year. At the end of the year, the students were given the money saved, which she indicated she used to "buy stuff for our house." This provided another example of taking on family responsibility. Zoraida and Maria discussed how their parents stress the importance of attending school. Students' relationship with *Self* involves attending school to better themselves so they can contribute to family. Thus, encounters with curriculum further an understanding of self as part of one's immediate and extended family.

The Role of Vietnamese Curriculum Encounters in Creating Life Purpose

When Heidi and Lý were asked about their early educational experiences, each replied that they enjoyed going to school up until high school. Lý explained,

> Elementary – little children, they don't know ... They're like, 'Oh we're friends in school!' And sometimes you just go to school for fun. And middle school, they know a little bit: 'Oh, ok, there are teachers that are fun. So I think I'm gonna go for that.' And in high school, [you] have to study for ... the most important exam in your life. And if you don't pass, just go home. You can't do anything.

What Lý referred to as *knowing* pertains to the understanding that education is one of the only two ways out of poverty and insecurity. The other is one's belonging to the communist party, which offers those who are privileged enough a chance of a life with relative financial stability. Throughout their narratives, Lý and Heidi reflected an acquiescence to the status quo amidst an unquestioning respect for authority and for their elders. For example, Heidi recalled an incident where the teacher asked her to come out so as to do something on the blackboard. She knew that Heidi, who had been daydreaming, would be embarrassed. When she failed, the teacher told her that her brain was small. Heidi concluded this anecdote with the following explanation: "[They] try to hurt you so you will feel bad and study. Study more to prove that you're not bad like they said." This anecdote is representative of many others recalled by both participants in that it shows a relationship between student and teacher that is not based on rapport but on unquestioning acceptance of the latter. The nature of students' relationship with *World* as presented in their relationships with Teacher is one of absolute acceptance. Students, on the other hand, feel accepted and validated if they pass "the most important exam" of their lives, which is the comprehensive high school/college entrance exam. Lý explained, "This is our culture: If you pass the exam, you're good. If not, you wasted your 12 years. And every year a lot of people, a lot of students that don't pass the exam, they try to kill themselves." The worst part of failing the exam is that children feel like a disappointment for their parents whose money and time they have wasted.

Regarding students' relationship with *Other*, both Heidi and Lý remembered how kids helped each other getting to school, which required maneuvering a scooter in the chaotically congested Vietnam traffic, and prepare for exams together. What stood out during our conversations was their focus on blending in. For example, with 40–50 students in a room, Heidi said people know your name "if you're special in class, special like you don't wanna study." Not wanting to study is shameful since it is a waste of parents' resources; hence, being "special" is undesirable.

Vietnamese children go to school and study knowing that their chances of getting a job are slim. Lý explained even if they get the perfect score on "the most important exam of your life," and if they get into a university and graduate, they need money to bribe officials to get a job unless they are part of the communist party. Membership is possible only if you are related or close to a government worker. She concluded, "I just don't understand ... we value our school but when we study for it and get a degree, you don't always use it. ... Just if your family belongs to the government, then you can work." Heidi reflected on this by reiterating a piece of wisdom all Vietnamese children learn from their parents: Life is not a path strewn with flowers. She concluded that a person's most important characteristic is fortitude. Her reflection on life sums up well how curriculum encounters influence the way Vietnamese students create purpose: "[M]y life has taught me three important things: how much you loved, how gently you lived, and how gracefully you let go of things not meant for you."

Discussion

This study explored how curriculum influences the way people create life purpose in Vietnam, Mexico, and the USA. The findings indicate that in Vietnam, curriculum is used to transfer knowledge, and the purpose of school is the successful passing of "the most important exam," which validates parents' sacrifices and determines a student's worth. In Mexico, the kind of purpose furthered by the curriculum is to better yourself for the sake of the family. In the USA, the purpose of school is to enable self-understanding and self-determination. The findings reflect a major difference between the two developing countries and the Western country: The point of origin in the USA seems to be the "I" who places him/herself in his/her communities. These communities are based on interest, which could be either natural strengths or the prospect of economic gains. By contrast, in Mexican and Vietnamese approaches to life purpose, the point of origin is the community one finds him/herself in, e.g., family or local social network. The individual thrives if the community thrives, for which reason the impetus derives from group needs while in the USA it is born out of individual needs (Fig. 2).

The findings indicate how a society approaches questions about purpose of school depends not solely on its culture but equally on its socioeconomic

Fig. 2 Point of origin for life purpose thinking

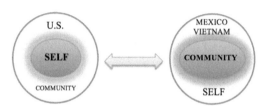

context. In the two developing countries, despite fundamental cultural differences, culture orients life purpose toward the community. By contrast, the purpose of school in the USA seems to be primarily directed at the self whose evolution remains at the center of curricular thinking. It appears that socioeconomic factors drive purpose more urgently than cultural ones.

While researching the education systems of Vietnam and Mexico, we encountered strong US American influence on both. For example, the 2016 NIEM Conference in Hanoi mentioned above invited US educational administrators from institutions of higher education to share their approaches to teacher accountability. Similarly, Mexico has begun to implement a high-stakes teacher evaluation system based on student test scores that mirrors that of the USA. One must wonder whether structural influences bring with them ideological ones. As part of this study, we tried to understand something about the evolving truths for the three countries. We concluded that US schools' underlying idea is that power is valuable and desirable. In Mexico, the implicit curriculum teaches that relationships are the nucleus of existence, and in Vietnam, a fundamental lesson children learn is that they have to prove their worth. This gives rise to the question: which human characteristics are nurtured by these truths? Under which circumstances does the desire for power enhance narcissism? What might the influence of this ideology be on the fortitude that results from a person's curricular experiences in Vietnam, or on the social caring that characterizes those who experienced the Mexican education system?

The purpose of this chapter was not to decide how each truth could best be capitalized on for the good of individuals, societies, or even the global picture. The intent was to make overt some of the complexities that make up the phenomenon school so that educators in each country can make informed decisions about the purpose of school and how it can be actualized.

CONCLUSION

The way in which a country's education system influences how life purpose is created and actualized derives from the complexities of its cultural and global contexts. This study was limited to three countries. Further research is needed to explore the influence of cultural and global contexts on non-Western education systems. While the body of research exploring Western and specifically the US American education system and curriculum theory is large and multifaceted, there appears to be paucity in curricular research for non-Western countries. Perhaps the philosophical explorations that curriculum theory brings about are the luxury of the rich and powerful who don't have to wrestle fundamentally with questions of survival. The danger of this is that existing truths might be undergirded and become dominant truths in a global context. Hence, a fundamental notion when thinking about purpose of school has to be the cultivation of critical consciousness necessary for a worldview that goes beyond the truths learned and experienced through the curriculum.

NOTES

1. Program for International Student Assessment: The PISA tests the reading, mathematics and science skills of 15-year-olds from 65 to 70 countries every three years. In the 2012 PISA, the USA ranked in the 36th place (OECD 2013). In the previous test, the USA ranked in the 17th place (OECD 2010), which is the place Vietnam occupies at present, while Mexico is in the 53rd place (OECD 2010).
2. Thomas and Julio are self-chosen pseudonyms.
3. Zoraida chose to use her given name, while Maria is a pseudonym.
4. Heidi is a self-chosen pseudonym. Lý chose to use her given name.
5. "In vivo" derives from the root for "live" and refers to words and phrases from the actual language of the participants in qualitative data (Saldaña 2009).

REFERENCES

Amanti, C. (2013). *International influence and the Mexican education system.* Doctoral dissertation. Retrieved from http://hdl.handle.net/10150/311475

Barton, P. E., & Coley, R. J. (2011). *The mission of the high school: A new consensus of the purposes of public education? Policy information perspective.* Princeton: Educational Testing Service.

Chinh, N. D., Linh, L. T., Quynh, T. H., & Ha, N. T. (2014). Inequality of access to English language learning in primary education in Vietnam. *Equality in Education,* 139–153. doi:10.1007/978-94-6209-692-9_11.

Darling-Hammond, L., Amrein-Beardsley, A., Haertel, E., & Rothstein, J. (2012). Evaluating teacher evaluation. *The Phi Delta Kappan, 93*(6), 8–15. Retrieved from http://www.jstor.org/stable/41497541.

Glesne, C. (2011). *Becoming qualitative researchers: An introduction* (4th ed.). Boston: Pearson.

Hằng, N. V., Meijer, M. R., Bulte, A. M., & Pilot, A. (2015). The implementation of a social constructivist approach in primary science education in Confucian heritage culture: The case of Vietnam. *Cultural Studies of Science Education,* *10*(3), 665–693. doi:10.1007/s11422-014-9634-8.

Huebner, D. (1975/1999). Poetry and power: The politics of curricular development. In V. Hillis (Ed.) *The lure of the transcendent: Collected essays by Dwayne E. Huebner* (pp. 231–240). Mahwah: Lawrence Erlbaum Associates.

Kincheloe, J. (2008). *Critical pedagogy* (2nd ed.). New York: Peter Lang Publishing.

Ladson-Billings, G. (2016). And then there is this thing called the curriculum: Organization, imagination, and mind. *Educational Researcher, 45*(2), 100–104. doi:10.3102/0013189x16639042.

Levinson, B. A. (2014). Education reform sparks teacher protest in Mexico. *Phi Delta Kappan, 95*(8), 48–45. doi:10.1177/003172171409500811.

Magaziner, J., & Monroy, C. (2016). Education in Mexico. *World Education News and Reviews.* Retrieved from http://wenr.wes.org/2016/08/education-in-mexico

National Institute of Education Management. (2016). *Proceedings from the international conference in 2016: Developing professional competency for teachers and managers: Vietnam and global trends.* Hanoi: Ministry of Education and Training.

OECD. (2010). *Pisa 2009 results: Executive summary.* Retrieved from www.oecd.org/pisa/pisaproducts/46619703.pdf

OECD. (2013). *PISA 2012 results: What makes schools successful? Resources, polices and practices* (Vol. IV). Pisa: OECD Publishing. Retrieved from http://dx.doi.org/10.1787/9789264201156-en

Patton, M. (2002). *Qualitative research & evaluation methods.* Thousand Oaks: Sage.

Polkinghorne, D. (1995). Narrative configuration in qualitative analysis. *International Journal of Qualitative Studies in Education, 8*(1), 5–23.

Puryear, J., Santibañez, L., & Solano, A. (2012). Education in Mexico. In *Emerging markets forum book chapters* (pp. 87–108). Washington, DC: Emerging Markets Forum.

Ravitch, D. (2016). *The death and life of the great American school system: How testing and choice are undermining education.* New York: Basic Books.

Saldaña, J. (2009). *The coding manual for qualitative researchers.* Thousand Oaks: Sage.

Santibañez, L., Vernez, G., & Razquin, P. (2005). *Education in Mexico: Challenges and opportunities* (Document number: DB-480-HF). Retrieved from RAND corporation website: http://www.rand.org/pubs/documented_briefings/DB480.html

U.S. Department of Education. (2016). *Testing: Frequently asked questions.* Retrieved from http://www2.ed.gov/nclb/accountability/ayp/testing-faq.html

U.S. Network for Education Information. (2008, February 22). Retrieved from http://www2.ed.gov/about/offices/list/ous/international/usnei/us/edlite-index.html

United Nations Educational, Scientific, and Cultural Organization. (2010/2011). *World data on education*. Retrieved from http://www.ibe.unesco.org/fileadmin/user_upload/Publications/WDE/2010/pdf-versions/Viet_Nam.pdf

World Bank Group. (2016). *Education in Vietnam: Development history, challenges, and solutions*. (n.d.). Retrieved from http://siteresources.worldbank.org/EDUCATION/Resources/278200-1121703274255/1439264-1153425508901/Education_Vietnam_Development.pdf

Sonja Varbelow is an assistant professor in the Department of Teacher Education at Angelo State University in Texas, USA. A native of East Germany, she moved to the USA as part of an exchange teacher program. Her research interests pertain to curriculum theory, the transformational role of education, and qualitative research. Her professional experiences include 14 years of teaching in grades 1–12 in Germany and at the high school level in the USA.For the past ten years she has been teaching pedagogy and methodology in higher education.

Donna Gee is a professor in the Department of Teacher Education at Angelo State University in Texas, USA.Her research interests pertain to how children learn mathematics, teacher professional development, and bridging the theory-praxis gap between academic research and politics.Her professional experience includes 9 years of teaching in public elementary and middle schools in the USA as well as 25 years of teaching in higher education.Part of her curriculum includes worldwide studies abroad, which focus on enhancing students' understanding of teaching and learning through global experiences.

Representation of World War II in Vietnam, China, and the USA: Political Ideologies in Secondary History Textbooks

Chau Vu

Any education, no matter how democratic, reflects the political and ideological perspectives of the society in which it serves. As argued by Apple (1992), school curricula are not neutral knowledge, instead, "what counts as legitimate knowledge is the result of complex power relations, struggles, and compromises among identifiable class, race, gender, and religious groups" (p. 4). Addressing the ideological dimension in education, Ginsburg & Lindsay (1995) suggested that the curriculum, classroom pedagogy, assessment, and educational outcomes are all influenced by the political agenda that a country advocates, as a consequence, teachers become "agents of political socialization" (p. 6) via the disciplines they teach.

As an indispensable part of the curriculum, textbooks have been used by all nations as "virtual icons of education" (Altbach, 1991, p. 242) to construct their pasts, represent their national collectivities and identities, as well as reinforce certain dynamics of the power-knowledge interrelationships

C. Vu (✉)
Louisiana State University, Baton Rouge, LA, USA

© The Author(s) 2018
C. Roofe, C. Bezzina (eds.), *Intercultural Studies of Curriculum*, Intercultural Studies in Education,
https://doi.org/10.1007/978-3-319-60897-6_8

(Apple & Christian-Smith, 1991; Brown & Da'Na, 2007; Ornstein, 1994). Particularly, history textbooks have been claimed by many researchers (Levesque, 2009; Phillips, 1998; Wineburg, 2001) to bear a significantly large amount of ideological and political discourses. Some scholars suggest that school history textbooks play a significant role in political socialization, promoting patriotism and the nation-building process (Han, 2007; Janmaat & Vickers, 2007; Pingel, 2006; & Zajda, 2015). School history texts, as both a source of curriculum and an instrument of ideological transformation, are currently closely monitored by the state, in countries like Japan, China, Taiwan, South Korea, and the Russian Federation, to name a few (Shin & Sneider, 2011; Zajda, 2015).

Much influential as they are, Altbach (1991) also depicted the world of textbooks as "an unequal world" (p. 242). Often times, he argued, economically and politically dominant Western countries such as Britain, France, Germany, and the USA gain a central role of producing and disseminating certain knowledge products through their multinational publishers to smaller, mostly "Third World" nations (p. 242). Among those left at a "peripheral position" (p. 242) of the knowledge production process, large countries like China and India can afford some autonomy in producing their own textbooks, while Mexico and Egypt attain a mediating role by working closely with multinational firms located in their countries and at the same time exporting textbooks to smaller nations in their regions (Altbach, 1991). What follows is comparative research in education tends to look at countries within the same position of either relative domination (Faden, 2015; Hardwick et al., 2010; LaSpina, 2003) or peripherality (Hsiao, 2011; Jones, 2011; Vickers, 2006), rather than those with vastly complex juxtapositions to one another. A look at the ideologically driven discourses in history textbooks from an intercultural lens deems necessary for the implementation of critical pedagogy in today's global context.

Various studies have been carried out on the ideological and/or political agenda of a country's curriculum (Apple, 1992, 2004; Bourdieu & Passeron, 1990; Dimitriadis et al., 2006) and on history education as a part of nation-building in a global culture (Shin & Sneider, 2011; Zajda, 2015). Likewise, studies have investigated the ideologies embedded in textbooks of singular countries (Hagai et al., 2017; Knain, 2001; Orr, 2001), but insights from a multinational perspective are missing. The study of such matters is significant because it will provide a unique standpoint comprised of diverse perspectives on which to construct truths and nurture empathy among people from different societies and cultures.

This chapter explores how ideologies are embedded in the secondary school history textbooks of three countries: the USA, China, and Vietnam, through the narratives of World War II, an event where the political, economic, and social contexts of the three intertwined and reset the world's order into what it is today. The USA, largely regarded as a "wartime victor" (Nicholls, 2006, p. 91), is also one of the dominant Western countries in Altbach's argument (1991). China, a "forgotten ally" (Mitter, 2013, p. 13), is considered by Altbach (1991) to have certain autonomy in producing its own textbooks. Vietnam endured serious effects from the war and now ranks among the lowest economically developed countries, a peripheral position compared to the other two. With the inclusion of a minority country's perspective, the study aims to provide a multifaceted representation of World War II and examine the ideological agendas of contemporary societies. Its focus is on answering the following questions:

1. How are different political ideologies embedded in the World War II narratives of secondary history textbooks being taught in the USA, Vietnam, and China?
2. What implications can be made regarding the teaching and learning of world history within the sociopolitical context of each country and globally?

Context of the Education System in the USA, China, and Vietnam

The three countries have a widely different context in terms of social, cultural, and political makings. The USA has the privilege of being one of the leading economies and military powers of the world. China is gaining firm establishment as a thriving economy, sharing the first position with the USA in Gross Domestic Product and Purchasing Power Parity, while Vietnam is one of the 80 smallest economies, sharing 1% in global wealth (International Monetary Fund, 2016).

The education system of the USA is unlike that of the other two countries. Both China and Vietnam implement a nine-year compulsory education covering grades one through nine, and it is the central government that formulates educational laws and policies, designs national curriculum standards, and supervises and guides educational reform (China's Ministry of Education, 2006; Vietnam's Ministry of Education, 1998). Schools in China used to have uniform textbooks published by government-designated publishing houses. However, for the past few years, they have employed textbooks that are more adjusted to local conditions while adhering to the respective national curriculums (Qun & Wanjin, 2007). Vietnam maintains a national curriculum and uses a unified set of textbooks for every local state and city, justifying the regional differences through the "bonus points" system. Within this system, students identified as residing in rural or remote areas are given from 0.25 to 0.5 points on a 10-point scale, on top of their total scores, when participating in the national high school graduation exam and the national university entrance exam ("Bonus point policy", 2015).

According to the US Network for Education Information (USNEI 2008), although there is no national curriculum in the USA, the US Federal government contributes almost 10% to the national education budget and states, school districts, and national associations do require or recommend that certain standards be used to guide school instruction. In addition, federal law mandates that state standards be developed and improved in order for states to receive federal assistance. It can be inferred that states are not totally unbounded by federal control.

IDEOLOGY AND IDEOLOGICAL PERSPECTIVE IN EDUCATION

From a cultural perspective, Geertz (1973/2000) considered ideology to be a cultural system of interacting symbols, without which social situations would become incomprehensible or meaningless. Speaking from the angle of discourse analysis, Barker (2000) explained that ideology is maps of meaning, which purport to be universal truth but are in fact specific understandings historically and intentionally constructed to obscure certain groups' power while maintaining the others'. These definitions share a common point that ideology is a belief shared by a group of people and has the same meaning to each of its members. Concurring with these definitions, Gutek (2014) further pointed out that ideology "serves to give theoretical legitimacy to a group's outlook, aspiration, program, and action" through an appeal to myth or history. In addition, it is used to "justify and determine the power relationships among contending groups" (p. 167). Looking at the educational significance of ideology in modern time, Gutek (2014) observed that "the advent of nationalism, the rise of modern nation-states, and an increased social-class consciousness stimulated by industrialization" (p. 168) have resulted in institutionalized education, a part of the national system that molds and regulates its citizens' thoughts and behaviors.

Regarding ideology and the curriculum, Apple (2004) proposed a series of guiding questions which, once answered in terms of ideological perspective, will help bring the curriculum into shape. These include: "What role does an educational system itself play in defining particular forms of knowledge as high status?" and "What role does it play in helping to create a credentialing process based on the possession (and non-possession) of this cultural capital, a credentialing system that provides numbers of agents roughly equivalent to the needs of the division of labor in society?" (p. 39). Also in Apple's words, "the school is not a passive mirror", but an "active force" that gives legitimacy to the ideologies so intimately connected to it. This means ideologies are not necessarily negative or oppressive, the matter lies in people's ability to recognize what they are and look for the alternative ones until genuine truths and values are discovered. This understanding is crucial in dissecting the ideologies embedded in history textbooks in this chapter.

METHODOLOGY

Ideological Discourse Analysis

The current study employed van Dijk's framework of ideological discourse analysis. The point of ideological discourse analysis is not merely to discover underlying ideologies, but to systematically link structures of discourse with structures of ideologies (Van Dijk, 1995, p. 143). He further claims, "the overall strategy of positive self-presentation and negative other presentation is a well-known way to exhibit ideological structures in discourse" (p. 144).

Narrative Analysis

In analyzing the content of the textbook samples, the current study employs Foster and Nicholls' (2005) method, which consists of three approaches to textual analysis and three areas of subject content. More specifically,

Textual analysis focused on story line and content analysis, narrative tone and perspective, and treatment of history from a disciplinary perspective.

The three content areas of focus for this study were the beginning of the Second World War, the main events and battles, and the end of the war. (Foster & Nicholls, 2005, p. 217)

This study aims to explore the underlying assumptions of the ideologies, predominantly political ones, that each textbook's narratives attempt to support. Though using the same method of content analysis as Foster & Nicholls (2005), the different countries, contexts, and texts chosen are expected to provide new findings and contribute to the literature as well.

The US textbook sample by Beck et al. (2012) was selected because it is considered "one of the five most popular and widely used world history textbooks, comprising about 80 percent of the textbook market" (Marino, 2011, p. 425). Note that this study begun in June 2016 and the edition analyzed was the second most recent publication dates available at the time of the analysis. Vietnam and China employed a national curriculum, and there was only one version of official textbook approved by the state, therefore, two samples of World History textbooks were selected for each country. World War II was first introduced in Vietnam's secondary history curriculum in Grade 8 while not until Grade 9 did it appear in China's. These samples were translated from the original language into English for the purpose of analysis. Given the arbitrary nature of comparative research, the author assumed that the difference in terms of grade level, and translation would not bring remarkable differences to the findings. All textbook samples are listed in the Appendix.[1]

FINDINGS

Findings are presented in the order of emergent political ideologies from the texts. All the three textbook samples consistently conveyed the political ideologies that each country believed to support the best form of government and the best economic system. These values are discussed both explicitly in textual form and implicitly throughout the texts' interpretations of the events in World War II.

Democracy as an American Ideology

Throughout the selected US World History textbook lessons on World War II, democracy was mentioned as a value strongly promoted by the USA. The representation of this ideal has been through various ways.

First, democracy was used as the righteous cause for US involvement in World War II. Second, it was referred to as the desirable political regime and social construction that USA stands for and that other countries should at least strive to resemble.

One prominent theme in the chosen American textbook excerpt on World War II was the evolving justifications for US involvement in the war, centering on justice and democracy. The unit started with a stage-setting of Hitler's aggression, which was seen as a threat to democracy. By associating democracy with hope and peace, the text suggested that any action against democracy is negative and needs to be prevented:

> During the 1930s, Hitler played on the hopes and fears of the Western democracies. Each time the Nazi dictator grabbed new territory, he would declare an end to his demands. Peace was guaranteed – until Hitler moved again. (AWH, p. 491)

In the majority of its content, AWH explained US policies before its involvement in the war, such as the Neutrality Acts or the Atlantic Charter. In addition, events surrounding the war, such as Pearl Harbor Attack and the Holocaust, preceded any discussion of US intervention, which, in turn, was viewed as the necessary last measure in response to a harmful or antidemocratic act of other nations. According to AWH, the USA was only "involved in an undeclared war with Hitler" after "a German U-boat fired on a U.S. destroyer in the Atlantic" (p. 496). Similarly, in one main idea sentence underneath the lesson titled *Japan's Pacific Campaign*, AWH stated:

> EMPIRE BUILDING Japan attacked Pearl Harbor in Hawaii and **brought the United States into World War II.** (AWH, p. 497, bold effect added)

Japan's attack of the US in the Pacific was explained in terms of their aggressive policies and imperialist intentions: "Like Hitler, Japan's military leaders also had dreams of empire. Japan's expansion had begun in 1931" (AWH, p. 497). By juxtaposing imperialist intentions next to the action of US government to strike back, the textbook suggested that the USA was trying to protect their democracy from the assault of an imperialist country.

A remarkable portion of the chapter on World War II in AWH was addressed to the Holocaust. Various details and emotive descriptions of the event with documentary-style visuals attempted to present the catastrophic and inhumane nature of fascism. This is in striking contrast to Chinese and Vietnamese history textbooks, which both left out the event with no single depiction of what happened. Since one of the major tenets of a democracy is the protection of human rights and maintenance of freedom, AWH brought the fascists' violation of democratic values under dire scrutiny, so as to delude to US involvement in the war in the lesson following it.

In describing the USA as having no choice but to enter the war, either to combat fascist Germany or to defend itself against imperialist Japan's aggressive assault on Pearl Harbor, AWH suggested that the USA had no imperialist intention in going to war, and the economic as well as political advantages that followed were natural consequences of taking the leadership role in international affairs.

Not only is democracy an ideal to be protected, AWH made clear that democracy is also a desirable form of governmental and social construction that other countries should adopt from the USA.

Apart from the depiction of the USA as a democratic nation who respects human rights and goes great lengths to protect freedom, AWH accentuated the problems associated with "old leadership", that is, undemocratic leadership, in Germany, Italy, and France: "Hitler's Nazi government had brought Germany to ruins. Mussolini had led Italy to defeat. The Vichy government had collaborated with the Nazis" (AWH, p. 515). Separated from these forms of leadership, communist leadership emerged as even more problematic:

> Also, in Italy and France, many resistance fighters were **communists**.
> After the war, the **Communist** Party promised change, and millions were ready to listen. In both France and Italy, **Communist** Party membership skyrocketed. The **communist** made huge gains in the first postwar elections. Anxious to speed up a political takeover, the **communists** staged a series of violent strikes. Alarmed French and Italians reacted by voting for anti**communist** parties. **Communist** Party membership and influence began to decline. And they declined even more as the economies of France and Italy began to recover. (AWH, p. 515)

Across the 40-page coverage of World War II in AWH, there are seven times when the words "communist(s)"/"Communist"/"Communism" appeared in explicit textual form, including "anticommunist". Notably, as can be seen from the above quote, all these seven words concentrate into one single paragraph. The intensive repetition of "communist" among the same lines with "resistance", "political takeover", and "violent strikes", as well as the observance of a decline in communist influence once the economy recovered, is highly indicative that communism is subversive in nature and feeds itself on economic instabilities. Ultimately, the message suggested from the American textbook is that communism is an antidemocratic ideal; communism and democracy are two irreconcilable sets of values and differences between the two cannot be compromised.

AWH further imparted the American democracy to its audience through a detailed account of the democratic manner in which the USA treated its former enemy, Japan, after the war. The text recapped the US occupation of Japan with General Douglas MacArthur at the center of the narrative:

> MacArthur was determined to be fair and not to plant the seeds of a future war. Nevertheless, to ensure that peace would prevail, he began a process of demilitarization, or disbanding the Japanese armed forces. He achieved this quickly, leaving the Japanese with only a small police forces. MacArthur also began bringing war criminals to trial. Out of 25 surviving defendants, former Premier Hideki Tojo and six others were condemned to hang.
>
> MacArthur then turned his attention to democratization, the process of creating a government elected by the people. In February 1946, he and his American political advisers drew up a new constitution. It changed the empire into a constitutional monarchy like that of Great Britain. The Japanese accepted the constitution. It went into effect on May 3, 1947. (AWH, p. 516)

The USA was described as showing a conscious attempt in helping another country set up a democratic system while still respecting its old order and traditions. The Japanese emperor was described as obsolete yet having decorative value for the new system:

> The emperor now had to declare that he was not divine. His power was also dramatically reduced. Like the ruler of Great Britain, the emperor became largely a figurehead – a symbol of Japan. (AWH, p. 517)

It is ambiguous whether the second sentence means figurehead is a symbol of Japan, or the emperor is a symbol of Japan. However, the general impression conveyed through this quote is that Japan was led to conform to a better political and social system. By broadening land ownership and increasing participation of workers and farmers "in the new democracy" even though he "was not told to revive the Japanese economy", MacArthur was seen as the savior of Japan, and it follows that the US military presence even after the signing of the peace treaty was legitimate (AWH, p. 517). The discussion questions presented alongside the main text, namely: "How would demilitarization and a revived economy help Japan achieve democracy?" (p. 516) and "Why did the Americans choose the British system of government for the Japanese, instead of the American system?" (p. 517), called specific attention to this matter, as if to emphasize once again the democratic treatment of the USA toward its former enemy, and the reasonable policies that the USA made to Japan as a nation in pursuit of democracy.

Socialism and Marxism-Leninism as Chinese and Vietnamese Ideologies

VWH portrayed World War II as the continuation of World War I, when "the imperialist nations could not resolve their conflicts in terms of the economic benefits and market conditions in their colonies", and war resulted from Italy, Germany and Japan's attempt "to re-divide the world's order in response to the economic crisis during 1929–1933" (VWH, p. 104). On the other hand, CWH saw the event as resulting from the selfish and greedy nature of Western countries at the cost of smaller countries. Socialism and Marxism-Leninism were not explicitly mentioned in either of the two texts at high frequency, but implied within the role of the Soviet Union as a nation willing to protect its fellow countries and liberate the world's peoples from fascist aggression and invasion.

In setting up the context of the war, VWH emphasized the mutual hatred that both axis countries and allied countries held toward the USSR, explaining that Britain, France, and the USA had shown compromises and lukewarm responses to Hitler's aggression with a view to pushing Germany against the USSR.

In between the imperialist nations formed two confronting groups: the Britain – France – United States versus the fascist Germany – Italy – Japan. They held dire conflicts against each other because of the market and the colonies, however, they both considered the U.S.S.R. a mutual enemy that needed to be eliminated. The Britain – France – United States group employed a compromising approach so that the fascist group could point their raging war spear toward the U.S.S.R. As a result of this, after joining

Austria into Germany, Hitler took Czech (March 1939). However, **feeling that he was not strong enough to invade the U.S.S.R., Hitler went for the European countries first**. September 1, 1939, fascist Germany attacked Poland. Right after that, Britain and France declared war against Germany. World War II broke out. (VWH, p. 104, bold effect added)

While American textbook saw the USA as a democratic and Japan as an imperialist country from the beginning, it can be seen in the above quote that all the six countries, Britain, France, USA, Germany, Italy, and Japan were considered imperialist from the Vietnamese perspective. By emphasizing the unresolvable economic conflicts between them, VWH pinpointed fascism as a classic consequence of capitalism, which could only be resolved through socialism. USSR, a socialist country with a world-top economy, was justified as the only suitable leader capable of stopping the aggressive wave of fascism from affecting the world's proletariats. The Soviet strike-back in Stalingrad was claimed to be "a turning point", which "led the world war out of stagnancy" by "opening up a series of other strike-backs across all other battles" (VWH, p. 107).

On the same note, CWH purposefully used the socialist discourse of "civilians and soldiers", or "the people" in the telling of combats between some Allied countries and fascist countries. While the image of "the fascist peoples" or "the American civilians and soldiers" was never constructed, that of "the Polish people", "the British people", or "the Russian people" was repeatedly employed. CWH also stressed the "unity" and "solidarity", typical socialist values, among the oppressed peoples in the world, regardless of their political regimes, in the shared fight against fascism. There recorded one instance where a Western country's government was separated from its people: "In June, 1940, France surrendered, but a lot of the French people persistently continued their fight against the invaders" (CWH, p. 36). This indicates that the governments of non-communist countries might compromise the nation's freedom for selfish benefits, but it is the peoples of these countries that could bring about revolutionary changes and protect the freedom for their nation. Besides, unlike the Allied or neutral countries in Europe, the USA was only mentioned as "US soldiers" or "US army", which suggests that this nation went to war not with its people first in mind, or for their benefits.

Both Chinese and Vietnamese textbooks embraced a strong Marxist orientation by presenting information in what appeared to be a scientific and dialectical order with events lining up chronologically. The narrating voices of the two texts were objective and impartial, which differs from American textbook with a high level of emotive language. Moreover, a Marxist/ Socialist attention to the general peoples, the proletariats, in other words, the masses, was illustrated through the constant use of countries' names more than individual leaders against each other, for example, "the Soviet Union" versus "Germany", instead of "Stalin" versus "Hitler", which highly differs from the narrating style in American textbook. In particular, VWH employed visuals of plural, unknown ordinary people instead of significant individuals' portraits which were also widely employed to illustrate world events.

Still within the dialectical flow of the narratives, both Chinese and Vietnamese textbooks represented World War II as a war of two contrasting ideologies, capitalism and socialism, which set the background for Cold War in the later chapters.

Exceptionalism as a Shared Ideology of Three Countries

The majority of the discourses inherent in three textbook samples served to characterize certain countries as uniquely virtuous protagonists. American exceptionalism was strongly promoted in AWH, while the USSR was portrayed by CWH and VWH as an exemplary world's leader and CWH specifically took a moralistic view in scrutinizing the actions of Western countries.

Captain America

The USA was narrated in AWH as entering the war to aid its allies once Britain and France encountered a deadlock situation with Germany. Apart from a passing discussion of Soviet and British contribution to the victory of the Allies, battles with US involvement received more detailed coverage. From the perspective of the AWH, Pacific, Western European and Mediterranean were considered the most crucial battle fields. Japan's Pacific Campaign received extensive coverage compared to the rest. Despite the use of the word "Allied", Britain and France were not mentioned in these battles while Australia appeared twice as a supporter for the USA in defeating the villain. AWH vividly accentuated the anti-democratic actions of the Japanese toward Allied prisoners as well as people of their colonies:

Before these conquests, the Japanese had tried to win the support of Asians with the anticolonialist idea of "East Asia for the Asiatics." After victory, however, the Japanese quickly made it clear that they had come as conquerors. They often treated the people of their new colonies with extreme cruelty. However, the Japanese reserved the most brutal treatment for Allied prisoners of war. (AWH, p. 498)

As pointed out in the previous analysis, democracy is a prevailing American ideology and the USA represents a good cause for humanity, therefore, any attempt against the USA is also against humanity and needs to be penalized. After painting Japan as the antagonist, AWH continued to introduce the USA as an invincible force that "made an important psychological point" to Japan, "shook the confidence of some" and finally left them "crippled", thus "turn[ing] the tide of war in the Pacific" after the Battle of Midway (AWH, p. 500).

Not only did the USA actively participate in the protection of democracy, it was also a tolerant hero who willingly cooperated with the USSR toward a common goal of eliminating fascism, although from the American perspective Stalin was considered "the Soviet dictator" (AWH, p. 491), not much unlike Hitler in his ruling approach. The USA's lenient treatment of Stalin's unreasonable demands manifested patience and generosity toward its temporary ally:

Churchill wanted Britain and the United States to strike first at North Africa and southern Europe. The strategy angered Stalin. He wanted the Allies to open the second front in France. The Soviet Union, therefore, had to hold out on its own against the Germans. **All Britain and the United States could offer in the way of help was supplies.** (AWH, p. 506, bold effect added)

US leaders, in particular, the presidents and generals in charge of orchestrating the war, also received excessive praise for their resourceful tactics and competent management of complex situations. Apart from Hitler and Churchill, MacArthur and Eisenhower had their portraits presented in AWH as key "history makers" of the entire war (p. 510).

In short, AWH positioned the USA as a peacekeeper and liberator, who was willing to go at great lengths to promote and protect freedom and equality. The construction of the USA as a reluctant "Captain America" highlights the USA' commitment to democratic freedom while in so doing, dimming the fact that the nation owed its privileged position in the global power to its military power and particular historical circumstances, most importantly, the developing of the military power to prepare for WWII did much to bring about the end of the Great Depression in America, which served to reinforce the greatness of capitalism.

The Heroic Soviet Red Army

In very brief description of the main events, VWH focuses on the USSR as the lone hero fighting against fascism and revolved the central axis of the war. Western countries were seen in the supporting roles, who were only able to win the war thanks to USSR's valiant attempts as the leader of the Anti-fascist International Alliance.

> On the Soviet – Germany battle, The Russian Red Army struck attack on large scale, swiping all German soldiers out of their homeland. Till the end of 1944, the entire Soviet territory was freed. **On the way chasing the Germans out, The Russian Red Army helped the peoples of East-European countries to free themselves from the clutch of fascism.**
> On the North Africa battle, in May 1943, facing with British – American attack, Germany and Italy had to turn in their arms. On the West-European battle, on June 6, 1944, the British – American Allies landed into North France, opening the second battle in West-Europe.
> **On the Asia – Pacific battle, the Russian Red Army destroyed the Japanese in Northeastern China.** On August 6 and 9, 1945, the US dropped nuclear bombs into Hiroshima and Nagasaki (Japan), causing the death of over 100, 000 people and injuring dozens of thousand people. (VWH p. 107-8, bold effect added)

During the five-page account of World War II, the name and image of Stalin were not presented in the chosen sample of Vietnamese history textbook. From an intertextual analysis of this matter in Vietnamese World History textbooks of other grades, it was found out that except for Lenin and his Bolshevik Party, only General Georgy Zhukov was mentioned directly in lessons about the Soviet Union. In the 11th Grade textbook, Stalingrad was followed by Volgograd in brackets as a note on the current name of the city. This phenomenon is different from that observed in the American textbook, which used Stalin among a variety of other war leaders' names. Whereas, in the Chinese textbook, Stalin is depicted as a great leader with exceptional military skills in bringing the world out of fascist oppression. It might be indicative of VWH's attempt to portray the Soviet Union as a holistic, inseparable entity whose audacious resistance served as a model for other nations to stand up and regain their freedom.

At the same time, the Chinese history textbook portrayed the USSR as the key figure, the major leader that brought the war to the end and settled the world's order into a state of peace and reconciliation. From the beginning of the war's outbreak, the USSR was seen as a lone hero, a similar image in VWH as well, who had to cope with multiple risks from both the aggressive fascist nations and the greedy, selfish Western nations to protect its own people and the fellow socialist countries. Later on, CWH reported the establishment of the United Nations at Yalta conference in Russia, with the presence of Stalin alongside Roosevelt and Churchill. This implied an influential peacekeeping role that the Soviet Union played in the global and international setting.

CWH frequently depicted Stalin as a great and inspiring leader and the Soviet Union as a mighty nation determined to protect their fatherland at all costs:

> June 1941, Germany aimed its army East ward, waging a war against the U.S.S.R. Within a few months, Germany occupied the majority of Russian land, directly pressing into Moscow the capital. The Russian soldiers and ordinary people, under Stalin's leadership, heroically defended themselves from the invaders, which failed Hitler's attempt to occupy Moscow.
>
> Stalin urged the people to fight against fascism, he said: Red Army, Navy and entirely every Soviet citizen have to protect every Soviet piece of land, fight till the last drop of blood over both cities and villages. (CWH, p. 38)

In covering the casualty of the Stalingrad, CWH highlighted the loss of German lives up to "1,500,000 people" out of the total number of "2,000,000 troops from both sides" (p. 41), which means that Russian troops, both dead and alive, were 500,000—a highly dominated number. This detail served to support an overarching image of the invincible Russian army. Moreover, the whole lesson on World War II ended with a glorious victory for the USSR against Germany, where "Hitler killed himself" and "the Soviet soldiers hung the red flag on top of the German parliament building", a classic ending in historical narratives of Vietnamese, Chinese, and other socialist/communist countries' textbooks.

Chinese Moralism

Chinese history textbook started the lesson with "The Munich Conspiracy", which showcased the ill intentions of "big Western countries" in protecting their own profits without caring for the wellbeing of small countries.

> After Hitler came to power, Germany was not at all reluctant in the arm race to prepare for wars, moreover, it conquered Austria without any prevention or restriction from world community. Germany's desires for invasion increased day by day. Meanwhile, Britain and France were counting on the benefits of sacrificing the Slovak Republic for a peaceful period. In September 1938, heads of the governments from all four countries – Germany, Italy, Britain and France in Munich, Germany signed into an agreement for Slovak to cut parts of its land in Sudetenland for Germany within 10 days. This is called "The Munich Conspiracy" in history. (CWH, p. 34)

While explaining the purpose of the Munich conspiracy, CWH elaborated on the undemocratic and unfair manner in which the decision was made, as well as the reluctance of Western countries in fighting against fascists' growing influence on the global scale, for fears of losing their own security. Further, it stressed the indifferent and irresponsible attitude of Western leaders toward "small countries":

> Although the Slovak Republic's benefits suffered heavy loss from the Munich conference, Britain's Prime Minister Chamberlain was very satisfied, telling British people: "This is our peaceful period, I ask that everyone should just sleep well every night". (CWH, p. 34)

AWH and VWH only presented one sentence to cover this event. On the other hand, a considerably large section of the CWH general coverage was dedicated to discussing the Munich Conspiracy. From the Chinese perspective, the action of Western countries was immoral, and by allowing itself to judge this action, China was then imagined at the other end of the spectrum, a moral and self-respected nation, who could see through the conspiracy and empathize with the "small countries" who were mere puppets of the "big countries".

> Wars broke out all over the world, some of these caused certain loss to Western countries. Big countries in the West did not approve of the fascist countries' invasion, but were afraid of their war threats at the same time.

They hence wanted to lead the invaders East ward, to aim Germany's attack spear at the U.S.S.R. Therefore, they did not strictly try to prevent the fascist invasion, instead, they counted on sacrificing small countries' benefits to calm down the invaders. They used a so-called "Pacifying Policy", which was pushed to the peak by the Munich Conspiracy. The Munich Conspiracy resulted in dire consequences, inflaming conquering intention within the fascist countries' bottomless greed while weakening anti-fascist countries at the same time. (CWH, p. 34)

Throughout the quote, CWH juxtaposed "big countries" against "small countries" and repeated the former's intention of "sacrificing" the latter to depict Western countries as powerful yet selfish empires, who only cared about accumulating capital even at the loss of others' wellbeing. This implies that the European allies are not trustworthy and not reliable; in other words, immoral; therefore, "small countries" would be better off by not joining their membership or risk being manipulated.

CWH did not clearly position China as either a big or a small country. However, given that CWH did not include Japanese invasion of Eastern China in this lesson on World War II, China appears to distance itself from the world's events to provide a seemingly impartial judgment of the other countries. This conveys a veiled sense of moralism, a Chinese ideology that has been widely promoted in many of its official educational policies.[2]

Nationalism as an Ideology of Othering

Despite the various discourses of democracy or socialism, among other ideologies, which are framed as the essential values that each country claims to support, it is highly telling that the purposeful narrations of historical events serve to protect the countries' power holders and benefit their particular agendas. Nationalism, then, emerges as the overarching political ideology strongly embraced in the three textbook samples.

US Nationalism

Seeing the USA as a democratic nation, AWH drew a clear line between the USA and the USSR. There were instances where a clear voice of hostility and aloofness was aimed at Stalin or the Soviets in general. For instance, while CWH and VWH portrayed the Stalingrad battle as heroic and sacred because Russian troops were protecting their fatherland, AWH painted it as Stalin's egotistical attempt to protect "the city named after him":

> The Battle of Stalingrad began on August 23, 1942. The Luftwaffe went on nightly bombing raids that set much of the city ablaze and reduced the rest to rubble. The situation looked desperate. **Nonetheless, Stalin had already told his commanders to defend the city named after him to the death.** (AWH, p. 507, bold effect added)

AWH went further to give remarks on the Allies' relation after the war:

> In the postwar world, enemies not only became allies; sometimes, allies became enemies. World War II had changed the political landscape of Europe. The Soviet Union and the United States emerged from the war as the world's two major powers. They also ended the war as allies. However, it soon became clear that their postwar goals were very different. This difference stirred up conflicts that would shape the modern world for decades. (AWH, p. 517)

By saying that the USA could forgive former enemy, Japan, and consider them an ally but could not tolerate the Soviet Union for the difference in postwar goals between the two, AWH was sending a message of American nationalism. The reason was not specifically discussed but could be inferred that America would consider the USSR, the other major power of the world, to be a threat to its exceptionalism and democracy.

AWH also promoted patriotism by dedicating a portion of the lesson to "The Allied Home Fronts", in which it mainly described how American citizens expressed the love for their army through economic measures, such as saving money, rationalizing their foods, producing war weapons and equipment, and buying wartime products "to help finance the war" (p. 509). This suggests that money, or capital, is an efficient way to support the nation, and to be patriotic means being able to contribute to the market. The overall emphasis of the AWH on the individuals and the economy seems to speak to a neoliberal agenda, which equates economic freedom with political freedom. By conflating capitalism and democracy, or to be exact, a democratic capitalism, AWH forwarded this agenda without blurring the image of an exceptional nation voluntarily guarding equality and freedom for the world. It is then in the USA's own best interest to make the world safer for democracy as well as capitalism because without other capitalist countries, the USA would not be able to trade freely and expand its market.

Chinese Nationalism

CWH narrated the happenings of the war from September 1, 1939 to December 7, 1941. Notably, discourses of the people together with their devoted political leaders persevering in the war against invaders to protect their nation are explicitly highlighted:

> May 1940, Chamberlain resigned, Churchill became the Prime Minister, and he encouraged the British people to be united in the fight against fascism. He said in his speech: "I do not have anything to sacrifice, but my blood, devotion, sweat and tears". In June, France surrendered, but a lot of French people remained persistent in fighting the invaders. (CWH, p. 35)

> Stalin encouraged his people to fight against fascism, he said: "The Red Army, the navy and citizens of the entire U.S.S.R. have to protect every piece of Soviet land, fight till the last drop of blood, protect every city and every village." (CWH, p. 35)

> The fascist countries' shameless invasion stirred up a wave of immeasurable anguish among the world's peoples. The U.S., Britain and the U.S.S.R. cooperated to confront the mutual enemies, gradually becoming each other's partner. (CWH, p. 36)

Through emphasizing the peoples of many nations, regardless of the side those nations were taking or their political regimes, CWH delivered a message of vehement nationalism and patriotism. At the same time, it suggested that the people can wield enormous power against enemies once they are united wholeheartedly as a nation, under the guidance of their political leaders.

Vietnamese Nationalism

Compared to the Chinese and American textbooks, Vietnamese textbooks gave the least coverage of the Pearl Harbor event and the US bombing of Japan, each accounted for through one sentence. This suggested that these events belong to a series of greater events taking place as a result of the conflict between the imperialist countries, for political and economic purposes. No discussion of democracy, humanity, or equality was observed. However, freedom is specifically depicted, in the context of the USSR and other countries gaining freedom for their nations, rather than freedom from the fascist regime.

DISCUSSION: "ONE HAS NO CHOICE BUT TO BE COMMITTED"

Overall, each country's textbook sample was densely embedded with political ideologies, namely, democracy, socialism, and Marxism-Leninism. At the same time, three countries shared similar attempts to promote exceptionalism and nationalism through the textbooks they produced. These findings have substantially illustrated that historical interpretation conveyed to students through textbooks in each country is not neutral; instead, textbooks have been granted too much power in deciding what is taught and how knowledge is constructed from a homogenous perspective of an epic nation-building story. Nicholls (2006) argued that textbook researchers can never attain a neutral position to observe the objects being researched from above, hence, they "will always be bound to a location, socially, politically and culturally enmeshed in relations of power and knowledge" (p. 105).

With that said, acknowledgment of the unavoidable biases and awareness of different international perspectives on history education does not necessarily mean we as teachers and teacher educators have to accept the power-knowledge structure as what it is. I would argue that the foremost course of action we could take is, as Apple (2004) proposed, "we must be honest about the ways power, knowledge, and interest are interrelated and made manifest, about how hegemony is economically and culturally maintained" (p. 151). Moreover, since our work already serves ideological interests, "one has no choice but to be committed" (Apple, 2004, p. 156)—committed to advocating critical pedagogy in and outside of the discipline and the classroom.

Regarding the perplexing perspectives on World War II from different countries, I support Nicholls' (2006) proposition to move beyond the national and the transnational and at the same time to disregard the relativistic view of including every viewpoint:

[T]o argue that "anything goes" is, at the same time, to limit the potential for critique to zero, stripping the subject-student, teacher, textbook researcher-of intent and purpose. Simply replacing single perspectives with multiple, without stipulating the grounds upon which critique is justified, mocks the very idea of going "beyond" the national and the transnational. (Nicholls, 2006, p. 95)

Rather than accepting any view without noticing the differences that make the difference, students need to have the ability to critically recognize, describe, and interpret those differences. One way to do this is allowing students the necessary time and space to interact with various sources of documents outside the parameters set by the textbook. Apple & Christian-Smith (1991) listed three ideal ways in which people would respond to a text, namely, dominated, negotiated, and oppositional. Whichever that response might be, students need to be able to read multiple authentic texts, gather and investigate non-textual evidences, dialogue with people inside their community or outside their country, and question their own background, before coming to a stance that then needs to be respected.

In short, while the focus of this study is on textbooks, it is really about what teachers make of them with the autonomy they are willing to enact. The possibilities of using multiple sources and the freedom to go beyond the text-book or outside the classroom could help students be exposed to alternative views about the world and themselves, make up their own minds, and draw their own conclusions from what they research, while always acknowledging their own biases. This approach is what I suggest to call the critical pedagogy of engagement, of learning that is created in the classroom and other spaces. This is what makes history an engaging and fascinating subject.

APPENDIX: TEXTBOOK SAMPLES

US Textbook (AWH)

Beck, R. B., Black, L., Krieger, L. S., Naylor, P. C., & Shabaka, D. I. (2012). *Modern world history: Patterns of interaction*. Orlando: Houghton Mifflin Harcourt Publishing Company.

Chinese Textbook

China's Ministry of Education. (2013). *History 9* (trans.). Beijing: People's Publisher.

Vietnamese Textbook

Vietnam's Ministry of Education. (2006). *History 8* (trans.). Hanoi: Hanoi Publishing Company.

NOTES

1. Each textbook was ascribed a code (i.e., AWH, CWH, VWH). Textbooks and their corresponding codes are listed in the Appendix. Each textbook sample is referred to in the Findings section by the code given.
2. **Article 5** Education shall serve the construction of socialist modernization, be combined with production and labor, and satisfy the needs of training constructors and successors with all round development of **morality**, intelligence, and physique for the socialist cause (Education Law of the People's Republic of China, 1995).

REFERENCES

Altbach, P. G. (1991). Textbooks: The international dimension. In M. W. Apple & L. K. Christian-Smith (Eds.), *The politics of the textbook* (pp. 242–258). New York: Routledge.

Apple, M. W. (1992). The text and cultural politics. *Educational Researcher, 21*(7), 4–11.

Apple, M. W. (2004). *Ideology and curriculum* (3rd ed.). London: RoutledgeFalmer.

Apple, M. W., & Christian-Smith, L. K. (1991). The politics of the textbook. In M. W. Apple & L. K. Christian-Smith (Eds.), *The politics of the textbook* (pp. 1–21). New York: Routledge.

Barker, C. (2000). *Cultural studies: Theory and practice*. London: Sage.

Beck, R. B., Black, L., Krieger, L. S., Naylor, P. C., & Shabaka, D. I. (2012). *Modern world history: Patterns of interaction*. Orlando: Houghton Mifflin Harcourt Publishing Company.

Bonus point policy for post-secondary exams. (2015). *Higher-Ed recruitment information*. Retrieved from http://www.thongtintuyensinh.vn/Cong-diem-uu-tien-va-diem-khuyen-khich-khi-xet-tot-nghiep-THPT_C272_D12044.htm

Bourdieu, P., & Passeron, J. C. (1990). *Reproduction in education, society and culture* (4th ed.). Thousand Oaks: Sage.

Brown, N., & Da'Na, S. (2007). The Palestinian national authority: The politics of writing and interpreting curricula. In E. A. Doumato & G. Starrett (Eds.), *Teaching Islam: Textbooks and religion in the Middle East* (pp. 125–152). Boulder: Lynne Rienner Publishers.

China's Ministry of Education. (2006). *Compulsory education law of the People's Republic of China*. Retrieved from http://www.moe.edu.cn/publicfiles/business/htmlfiles/moe/moe_2803/200907/49979.html

Dimitriadis, G., Weis, L., & McCarthy, C. (2006). Introduction. In L. Weis, C. McCarthy, & G. Dimitriadis (Eds.), *Ideology, curriculum, and the new sociology of education: Revisiting the work of Michael Apple* (pp. 2–13). New York: Routledge.

Education Law of the People's Republic of China of 1995, 45 Chinese Code. §§1-84. (2006).

Faden, L. Y. (2015). Globalisation and history education: The United States and Canada. In J. Zajda (Ed.), *Nation-building and history education in a global culture* (pp. 51–65). Dordrecht: Springer.

Foster, S., & Nicholls, J. (2005). America in World War II: An analysis of history textbooks from England, Japan, Sweden, and the United States. *Journal of Curriculum and Supervision, 20*(3), 214–233.

Geertz, C. (2000). *The interpretation of cultures: Selected essays*. New York: Perseus Books Group. (Original work published 1973).

Ginsburg, M. B., & Lindsay, B. (1995). Conceptualizing the political dimension in teacher education. In M. B. Ginsburg & B. Lindsay (Eds.), *The political dimension in teacher education: Comparative perspectives on policy formation, socialization, and society* (pp. 3–20). London: Psychology Press.

Gutek, G. L. (2014). *Philosophical, ideological, and theoretical perspectives on education*. London: Pearson Education, Inc.

Hagai, S., Kitamura, Y., Ratha, K. V., & Brehm, W. C. (2017). Ideologies inside textbooks: Vietnamization and Re-Khmerization of political education in Cambodia during the 1980s. In M. J. Bellino & J. H. Williams (Eds.), *(Re)constructing memory: Education, identity, and conflict* (pp. 49–73). Rotterdam: Sense Publishers.

Han, C. (2007). History education and 'Asian' values for an 'Asian' democracy: The case of Singapore. *Compare: A Journal of Comparative and International Education, 37*(3), 383–398.

Hardwick, S. W., Marcus, R., & Isaak, M. (2010). Education and national identity in a comparative context. *National Identities, 12*(3), 253–268.

Hsiao, H. M. (2011). One colonialism, two memories: Representing Japanese colonialism in Taiwan and South Korea. In G. Shin & D. C. Sneider (Eds.), *History textbooks and the wars in Asia: Divided memories* (pp. 173–190). New York: Routledge.

International Monetary Fund. (2016). *World economic outlook database* [Database]. Retrieved from http://www.imf.org/external/pubs/

Janmaat, J., & Vickers, E. (2007). Education and identity formation in post-communist Europe and East Asia: Introduction. *Compare: A Journal of Comparative and International Education, 37*(3), 267–275.

Jones, A. (2011). Toward pluralism?: The politics of history textbooks in South Korea, Taiwan, and China. In G. Shin & D. C. Sneider (Eds.), *History textbooks and the wars in Asia: Divided memories* (pp. 208–229). New York: Routledge.

Knain, E. (2001). Ideologies in school science textbooks. *International Journal of Science Education, 23*(3), 319–329.

LaSpina, J. A. (2003). Designing diversity: Globalisation, textbooks, and the stories of nations. *Journal of Curriculum Studies, 35*(6), 667–696.

Levesque, S. (2009). *Thinking historically: Educating students for the 21st century.* Toronto: University of Toronto Press.

Marino, M. P. (2011). High school world history textbooks: An analysis of content focus and chronological approaches. *The History Teacher, 44*(3), 421–446.

Mitter, R. (2013). *Forgotten Ally: China's World War II, 1937–1945.* London: Houghton Mifflin Harcourt.

Nicholls, J. (2006). Beyond the national and the transnational: Perspectives of WWII in U.S.A., Italian, Swedish, Japanese, and English school history textbooks. In S. J. Foster & K. A. Crawford (Eds.), *What shall we tell the children? International perspectives on school history textbooks* (pp. 89–112). Charlotte: Information Age Publishing.

Ornstein, A. C. (1994). The textbook-driven curriculum. *Peabody Journal of Education, 69*(3), 70–85.

Orr, J. J. (2001). *The victim as hero: Ideologies of peace and national identity in postwar Japan.* Honolulu: University of Hawai'i Press.

Phillips, R. (1998). *History teaching nationhood and the state: A study in educational politics.* London: Cassell.

Pingel, F. (2006). Reform or conform: German reunification and its consequences for history schoolbooks and curricula. In J. Nicholls (Ed.), *School history textbooks across cultures: International debates and perspectives* (pp. 61–82). Oxford: Symposium Books.

Qun, G., & Wanjin, M. (2007). China's new national curriculum reform: Innovation, challenges and strategies. *Frontiers of Education in China, 2*(4), 579–604.

Shin, G. W., & Sneider, D. C. (2011). *History textbooks and the wars in Asia: Divided memories.* New York: Routledge.

U.S. Network for Education Information. (2008). *Structure of U.S. education.* Retrieved from https://www2.ed.gov/about/offices/list/ous/international/usnei/us/edlite-structure-us.html

Van Dijk, T. A. (1995). Discourse analysis as ideology analysis. In C. Schäffner & A. L. Wenden (Eds.), *Language and Peace.* Amsterdam: Harwood.

Vickers, E. (2006). Defining the boundaries of "Chineseness": Tibet, Mongolia, Taiwan, and Hong Kong in mainland history textbooks. In S. J. Foster & K. Crawford (Eds.), *What shall we tell the children?: International perspectives on school history textbooks* (pp. 25–48). Greenwich: Information Age Publishing.

Vietnam's Ministry of Education. (1998). *Education law*. Retrieved from http://vbpl.vn/TW/Pages/vbpqen-toanvan.aspx?ItemID=1275&Keyword=educatio n+law

Wineburg, S. (2001). *Historical thinking and other unnatural acts: Charting the future of teaching the past*. Philadelphia: Temple University Press.

Zajda, J. (2015). Globalisation and the politics of education reforms: History education. In J. Zajda (Ed.), *Nation-building and history education in a global culture* (pp. 1–14). London: Springer.

Chau Vu studied English Teacher Education at Vietnam National University and worked as a lecturer at University of Languages and International Studies, Vietnam, before gaining her Master's in Curriculum & Instruction from Louisiana State University (LSU). She is now pursuing her doctoral degree in Curriculum & Instruction also at LSU.

The Grammar of Neoliberalism: What Textbooks Reveal About the Education of Spanish Speakers in Mexico, Colombia, and the United States

Andrés Ramírez and Cristobal Salinas

INTRODUCTION

Educators serving Emergent to Advanced Bilingual students (EABs) across the USA use a variety of approaches to address their students' English language and academic needs. Out of these programmatic options, dual language programs have gained in popularity nationally as they support the integration of EABs and English-speaking children, unlike other approaches that segregate EABs students like traditional English as a Second Language (ESL) programs. Furthermore, during the past 25 years, national research has undoubtedly positioned dual language instruction (also called two-way immersion or two-way bilingual) as the most effective approach. In the most comprehensive study of EABs to-date, Collier and Thomas (2009) examined over 6.2 million English Learners students (ELs) for nearly

A. Ramírez (✉) • C. Salinas
Florida Atlantic University, Boca Raton, FL, USA

© The Author(s) 2018
C. Roofe, C. Bezzina (eds.), *Intercultural Studies of Curriculum*, Intercultural Studies in Education,
https://doi.org/10.1007/978-3-319-60897-6_9

25 years and found dual language programs had the greatest long-term positive impact on both the academic achievement and English proficiency for EABs, compared to all the other program approaches. This research illustrates that EABs in dual language programs not only outperform other EABs not enrolled in dual language classes, but *they also outperform English-speaking children* on standardized tests.

Indigenous communities in Mexico and Colombia often do not have access to bilingual programs that use their indigenous language and Spanish. These programs either do not exist at all, are marginal and unstructured, or in general terms, reproduce by and large the nationalist values of a common nation state that promotes upward mobility both through cultural and linguistic assimilation and through valuing Spanish and Spanish literacy as their most precious cultural capital, whereas their own native languages are not considered suitable for academic activities (Hamel 2008). A parallel but completely different kind of bilingual education exists not only in Mexico and Colombia, but throughout Latin America. This kind of bilingual education involves the teaching of Spanish and another European language (which overwhelmingly means English), and it is offered mostly in private primary and secondary institutions. Most of these schools brand themselves as bilingual institutions, but in fact the term "bilingual school" covers a wide spectrum of institutions that range from instruction of only a few hours a week of foreign language classes to elite institutions that teach content through English (Sayer and Lopez Gopar 2015).

One key constant that transcends geographical location or type of program (bilingual or not) is the prominent role of the textbook in instruction. As it is the case in regular English-only and dual language programs in the USA (Milner 2014) and elsewhere, the content that reaches students is highly mediated by textbooks. Our objective is not to evaluate the worthiness of the textbook in instruction. Rather, we contend that its prominence in instruction makes it worth its study in detail as attempted in the present chapter. This is so because in the particular case of Mexico, for example, textbooks have not only been key factors in the educational policies in the country, but because of its relevance and presence in the educational process for decades, textbooks have indeed been *the main agent in educational reform* (Chamizo 2005, p. 272).

The key nature of textbooks in dual language programs in the USA occupies the central concern of this chapter. Overwhelmingly, EABs who are fortunate to receive quality bilingual education in the USA receive instruction from *mirror texts*, that is, texts that are direct translation from their English counterparts (Ramírez et al. 2016). Since these textbooks are literal translations from English, the language demands found in the Spanish translations are those that are particular to the English source text and not to the unique meaning making potential of Spanish as an autonomous linguistic system. Before exploring in detail the implications for the prominent use of mirror texts with Spanish-speaking students enrolled in dual language programs in the USA and the contrasts with the texts written for Spanish-speaking students enrolled in regular (not bilingual) classrooms in Colombia and Mexico, we examine some general features of the educational systems in these countries as they pertain to textbooks' policies and education spending.

EDUCATION SPENDING IN THE USA, COLOMBIA, AND MEXICO

A telling indicator of the macropolitics regarding education in any given country is the general government expenditure on education. The World Bank defines this indicator as a percentage of total general government expenditure on all sectors (including health, education, and social services). As reported by the UNESCO, since 2002 the public spending in education in relation to the total percentage of government spending has steadily dropped in the USA, from 16.55% in 2002 to 13.05% in 2011. This contrasts sharply with a steady increase of public spending in education in the same indicator for Colombia and Mexico. Colombia's spending in education has steadily risen from 12.48% in 1998 to a high percentage of 16.91% in 2013. For Mexico, the increase in spending in education has even been more pronounced. Mexico's expenditures in education have averaged a high percentage of 19.81 from 1998 to 2011 with a *minimum of 15.79% in 1998*, and a *maximum as high as 22.44% in 2003* (UNESCO 2016). Expenditures in education for the three countries are heavily placed in public institutions, with the USA as the one that spends a less percentage of its budget in public educational institutions—an average of 89% as compared to 90% and 96.5% for Colombia and Mexico respectively, in the 2003–2013 period (UNESCO 2016).

When analyzing these percentages in more detail for the three countries, it is noticeable that the expenditure of primary education as a percentage of government spending on education is even wider in relation to the expenditure on primary education for Mexico and Colombia. While the

USA has spent a total average of 31% in primary education in the period between 1999 and 2015, Mexico and Colombia have spent a total average percentage of 39% and 40% in the same period, respectively (UNESCO 2016). The above numbers suggest that neoliberal policies of less government involvement with public institutions as it relates to education were much more pronounced and successful in the USA than in Colombia and Mexico during the time period between 1999 and 2015. After a brief look at the evolution of textbooks in education in general and in the three focus countries, we address the issue of how neoliberalism and neoliberal reforms in education in particular has affected the work of teachers who use these textbooks to teach EABs.

THE EVOLUTION OF TEXTBOOKS IN EDUCATION

For most of the pre-modern era (roughly from the fourth century A.D. until well into the nineteenth century), the deductive style of textbooks, consisting of a series of questions and answers that originally related to religion, was the dominant paradigm (Elson 1964). Regardless of the fact that textbooks became more secular after this period, the catechetical textbook structure remained, and its original design was intended "for the minimum classroom, that is, one consisting of the barest elements: a master reading...with no further necessary equipment such as blackboard or writing equipment- desks, pens, ink, and paper" (Bowen 1975, p. 408). In his historical account of American schoolbooks, Carpenter illustrates how what maintained the use of this kind of textbook structure was the absence of teachers who were appropriately trained. All that was required (and desirable) was an instructor literate enough to simply follow the structure given by the textbook. John Swett, a well-known author of a reading series popular at the end and beginning of the nineteenth and twentieth centuries, contended the main job of the teacher was to "ask the textbook questions without note, comment or explanation" (Swett as cited in Wakefield 1998, p. 8).

By the mid-nineteenth century, and through the influence of Swiss pedagogue Johann Pestalozzi (1898) (often called father of modern education), the catechetical structure fell out of favor and transitorily gave way to more aesthetically appealing textbooks with inductive questions that sought to promote understanding in students as opposed to simple rote memorization. Object teaching, a particular teaching method developed by Pestalozzi, emphasized the importance of children's direct experience of the world and the use of natural objects in teaching. Object teaching encouraged teacher training as teachers' roles changed from following catechetical scripts to designing and guiding lessons that promoted discussion and discovery.

Despite Pestalozzi's (1898) developments, the profound influence of the catechetical textbook, with its highly scripted and narrow curricular focus, manifested itself with special strength in the USA as opposed to Mexico and Colombia as evidenced in Project *Follow Through*, a US federal initiative from President Lyndon Johnson's "War on Poverty" designed to extend Head Start and provide educational, health, and social services to typically disadvantaged kids and their families. The direct instruction model, DISTAR (Direct Instruction System for Teaching Arithmetic and Reading), was an important part of Project *Follow Through* that specified precisely what the teacher must say and what the students' responses should be. Instruction was carefully sequenced so students could not progress to higher-order skills unless they had mastered prerequisite basic skills.

Direct instruction, and prescribed methods of teaching, continued to resurface years later with more strength and prominence. The basal literacy component of DISTAR was rebranded as Reading Mastery and has been used by thousands of schools across the USA in the last 35 years. The timing of this rebranding roughly and non-coincidentally concurs with the emergence of neoliberal capitalism in the USA. While the approaches in Reading Mastery have been changed, and updated, the direct instruction spirit from DISTAR remains, as expressed in the website for the National Institute for Direct Instruction: "fully scripted lessons to guide teachers through carefully constructed instructional steps" (National Institute for Direct Instruction 2016). During the past three decades, major publishing companies have not only successfully expanded and rebranded direct instruction methodology, but have also managed to align their program to the mandates and standards of the corresponding period including Goals 2000: Educate America Act, No Child Left Behind Act, Race to the Top, Common Core Standards, and the recent Every Student Succeeds Act.

During the same period that the US private publishing companies successfully rebranded direct instruction and aligned it to federal program mandates, Mexico was moving in the opposite direction, away from market imperatives and toward meeting the educational needs of students in the system. M.A. Vargas, a researcher from the *Departamento de Investigaciones*

Educativas (Department of Education), argues that the increased role that the *Secretaría de Educación Pública* (SEP; Public Education Ministry) has had in textbook quality and redesign has been significant, surpassing quality standards of textbooks produced by private publishers.

> Graphic quality was substantially improved in the edition of the new materials, with a clearly higher level than most textbooks marketed by private publishing houses. And the relevance lies on the fact that the SEP improved the quality of the material not as a market-competition move, but obeying a strictly educational need: to encourage the children of the country to experience an enriching approach to the world of books. (Vargas as cited in Chamizo 2005, p. 279)

What Vargas finds most relevant is what also remains as key for the argument up to this point. As stated by Vargas, unlike in the USA, market-based economics were not imperatives for textbook distribution and design in Mexico. In fact, the Public Education Ministry (SEP) in Mexico, through the government's high investment in education, has included a SEP free textbook program since 1960, which was later ratified in the educational reform launched in the early 1990s (and still is in place today). This textbook program provides each student in Mexico with as many as 40 textbooks throughout their elementary years at a little less than a dollar per textbook (Chamizo 2005). This contrasts sharply with the situation in the USA under neoliberal capitalism where public institutions, education agencies included, are considered "black holes" and thus were targeted for obliteration and defunding. The confirmation of Donald Trump's Education Secretary Betsy DeVos in February of 2017 is sure to exacerbate this trend, as Secretary DeVos has been a strong advocate of neoliberal educational reform in the form of school vouchers, charter schools, and school choice.

Colombia is a different case from the USA and Mexico in terms of the textbook market. Colombia's schools and teachers have the freedom to adopt textbooks. Also, highly relevant is the fact individual finances of families play a significant part in access and dissemination of textbooks. As in the USA, for the most part, textbooks in Colombia are not developed by any governmental agency. The overwhelming majority of textbooks come from publishers established in Colombia or from foreign firms. However, similar to Mexico, the *Instituto Colombiano de Pedagogía* (ICOLPE) (Colombian Institute of Pedagogy) of the Ministry of

Education has developed free primers, called *cartillas,* to enhance elementary school teachers' pedagogical skills and to provide materials and suggestions to facilitate their daily work. Unlike Mexico and the USA, it is the responsibility of Colombian parents, not schools or districts, to purchase all school supplies, including textbooks, according to the preferences of schoolteachers or administrators. To avoid speculation with the risen cost of textbooks, the Colombian congress has established that once a school adopts a textbook, the school must use it for a minimum of three years.

As individual schools and even teachers have liberty to choose their books, often and frequently due to the financial burden that this causes to families, only some parents are able to get all the materials, while others can only get a part of them. On a frequent basis, parents recur to the expanding and widely available second-hand textbook market where textbooks are often acquired at a fraction of their cost. It is also not uncommon at all for parents without sufficient means to make copies of the material or to find the textbook on the internet. Indeed, according to the *Cámara Colombiana del Libro* (Colombian Chamber of Books), in 2015 publishers in Colombia reported sales for less than one textbook per student or no more than 10 million textbook copies sold to the more than 11 million of students attending Colombia's schools (Romero 2016). Compared to the $28 billion market in 2014 reported in the USA. (Bluestone 2015), the textbook market in Latin America, let alone Colombia and Mexico, is insignificant. In Mexico, this is almost a non-issue; as textbooks are provided free of charge to students. Since individual finances are a key factor in Colombia, the Colombian government, through its new initiative *Colombia Aprende* (Colombia Learns), has begun to make educational materials available online and free of cost for parents. This effort is not as comprehensive as it has been in Mexico, but experts feel that with this small step the door toward open access materials has opened (Romero 2016).

SYSTEMIC FUNCTIONAL LINGUISTICS AS THEORETICAL FRAMEWORK

Systemic Functional Linguistics (SFL) (Halliday and Matthiessen 2004) holds the view that language is a social construct and that language itself is structured as it is due to what it seeks to accomplish (Martin and Rose 2007). Systemic organization is concerned with grammatical structure as a realization of a set of options and a reservoir of interrelated grammatical resources for meaning potential (paradigms) available to the speaker to express meaning. Using SFL-specific tools for linguistic analysis, one curricular unit is compared across popular school textbooks used in Mexico, Colombia, and the USA.

Following decades of successful research and classroom application inspired by the "Sydney School" in Australia and in many parts of the world (see, e.g., Deyfus et al. 2016), Systemic Functional Linguistics is increasingly becoming a favored alternative to traditional linguistics in the US context and abroad (Brisk 2015; Gebhard and Harman 2011; Moore and Schleppegrell 2014; de Oliveira and Iddings 2014; Figueredo 2014, 2015; Kartika Ningsih 2015; Ramírez 2014; Ramírez et al. 2016; Ramírez et al., in preparation). Researchers who work in SFL view language as a social construct, and maintain that language itself is structured as it is because of what it seeks to accomplish. In other words, systemic organization is concerned with grammatical structure not as a prescriptive set of rules as in modern formal grammar but as a realization of a set of options; a reservoir of interrelated grammatical resources for meaning potential (paradigms) available to the speaker to express meaning.

The set of choice points capturing paradigmatic relations are called systems or system networks. System networks make it possible to capture simultaneous meaning making in a clause or expression. In SFL theorization, language is organized into different modes of meaning or metafunctions: ideational, interpersonal, and textual. For example, a clause from one of the curricular units that comes from the Mexican focus texts to be examined here reads: *¿Cómo son los materiales y sus interacciones?* (How is matter and its interactions?) simultaneously talks about something (ideational meaning), positions the reader in certain way (interpersonal meaning), and does so in a specific mode (textual meaning). That is, because language is conceived as a set of interrelated choices available to the speaker, the clause above could have been about anything else other than matter, it could have been expressed not through a question but through a command or declarative statement (thus positioning the reader differently), and it could have been in an oral mode instead of a written one.

METHODOLOGY

Materials and Setting

This chapter features a linguistic analysis of text excerpts from the Florida *Fusión* science textbook in Spanish for 3rd grade published by Houghton Mifflin Harcourt Publishers used in the USA, the *Enlaces* Science textbook in Spanish for 3rd grade published by Santillana Publishers used in Colombia, and the *Ciencias Naturales* (Natural Sciences) textbook for 3rd grade used in Mexico. The Spanish *Fusión* science textbook is the translated text version of the English Florida *Fusión* science textbook mandated for 3rd grade Science subject area teaching in the Palm Beach and Broward County Public School System in Florida. The content of the book is written to be aligned with Florida's Science Next Generation Sunshine State Standards. All designs, content, and page layout in both the English and Spanish texts are the same, but the book was originally written in English. The translated Spanish *Fusión* science textbook is only used in dual language programs in these school districts.

The *Enlaces* Science text from Santillana Publishers is a textbook series, commonly used in primary classrooms throughout Colombia and other Latin American countries. Just as the Ciencias Naturales textbook used in Mexico, the *Enlaces* series was originally written in Spanish and does not include any translated content or mirrored elements of design that was mirrored from another text as was the case with the Florida *Fusión* Spanish textbook. The three focus texts are in the same language (Spanish) and share same topic (matter), the same grade level (3rd grade), and the same register (informational texts).

Data Collection and Analysis

In this analysis, we selected the units dedicated to the subject area of "Matter" in the USA particularly from the state of Florida and the Colombian and Mexican science textbook because the subject area of "Matter" is part of core for the 3rd grade science curriculum in the three countries. The unit dedicated to "Matter" exclusively in each textbook is treated similarly across textbooks. This consisted of Unit 3 in the Spanish Florida *Fusión* textbook, Unit 4 in the Science Santillana textbook, and unit 3 in the *Ciencias Naturales* textbook. The analysis focused on the academic language structures of authentic and translated Spanish academic texts. The written text portion within these units, inclusive of titles, subtitles, and main text with less but sufficient attention to pictures, sidebars, and other auxiliary information were the units of analysis.

We conducted a linguistic analysis using Martin and Rose (2007) SFL Framework in order to discern how the language structures and macro-structures in each textbook were organized to describe, report, and inform on the subject area of "Matter." By using an SFL-informed analytical approach which recognizes that language is structured according to meaning, we were able to discern and compare the academic language choices in each text across a common genre and purpose both within and beyond the clause. Following this framework, the authors identified and labeled the participants (the subject, object, and other nouns), processes (the verbs), and circumstances (the adjectival and adverbial groups) of each clause. We also used the logical component of the ideational metafunction as we focused on the level of interdependence of clauses (system of TAXIS) and the logico-semantic relations that either project or expand meaning within and across clauses. We were strategic in choosing to analyze solely the ideational metafunction as this provided a snapshot into how the content and logic relations of the text were communicated through the language. Due to space constraints and the importance to address how content is treated in each of the countries, this chapter only reports on a small set of the findings, specifically those that pertain to the first pages of the curricular units as they are important for the analysis of macrothemes.

FINDINGS

This section presents findings from a linguistic analysis using SFL framework to compare three science units dedicated to the subject area of "Matter" in the school textbooks used in Mexico, Colombia, and the USA. The findings are presented as sematic waves and macrothemes. Macrothemes (Martin and Rose 2007) are semantic waves of information at the textual level (as opposed to clauses) that foreground essential premises providing overarching content statements prospectively, that is, in a fashion that will be elaborated later in the text as a whole.

Semantic Waves and Macrothemes

At first sight, the first two introductory pages for the unit in the three texts project a remarkably similar macrotheme. Upon closer examination, the differences are clear. Text 1 (mirror text translated from the English version) is labeled *Las Propiedades de la Materia* (Properties of Matter). This unit starts with a page depicting a large picture of a scuba diver submerged in the ocean surrounded by colorful corals. The picture caption identifies the place as a coral reef in Key Largo, Florida. To the right side of the picture and the large title, two text boxes identify what they call *La gran idea 8 and 9* (The great idea 8 and 9). Both great ideas 8 *Las Propiedades de la Materia* (properties of matter) and 9 *Cambios en la materia* (changes in matter), end up being not ideas but simply topics. The right bottom of the page displays a close up of one of the fish that appears in the main picture. The title of this section reads *Me pregunto porqué* (I wonder why) accompanied by the following text: *Los colores de los peces y de los corales nos pueden ayudar a aprender a usar las propiedades de la materia. ¿A qué se debe esto? Da vuelta a la pagina para descubrirlo* (Fish and coral colors can help us learn to use the properties of matter. Why is this? Turn the page to discover it). At the top of the next page (which is visible when the previous page is open without need to turn it), the subtitle *Por Esta Razón* (for this reason) is written. The answer to the previous question is given by referring to the fact that color is a physical property of matter and that we can use color to classify corals and fish into groups. After a table of contents in the center of the page describing the 5 lessons for the unit, the same text boxes with the great ideas 8 and 9 show up again, but this time much smaller. Without any further explanation, a prominent text box announces *¡Ya Entiendo la gran idea!* (Now I understand the great idea!).

Similar to the just described mirror text, text 2 (the non-translated text for native Spanish speakers) depicts a large, colorful picture and the title *Entorno Físico: La Materia* (Physical Environment: Matter). The picture shows a large colony of penguins divided into three groups standing on huge ice caps along a body of water in what appears to be Antarctica. A caption on the bottom left reads: *El calentamiento de nuestro planeta esta derritiendo los polos, que son el habitat de animals como los pinguinos y las morsas* (Global warming is melting the poles which serve as habitat for animals such as penguins and Walruses). The next page (as with the mirror text also visible when the previous page is open) lists what students will be learning (i.e., what is matter and what are its properties).

The *Enlaces* textbox used in Colombia asks students for their opinion using different questions ranging from simple to more complex factual questions (i.e., what do you observe in the images? What kind of substance is water and in what states can it be found in nature?). The third text, coming from the *Ciencias Naturales* textbook used in Mexico, depicts a full-colored page graph displaying a dominant anvil close to a small white feather. The small caption on the next page after the big title for the unit reads: *Un Yunque, bloque macizo y pesado de hierro, y una pluma, muy ligera* (An anvil, solid and heavy block of iron, and a very light feather). The title next to this caption reads ¿*Cómo son los materiales y sus interacciones?* (How is matter and its interactions?).

Important points can be gathered from the described texts above. The first two pages of the unit in text 2 used in Colombia set up a wave of information or macrotheme that is concerned with disciplinary knowledge at the heart of scientific inquiry set up at a global stage. Significantly, the issue of global warming is treated as a fact that is threatening the habitat of different animals across the globe and implicitly connected to the unit of matter. The picture from Antarctica depicting colonies of penguins not only frames and reinforces the global point but attempts to build affiliation with distant non-human participants through the reality presented in this page. The request for the student's opinion on the next page on the kind of materials that form water, rocks, and living beings (in addition to other similar questions) serve as an attempt to provide students' with a sense of the kind of information that will be covered in the unit. It is worth noting that the integrity and felicitous nature of questioning is not transgressed as the text does not seek to answer such questions, at least not immediately. Similar to this text 2 *Enlaces*, text 3—*Ciencias Naturales* used in Mexico, foregrounds disciplinary knowledge in an implicit way by contrasting two objects that differ significantly in terms of mass and volume (anvil and feather), which are the central concepts in this unit. Although global connections are not explicit as in text 1, the disciplinary nature and priority of the unit is highlighted through non-human participants and reinforced with the image of a full-page balance with a caption on the next page that reads: *La balanza es un instrumento que se utiliza para medir la masa de los objetos* (The scale is a tool used to measure the mass of different objects).

Unlike the previous two texts, the translated mirror text used in the USA displays an overall concern with human participants interacting in the immediacy of the here and now. The illustration depicts a human participant (scuba diver) as the central participant not only in interaction with the underwater maritime environment in which s/he is acting. Crucially, the interaction is also with the intended reader (a 3rd grade child living in Florida). As such, the picture of the coral reefs in Key Largo Florida is a strategic choice to promote geographical affiliation with the Florida consumers of the text. This is evident not only by the fact that most pictures in the book series seek to build such personal affiliation, but that the same series in other parts of the country displays pictures relevant to the clients in that part of the country. This is a strong indication that marketing imperatives guide the choice of pictures for the series.

Ironically, the efforts to build affiliation between human participants are minimized and trivialized when it comes to germane communication exchange patterns, arguably the most important way we build or at least seek affiliation with others. As you may recall, this text asks EAB students at the bottom of the page how is it that fish and coral colors could help people learn to use the properties of matter. Following this, the text invites EABs to "discover" only to provide the answer in the next sentence. In fact, this pattern of asking questions right after a very small piece of information continues through the whole unit promoting a fabricated conversational tone that not only pretends to take over the role of the teacher in promoting academic talk but that dilutes the supposed disciplinary focus of the unit. Coming back to the example already alluded to, the explicit proposed action by the text that leads to the "discovery" is simply to turn the page, an action that in no way resembles that of scientists attempting to discover. In addition, as already described, the big ideas 8 and 9 "Properties of Matter" and "Changes in Matter," described in some detailed before, are not truly ideas but simply topics. Even if this detail is not as telling, what is worth examining is that at the end of the next page, only after having provided the learner with the fact that color can be used to classify corals and fishes, it is announced that students *now I understand the big idea!* Such is an unsophisticated assumption without any kind of qualification that responds more to the feigned interactional patterns promoted in the unit than to a convincing effort to advance understanding of the topic.

The trivialized nature of the discovery as proposed in the mirror text targeted for EABs' is perhaps best illustrated by contrasting it with the notion of discovery through experimentation in the Mexican curricular unit intended for monolingual Spanish students, a focus that runs through the whole unit. After a brief general explanation about matter and how all objects that surround us have specific properties (i.e., color, hardness),

204 A. RAMÍREZ AND C. SALINAS

Mexican students are not only shown a beam balance and told how this tool is used to measure the mass of objects, but they are given specific directions to build a beam balance themselves using a stick, some string, and two lids or recipients of equal characteristics. Using their recently built balance, these students are then directed to place different wood cubes with different mass into the beam balance and are asked to record the results. Following this, students are asked yet again to use the beam balance to explore the relationship between mass and size. In the final experiment, students are asked to take three equal portions of clay, shape them differently, and explore the relationship between mass and shape. The next section explains volume and leads the students to complete three curricular tasks to discover the properties of volume once again through experimentation.

The prominence of experiments in the *Ciencias Naturales* text is hardly surprising. After systematic ethnographic observation of different science classrooms throughout Mexico, Gabriela Naranjo, and Antonia Candela (2006), research members from the federally funded *Centro de Investigaciones y Estudios Avanzados* (CINVESAV) concluded that in science classes, teachers show concern for their students' learning by promoting thinking processes through experimental activities proposed in textbooks as well as other additional ones. The most favored routes to reach success in this regard was by building up on students' thoughts, accepting alternative paths, asking for coherence in actions, returning questions, asking for arguments, accepting challenges, and seeking for consensus instead of imposing one's point of view (Naranjo and Candela 2006, p. 822). As already shown, this concern with experimentation is well represented in the *Ciencias Naturales* text. Unlike the contrived and fabricated interactional patterns described with the mirror text in which the role of the teacher was not simply minimized but hijacked, the Mexican text needs a skillful teacher to guide students through meaningful interaction in the context of shared ideas (Rose and Martin 2012).

The clearly distinct macrothemes that these different texts present stand in stark opposition to their similarities in genre and register. The genre of the text can be better defined in relation to its purpose: to instruct. As for register, in terms of field, all three texts are on the same topic of matter. In terms of tenor, texts assume a hierarchy between the authors (experts in the field) and the readers (3rd graders). In terms of mode, texts are written to be read in the context of a classroom. To recap, the analysis of the macrothemes from these three texts provided evidence that while text 1 was structured in such a way as to building interpersonal affiliations, text 2 and 3 are more concerned with building disciplinary knowledge; the kind of knowledge needed by all students (including EABs) to advance academically.

DISCUSSION

The fact that education has traditionally been a site of struggle is nothing new to neoliberal times. Just as many classic and determinant theorists on US education (i.e., Dewey 1938; Giroux 1981) did, Basil Bernstein (2000) conceived education as a battleground where different actors set out to carve out intellectual and institutional territory in search of power and legitimation that "tilt the field in their favour" (Maton 2014). In the education battleground, different actors fight for control over what Bernstein called the pedagogic device (Bernstein 2000), or the ensemble of procedures via which knowledge is recontextualized or converted from knowledge into pedagogical communication (classroom talk, textbooks, and curriculum).

Two fields regulate the recontextualization field. The first is the Official Recontextualizing Field (ORF), controlled by the state, selected agents, and ministries in charge not only of transforming specialist knowledge through the development of syllabi, curricula, and assessment regimes, but importantly, responsible for legitimizing through standards and mandates what is to be learned in schools. The second is the Pedagogic Recontextualizing Field (PRF) which is responsible for providing interactional structures capable of distilling specialized knowledge into manageable appropriate chunks for specific students. As such, the pedagogic device materializes symbolic control; therefore, it is the object of struggle for possible domination as it attempts to shape and distribute forms of consciousness, identity and desire.

As shown in this chapter, the educational context of the USA is a context that has responded to the global economic and political restructuring in the service of free market imperatives. This is the Official Recontextualizing Field. Its marketization efforts have resulted in the intensification of teachers' work that in turn has led to degeneration of teacher professionalism, where teachers are less trusted as qualified candidates to make value judgments on the best learning paths for students who they know best. This "distrust" was found to be operationalized in the Pedagogic Recontextualizing Field through the textbook contents. As revealed in the analysis, even though the texts share the same topic (matter), the same grade level (3rd grade), and the same register (informational texts), they are indeed very different texts with distinct consequences for students and teachers. The mirror text used in the USA was found to miss important lexical connections between the everyday and the academic register in Spanish and impose an English dominant syntactical straightjacket on Spanish, not present in the other two texts. More importantly, the text was found to assume a burdening interactional pattern that foregrounds interpersonal affiliation at the expense the disciplinary knowledge EAB students require for success in academic settings.

CONCLUSION

The analysis of the three school textbooks in these three distinct countries shows that even though the texts share the same topic (matter), the same grade level (3rd grade), and the same register (informational texts), they are indeed very different texts. Contrary to the texts used in Colombia and Mexico, the text used in the USA is a direct translation from its English counterpart; it misses important lexical connections between the everyday and the academic register in Spanish and imposes an English dominant syntactical straightjacket on Spanish. More importantly, explored at the micro level, the text assumes a burdening interactional pattern that foregrounds interpersonal affiliation at the expense of the disciplinary knowledge EAB students require for success. Explored at the macro level, it serves as yet another illustration of the intensification of teacher's work with dire consequences for the education of all students, including EABs.

Findings of this analysis strongly suggest that EABs enrolled in bilingual programs across the USA may benefit from having access to texts that are originally written in Spanish. Indeed, and as part of Mexico's Free Textbook Distribution Program, the Secretary of Public Education and the Secretary of Foreign Relations (through the Mexican Cultural Center) have begun to provide the state of Colorado in the USA with resource books for 1–6 grades that are used for Mexico's national curriculum, as a resource for binational students. Policy makers, educators, and research must continue to advocate for quality education for all EAB students.

REFERENCES

Bernstein, B. B. (2000). *Pedagogy, symbolic control, and identity: Theory, research, critique.* Lanham: Rowman & Littlefield Publishers.

Bluestone, M. (2015). *U.S. publishing industry annual survey reveals $28 billion in revenue in 2014.* Association of American Publishers. Retrieved September 18, 2016, from http://publishers.org/news/us-publishing-industry%E2%80%99s-annual-survey-reveals-28-billion-revenue-2014

Bowen, J. (1975). *A history of western education: Civilization of Europe, sixth to sixteenth century* (2nd ed.). New York: St. Martin's Press.

Brisk, M. E. (2015). *Engaging students in academic literacies: Genre-based pedagogy for K-5 classrooms.* New York: Routledge.

Chamizo, J. (2005). The teaching of natural sciences in Mexico: New programs and textbooks for elementary school. *Science Education International, 30*(4), 271–279.

Collier, V. P., & Thomas, W. P. (2009). *Educating English learners for a transformed world.* Albuquerque: Dual Language Education of New Mexico – Fuente Press.

de Oliveira, L. C., & Iddings, J. (2014). *Genre pedagogy across the curriculum: Theory and application in U.S. classrooms and contexts.* Sheffield/Bristol: Equinox.

Dewey, J. (1938). *Experience and education.* New York: The Macmillan company.

Deyfus, S. et al. (2016). *Genre pedagogy in higher education.* The SLATE project. London: Palgrave.

Elson, R. M. (1964). *Guardians of tradition, American schoolbooks of the nineteenth century.* Lincoln: University of Nebraska Press.

Figueredo, G. (2014). Uma metodologia de perfilhação gramatical sistêmica baseada em corpus. *Letras & Letras, 30* (2), 17–45.

Figueredo, G. (2015). Um estudo do conjunto multilíngue Interpessoal português brasileiro/inglês Subsidiado pelos estudos da tradução e pela Linguística sistêmico funcional. *Florianópolis, 35*(1), 139–166.

Gebhard, M., & Harman, R. (2011). Reconsidering genre theory in K-12 schools: A response to school reforms in the United States. *Journal of Second Language Writing, 20,* 45–55.

Giroux, H. (1981). *Ideology, culture and the process of schooling.* Philadelphia: Temple University Press.

Halliday, M. A. K., & Matthiessen, C. M. I. M. (2004). *An introduction to functional grammar* (3rd ed.). London/New York: Arnold.

Hamel, R. (2008). Bilingual education for indigenous communities in Mexico. In N. Hornberger (Ed.), *Encyclopedia of language and education* (pp. 1747–1758). New York: Springer.

Kartika Ningsih, H. (2015). *Multilingual re-instantiation: Genre pedagogy in Indonesian classrooms*. Sydney: University of Sydney.

Martin, J. R., & Rose, D. (2007). *Working with discourse: Meaning beyond the clause* (2nd ed.). London/New York: Continuum.

Maton, K. (2014). *Knowledge and knowers: Towards a realist sociology of education*. Oxon: Routledge.

Milner, R. (2014). Scripted and narrowed curriculum reform in urban schools. *Urban Education, 49*, 743–749.

Moore, J., & Schleppegrell, M. (2014). Using a functional linguistics metalanguage to support academic language development in the English language arts. *Linguistics and Education, 26*, 92–105.

Naranjo, G., & Candela, A. (2006). Saberes docentes en las clases de ciencias en las que se integra un alumno ciego. *Revista Mexicana de Investigación Educativa, 11* (30), 821–845.

National Institute for Direct Instruction. (2016). *Reading mastery signature edition*. Retrieved December 16, 2016, from http://www.nifdi.org/programs/reading/reading-mastery

Pestalozzi, J. H. (1898). *How Gertrude teaches her children: An attempt to help mothers to teach their own children and an account of the method*. London: C.W. Bardeen.

Ramírez, A. (2014). Genre-based principles in a content-based English as a second language classroom. In L. C. de Oliveira & J. Iddings (Eds.), *Genre pedagogy across the curriculum: Theory and application in U.S. classrooms and contexts*. Sheffield/Bristol: Equinox.

Ramírez, A., Sembiante, S., & de Oliveira, L. (2016, July). *Multilingual meaning potential: Spanish/English academic texts in dual language programs in the U.S. International Systemic Functional Linguistics*. Paper presented at Universitas Pendidikan Indonesia. Bandung.

Ramírez, A., Sembiante, S., & de Oliveira, L. (in preparation). The textbook and the deskilling of teachers' work: An English-Spanish comparative functional linguistic analysis.

Romero, L. (2016). Textos Escolares: Un Negocio en Debate. *El Espectador. Bogotá*. Retrieved December 15, 2017, from http://www.elespectador.com/noticias/educacion/textos-escolares-un-negocio-debate-articulo-610781

Rose, D., & Martin, J. R. (2012). *Learning to write, reading to learn: Genre, knowledge and pedagogy in the Sydney school*. Sheffield/Bristol: Equinox.

Sayer, P., & Lopez Gopar, M. (2015). Language education in Mexico. In W. E. Wright, S. Boun, & O. García (Eds.), *Handbook of bilingual and multilingual education* (pp. 578–591). Oxford: Wiley.

UNESCO. (2016). Education: Expenditure on education as % of GDP. *Institute for statistics*. Retrieved December 15, 2016, from Data.uis.unesco.org

Wakefield, J. (1998, June). *A brief history of textbooks: Where have we been all these years?* Paper presented at the Meeting of the Text and Academic Authors. St. Petersburg.

Andrés Ramírez is an assistant professor in the Curriculum, Culture, and Educational Inquiry Department at Florida Atlantic University. He teaches courses in Teaching English to Speakers of Other Languages (TESOL), Bilingual Education, and Applied Linguistics. His scholarly work explores the linguistic, cultural, and economic conditions constraining and enabling the academic literacy achievement of culturally and linguistically diverse students in the United States. He anchors his academic work on poststructural materialism and critical discourse studies. His current scholarship focuses on the intersection between bilingual language development theory and practice and Systemic Functional Linguistics (SFL).

Cristobal Salinas Jr is an assistant professor in the Educational Leadership and Research Methodology Department at Florida Atlantic University. He coauthored the book *Iowa's Community Colleges: A Collective History of Fifty Years of Accomplishment.* Cristobal is the co-founder and managing editor for the *Journal Committed to Social Change on Race and Ethnicity.* His research promotes access and quality in higher education, and explores the social, political, and economic context of educational opportunities for historically marginalized communities, with an emphasis on Latino/a communities.

The Secondary Arts Curricula in Australia, Canada and Malaysia: Issues of Policy and Culture

Sharon Lierse

INTRODUCTION

The Arts are an integral part of society. How they are taught and represented in the school curriculum is a reflection of their aesthetic values and cultural significance. Moreover, they can reveal how society represents current themes and issues such as indigenous cultures, globalisation and the environment (Robinson and Aronica 2009). The three countries selected for the chapter are Australia, Canada and Malaysia. They were chosen due to their similarities in population, English as a language priority, connections to the monarchy and indigenous populations. According to the 2014 Human Development Index (HDI), Australia and Canada are classified as Very High with Australia second in the world to Norway (2016, List of Countries by Human Development Index). Canada is ranked in the top ten, at number nine. Malaysia is classified as High, classifying it as

S. Lierse (✉)
Charles Darwin University, Melbourne, VIC, 3000, Australia

© The Author(s) 2018   211
C. Roofe, C. Bezzina (eds.), *Intercultural Studies
of Curriculum*, Intercultural Studies in Education,
https://doi.org/10.1007/978-3-319-60897-6_10

a developing country and is ranked 62 in the world. Consequently, it is expected that The Arts curricula would be similar in Australia and Canada with a marked contrast to Malaysia.

Understanding curricula of different cultures is complicated and many factors need to be taken in account in order to appreciate variances amongst them. Curriculum documents are fundamentally important yet this is only one lens in which to understand aspects of culture. For the purpose of the chapter, the secondary arts curriculum documents were examined from Australia, Canada and Malaysia, then cultural differences were considered using Geert Hofstede's Six Dimensions of National Cultures (Hofstede 2016). Hofstede conducted research into cultural structures with an aim to explain how people from different nations think, feel and act. From his research over 40 years and examining 70 countries, he constructed six dimensions in which to better understand different culture. The six dimensions are *Power Distance, Individualism, Masculinity, Uncertainty Avoidance, Long-Term Orientation* and *Indulgence*. Through these lenses, a deeper understanding of "difference" can be gained in order to reveal more insight into how these factors influence educational systems and The Arts, in an increasingly complicated world.

Australia

Australia is situated in the Southern Hemisphere in the Asia Pacific. Colonised by the British in the eighteenth century, it is a Commonwealth country with a culturally diverse population of approximately 24 million people (Australian Bureau of Statistics 2017). There are six States and two Territories with the majority of people residing in capital cities. The formal language spoken is English. Australia has one of the oldest indigenous populations in the world with over 100 Aboriginal and Torres Strait Islander cultures. Education is compulsory for students from the ages of 5 to 15 and is founded on the British system of public schools, church schools and government schools (Cameron 1969). Government schools are secular, compulsory and free, and students are zoned to a school depending on their geographic location (Education Act 1972). There are differences between schools depending on their geography, location, funding and areas of specialty.

Australia's Western arts heritage was initially borrowed or imported from overseas, notably the United Kingdom. The Arts are still influenced by Europe and more recently Asia and the United States of America. Australia is still developing its own cultural identity in terms of musical and artistic traditions.

In 2011, the Australian Curriculum was introduced for students from Foundation year which is for four- to five-year olds to Year 10 which is for students who are 15 or 16 years old. The curriculum has undergone a series of revisions and many consultation sessions and is now at the stage of being implemented in some of the States and Territories although some schools prefer their old local curriculum. For students in Years 11 and 12, they still have their own State or Territory curricula.

The Arts form one of the compulsory learning areas in the Australian Curriculum, Assessment and Reporting Authority 2011 and is divided into five subjects. These are visual art, media art, dance, drama and music. Each of the subjects offers content descriptors such as "Structure compositions by combining and manipulating the elements of music using notation" in Year 7 music (Australian Curriculum, Assessment and Reporting Authority 2016). This enables scope for any school to deliver this component of The Arts curriculum. However, the information in the documents is descriptive rather than prescriptive. For students in the secondary years of schooling, that is, from Years 7 to 12, The Arts are encouraged but not compulsory as stated below:

> From the first year of secondary school (Year 7 or 8), students will have the opportunity to experience one or more arts subjects in depth. In Years 9 and 10, students will be able to specialise in one or more arts subject. Subjects offered will be determined by state and territory school authorities or individual schools. (Australian Curriculum, Assessment and Reporting Authority 2016)

The Arts curriculum is available but not mandated in schools. An issue of concern is that students may not receive a secondary arts education at all depending on the resources available at that particular school. The rationale for The Arts in the Australian Curriculum is as follows:

> Through The Arts curriculum students pursue questions regarding intended meaning, audience understanding, cultural context and the beliefs and values reflected in artworks. There is opportunity to engage with artists' influence on society, the effect of technology on presentation and audience engagement with artwork. (Australian Curriculum, Assessment and Reporting Authority 2016)

The strands of The Arts curriculum are as follows: "(1) making which includes learning about and using knowledge, skills, techniques, processes, materials and technologies to explore arts practices and make artworks that communicate ideas and intentions and (2) [R]esponding which includes exploring, responding to, analysing and interpreting artworks" (Australian Curriculum, Assessment and Reporting Authority 2016). These strands are found throughout The Arts curriculum from Foundation to Year 10.

There are three cross-curriculum priorities in the Australian Curriculum which are Aboriginal and Torres Strait Islander Histories and Cultures, Asia and Australia's Engagement with Asia and Sustainability (Ministerial Council on Education, Employment, Training and Youth Affairs 2008). These have been developed from the Melbourne Declaration on Educational Goals for Young Australians. This was jointly published by Australian Education Ministers in 2008. The preamble states:

> As a nation Australia values the central role of education in building a democratic, equitable and just society—a society that is prosperous, cohesive and culturally diverse, and that values Australia's indigenous cultures as a key part of the nation's history, present and future. (Ministerial Council on Education, Employment, Training and Youth Affairs 2008, p. 4)

The three priorities are intended to be addressed through the curriculum rather than being a stand-alone subject with the aim to "add depth and richness to student learning" (Ministerial Council on Education, Employment, Training and Youth Affairs 2008). In this context, indigenous arts can be incorporated into the curriculum through using examples of indigenous arts works and learning and the techniques and processes. Likewise, globalisation is addressed with the Engagement with Asia through an inclusion of Asian arts. Environmental issues may be incorporated through learning about sustainability and recycling arts materials. These three priorities are up to the teachers and schools in how these are manifested.

The secondary arts curriculum in Australia is current and relevant to themes and issues found in Australian society. As they are descriptive, the documents are up to interpretation. The Arts, however, are not mandated, and the implementation of The Arts varies between classes and schools. Consequently, each student has a different experience of The Arts depending on the class, school, geographic location and cultural background.

Canada

Canada is a federation and ruled by a constitutional monarchy. There are ten provinces and three territories with a total population of approximately 33 million people. Situated north of the United States of America, it is the second largest country in the world with the largest portion of fresh water lakes. Due to its proximity to the Arctic Circle, they experience very cold winters. The main languages spoken are English and French in some provinces. There are also recognised indigenous populations and Canada is multi-cultural with migrants representing many overseas countries. According to the Organisation for Economic Co-operation and Development (OECD) Canada is number one in the world for adults holding a tertiary qualification (Canada 2016).

Each province has autonomy over programs including education, healthcare and welfare. As a result, there is no national curriculum; rather each province is responsible for writing and implementing their curricula. For the purpose of this chapter, the province of Ontario has been examined due to its large population size with approximately five and a half million people living in its capital, Toronto.

The Arts Curriculum document known as *The Arts* covers Grades 1–8 and includes the rationale and practice in its holistic environment. In Canada, the class level is referred to as a "Grade", whereas in Australia they are known as a "Year". The chapter focuses on Grades 7 and 8 as well as Grades 9–12 in the Senior Curriculum. The four arts subjects are similar to Australia, that is, dance, drama, music and visual art. A unique feature of The Arts curriculum is the expectation that "Teachers in the intermediate division should explicitly teach and model the use of arts knowledge, skills, and strategies across all subject areas" (Ontario Curriculum: Elementary. *The Arts* 2009a, p. 131). Arts education here is connected to their overall lives:

> The expectations encourage students to explore issues related to personal identity and community concerns as they interact with increasingly complex and/or challenging media; to critically analyse and evaluate perspectives in works of dance, drama, music, and visual art; to use inquiry and research skills to extend their interpretive and creative abilities; and to use The Arts to explore and comment on topics of relevance that matter in their daily lives. (Ontario Curriculum: Elementary, *The Arts* 2009a, p. 131)

There are three overall expectations in each of The Arts which are similar to Australia's strand of making and responding. The strands in the Ontario arts curriculum are: creating and presenting; reflecting, responding and analysing; and exploring forms and cultural contexts. The curriculum document is more prescriptive with more detailed information of the elements of The Arts forms with teacher prompts as starting points and ideas for lessons plans and course development. However, there is no compulsory content or repertoire.

In Grades 9 and 10, there is an arts curriculum covering courses in dance, drama, media arts, music and visual arts. There is also a new integrated arts unit in which students may commence in Grades 9 or 10 making a choice of five arts subjects:

> Through studying works of art from various cultures, students deepen their appreciation of diverse perspectives and develop the ability to approach others with openness and flexibility. Seeing the works of art produced by their classmates also helps them learn about, accept, and respect the identity of others and the differences among people. The openness that is fostered by study of The Arts helps students to explore and appreciate the culture of diverse peoples in Canada, including First Nations and francophones. (Ontario Curriculum: Grades 9 and 10. *The Arts* 2009b, p. 3)

There is an emphasis here on knowing the local culture including indigenous cultures and First Nations. In Grades 9 and 10, the strands of making, creating and responding are similar to the earlier years. The curriculum is based on four central ideas "developing creativity, communicating, understanding culture, and making connections" (Ontario Curriculum: Grades 9 and 10. *The Arts* 2009b, p. 5). Similarly, in grades 1–8, there are the three strands of: Creating and Presenting or Creating and Performing or Creating; Presenting, and Performing (depending on the art subject); Reflecting, Responding; and Foundations (Ontario Curriculum: Grades 9 and 10. *The Arts* 2009b, p. 14).

There are two features of the Grade 9 and 10 arts curricula which are unique. The first is the introduction of an Integrated Arts subject where they can present from two or more of The Arts discipline in an arts work production. The other is "open" courses where there are no prerequisites to enrol and complete a subject. Students may also commence an arts' subject in Grade 10. This flexibility would not occur in other subjects such as mathematics, languages or science. In the Grades 11 and 12 curricula in The Arts, students experience a similar curriculum structure and framework:

Through studying works of art from various cultures, students deepen their appreciation of diverse perspectives and develop the ability to approach others with openness and flexibility...the openness that is fostered by study of The Arts helps students to explore and appreciate the culture of diverse peoples in Canada, including First Nations and francophones. (Ontario Curriculum: Grades 11 and 12. *The Arts* 2009c, p. 3)

In the Grade 11 and 12 arts curriculum, the subjects dance, drama, visual art and music are offered with two streams. These are for students who wish to continue to arts at university or college with a prerequisite of The Arts subject from grades 9 and 10. The other option is to study The Arts as an open subject with no prerequisites (Ontario Curriculum: Grades 11 and 12. *The Arts* 2009c, p. 10).

The Ontario secondary arts curriculum is similar to Australia with the selection of subjects and strands. There is an emphasis on local rather than global issues and a focus in Canadian indigenous culture to reflect the aims of understanding their own society.

Malaysia

Situated in Southeast Asia, Malaysia is a country with a population of approximately 30 million people. Within Malaysia, there are three cultures with their associated languages and religions. Approximately 60 per cent of the population are Malay in which their first language is Bahasa Melayu and are Muslims (Malaysia 2016). Around 30 per cent of the population identify themselves as Chinese Malaysian and mostly practise Buddhism. There are also Tamil Indians who are Hindus. The country is unique in that there are three distinct languages, religions and cultures co-existing.

The country has undergone a transformation in the school curriculum which impacts what is taught in schools in order to strive for improvement in standards. The inclusion of an arts programs in secondary schools is dependent on each school's rationale.

Malaysia offers educational opportunities from Early Learning Centres to universities. Secondary school education is available to students with some schools offering specialised programs such as arts programs (Ministry of Education 2016). To address the issue of three distinct cultures and languages, there are schools specifically for the Malays, Chinese Malaysians and Indians. The main language of instruction is Bahasa Melayu with

English as the second language. English is considered as a priority as the international language of communication.

The education system has been experiencing a transformation with the goal of improvement to reflect international trends. The Malaysia Education Blueprint 2013–2025 is the plan for educational transformation up to 2025. In the forward from the Minister of Education, Yb Dato' Seri Mahdzir Bin Khalid "encapsulates the essence of the United Nations development plans such as Education for all and the Millennium Development" (Ministry of Education 2016, p. 5). This is a big picture transformation in which The Arts are not an area of priority. The following stages will describe how The Arts are manifested into the curriculum.

Wave one from 2013 to 2015 was to "turn around the system by providing support to teachers and focusing on core skills" (Ministry of Education 2016, p. 5). The Arts were a focus at this point due to the priority of improving the quality of standards of teaching, specifically in rural areas and at the early learning stages.

Wave two of the transformation is continuing Early Childhood education, attracting top quality teachers, bilingual education in Bahasa Melayu and English and Science, Technology, Engineering and Mathematics known as "STEM" (Ministry of Education 2016, p. 15). The changes in the classrooms are to upskill teachers in Information and Communication Technologies (ICT), Higher Order Thinking Skills and an approach to Problem-based learning. Malaysia is also catering to the Orang Asli and indigenous students with support in the infrastructure with teacher support and training (Ministry of Education 2016, p. 19). There is also a focus on bringing together students from different backgrounds through cultural and sports-related activities (Ministry of Education 2016, p. 21). Known as Rancangan Integrasi Murid Untuk Perpaduan (RIMUP), the student integration has The Arts as a mean for integrating different ethnic groups. "Every Malaysian child deserves equal access to an education that will enable to child to achieve his or her potential. The Ministry aspires to ensure universal access for all Malaysian children from preschool to upper secondary school by 2020" (Ministry of Education 2016, p. 26).

The Ministry of Education labels The Arts as "co-curricular" bundled in with sport. In the Ministry of Education report, there was more focus on sports activities with their respective achievements (Ministry of Education 2016, p. 89). The Arts are not mandated in secondary schools but are valued in society. The Malaysian Education Blueprint states: "Arts schools at the secondary level are important in developing artistic talents. With an addition of a new arts school, there are currently three art schools with a total of 755 students" (Ministry of Education 2016, p. 40). The three schools are Sekolah Seni Malaysia Johor (SSeMJ), Sekolah Seni Malaysia Johor (SSeMJ), Sekolah Seni Malaysia Sarawak (SSeMS) and Sekolah Seni Malaysia Kuala Lumpur (SSeMKL). In contrast, there are four sports schools and 237 secondary schools which specialise in Islamic instruction Sekolah Menengah Kebangsaan Agama (SMKA).

Teaching The Arts in secondary schools is up to the individual school, and what is offered from school to school varies. For instance, some schools may have an emphasis on visual art, whereas other schools may have a guitar or singing programs. In regard to Western art traditions, Malaysia does have a symphony orchestra called the Malaysian Philharmonic and also regional theatre and dance companies, museums, art galleries but no opera house.

There are arts curriculum documents which are separated into art and music. The forward of the music curriculum has been translated to English and describes:

> Music Education in the secondary school curriculum aims to build knowledge and skills for music students, to enable them to have the awareness and aesthetic appreciation of music from various cultures and for students to develop their potential in generating creative ideas through musical activities. (Kementerian Pendidikan Malaysia 2015, p. 2)

The curriculum is divided into subject areas including ensemble, theory, singing, reading and notation, history and appreciation. The curriculum is more descriptive than prescriptive and can be adapted to each school depending what the teacher chooses as the focus. Additionally, there are different types of music depending on the background and culture of the students.

The author lectured in Malaysia from 2010 to 2012 at a local Educational university where she prepared pre-service teachers for the secondary music curriculum. The students comprised Malay, Chinese Malaysian and Indian students and the languages of instruction were Bahasa Melayu and English with a focus on English for internationalisation. Each semester, students were provided with an overview of how to teach instruments in the Western tradition as well as traditional Malaysian music. The semester subjects were Western orchestral instruments, choir, composition, popular music, Western music history, music theory as well as the traditional Malay instruments. This approach reflected the secondary music curriculum documents where it was up to each school to determine what type of music they wished to teach. At the university, the traditional Malaysian culture was still strong, vibrant and part of their lives. The performing arts faculty also taught traditional Malay dance, drama and shadow puppetry known as "Wayang Kulit".

The Arts are an important fabric of Malaysian culture, but due to the current transformation of its education system, they are not a priority. In the future, this may change when the stages of transformation are met.

HOFSTEDE'S SIX DIMENSIONS OF NATIONAL CULTURE

This chapter centres on how The Arts are manifested in educational systems when comparing programs in Australia, Canada and Malaysia. Each country has its own language, traditions and practices. This is reflected in what is valued, how people communicate and how their organisations are structured. Through studying particular aspects of a nation, cultural differences can be better understood. Geert Hofstede created the Six Dimensions of National Culture. This was developed from a study in which he compared data from 76 countries. This reflected what the country valued by its population and how this was demonstrated through their cultural behaviour. The six dimensions formulated by Hofstede are Power Distance, Individualism, Masculinity, Uncertainty Avoidance, Long-Term Orientation and Indulgence. Through examining these dimensions, these provide some insights into what is valued and prioritised by society. Furthermore, they reflect the decisions governments make in relation to education and The Arts. These values are sometimes overtly expressed, but more often than not, these cultural assumptions are ingrained into the nation's psyche. Arts education and how it is manifested in the secondary education curriculum is one aspect of what is valued as culturally important (Hofstede 2016).

The approach to culture and cultural difference was developed from the notion that societies face the same problems. It is how they address and answer these, which sets nations apart (Hofstede et al. 2010, p. 29). Additionally, difference is manifested by what is desired or valued by members of society.

Understanding culture is multi-dimensional and complex, and to fully grasp why nations function in a particular way requires several indicators as well as cultural immersion. Hofstede was provided with survey data from

Table 1 Comparison of Australia, Canada and Malaysia

	Australia	*Canada*	*Malaysia*
Power Distance	36	39	100
Individualism	90	80	26
Masculinity	61	52	50
Uncertainty Avoidance	51	48	36
Long-Term Orientation	21	36	41
Indulgence	71	68	57

International Business Machines (IBM) where employees from around the world were asked to agree or disagree with statements. The statistical average of the answers from each country was analysed which highlighted the differences in their value systems. These value systems were then developed to be known as Dimensions of National Cultures.

Australia, Malaysia and Canada are compared on the six indicators with the French-Canadian province of Quebec also discussed to highlight that within a nation, there can be some notable differences. In Hofstede's research, he graded each dimension on a continuum rather than out of 100. Below is a table of the comparison of the three countries:

Table 1 shows a general similarity between Australia and Canada, whereas Malaysia displays difference in cultural values. Even though Australia and Malaysia are Commonwealth countries, are relatively close geographically and have similar population sizes, there are fundamental differences which need to be taken into consideration. Australia and Canada are similar except in the dimensions "Masculinity" and "Long-Term Orientation", whereas Canada and Malaysia are similar (Hofstede 2016).

Power Distance

Power Distance is described as "the degree to which the less powerful members of a society accept and expect that power is distributed unequally" (Hofstede 2016). A society with high Power Distance classify people according to their hierarchy and status. Royalty or heads of state generally would be inaccessible to the general public. In contrast, in nations where there is low Power Distance, one would find people in positions of power walking down the street alongside the general public.

Malaysia has one of the highest Power Distance scores and in 2009 was the highest in the world according to Hofstede (Hofstede et al. 2010, p. 57). In Malaysia, titles and positions are of extreme importance and people in positions of authority such as royalty and politicians are revered. How this potentially translates in an educational context is that students would not question the teacher, and teachers would not challenge the principal if they wanted to evoke change. Meetings between staff members are very formal and titles would be used to reinforce who was in power. Teachers are treated with respect and fear and what the school dictates is taken as gospel and not challenged. In a secondary school system, an arts teacher who wanted to start or develop an arts programs would require the principal to be fully supportive otherwise it would be very difficult to achieve this. Australia and Canada in contrast have a low Power Distance score in which the teachers and principals would treat each other as equals. Students may challenge the teacher and can even have a say in the direction of The Arts programs. Interestingly, the French-Canadians in the province of Quebec have a higher Power Distance score of 54 compared to 39 in the English-speaking provinces which reflects their more hierarchical, formal culture. In 2009, Malaysia had the highest Power Distance Index rating of 104 with Austria as the lowest with 11.

Individualism

In a society with a high level of Individualism, people look after themselves and their immediate families. They perceive themselves as "I" rather than "we". A low level of Individualism is known as collectivism where groups look after each other and are loyal to the beliefs. Australia was perceived as a highly individualistic society with a scoring of 90 where people work independently and look after themselves and their immediate families. In 2009, the top four Individualistic countries were the United States of America, Australia, Great Britain and Canada (Hofstede et al. 2010, p. 95). They would be rewarded for showing initiative and promotions would be based on merit and evidence of past work-related achievements. Canada is also high on the ratings of 80 where they are perceived as individualistic but groups still exert some influence. The French-Canadian province has scored 73 which reveals a slightly more collective nature. Malaysia in contrast is seen as more collective with a score of 26. Individuals would be influenced more by group decisions to keep the collective wider community happy. Background and status would have an influence on promotion and how it would impact the group in general. Interestingly in 2009, the nation with the lowest level of Individualism was Guatemala with a score of 6.

In an educational setting, teachers from a country with a high rating in Individualism would more likely be promoted based on their ideas and initiative rather than their background and status. Arts programs in a secondary school would succeed with an influential arts educator with initiative and strong leadership skills. In Malaysia, the success and future of an arts programs would be determined by the teachers and families. If The Arts curriculum was valued in schools, the programs would be supported by the school and the wider community.

Masculinity

Masculinity refers to how some societies value achievement. Assertiveness, heroism and material rewards in a competitive atmosphere are manifestations of a masculine society. In a feminine society, people are more caring towards each other, look after the weak and needy, work in a co-operative way and are concerned about their quality of life. Hofstede has adopted the term "tough versus tender" cultures. Australia is rated as a masculine society with a score of 61 where individuals are competitive. Canada scored moderately at 52 and 45 for Quebec here with a high standard for work, but also striving for a work-life balance. Malaysia is also perceived as a moderately masculine society. In 2009, the most masculine society was Slovakia with Norway, Sweden and Latvia as the most feminine (Hofstede et al. 2010, p. 141). In a secondary school arts curriculum, a feminine culture would be more effective where staff, students, parents and the community would work together in a co-operative way.

The Arts play an important role at schools for students whose sense of well-being and acceptance are linked to their creativity. An observation which the author has heard frequently in school settings is that arts teachers discover hidden artistic talents of students who otherwise would not be aware of their extraordinary gifts. This discovery usually occurs in a feminine class environment where there was a co-operative environment and class support. An arts curriculum encourages co-operation in a supportive environment which may contribute to the students' well-being and more importantly, an aesthetically rich society.

Uncertainty Avoidance

This dimension refers to how nations deal with uncertainty for the future and the unknown. Hofstede has described this as "what is different is dangerous." A nation which receives a high score is more set in their beliefs and resistant to change, whereas countries which score low have a more relaxed attitude towards change and goes with the flow. They are more concerned with practice than principles. Globally, Greece scored the highest and Singapore the lowest (Hofstede et al. 2010, pp. 193–4). Australia and Canada scored a medium in this dimension, whereas Malaysia scored lower. This may be surprising for a conservative society; however Malaysia is one of the few nations where they have not had a change in government since the formation of the country in 1963. There has been political stability and a degree of trust in their governance where the peoples' needs are addressed. Generally, in secondary arts education, schools and students can adapt to changes in the curriculum without great fear or resistance. A curriculum from a nation which rates highly would have a structured curriculum with little room for change. Direct instruction rather than project-based learning would work well here. An issue in The Arts curriculum is the necessity to have a safe, creative environment where students can experiment and are not afraid for their creation to fail. Unstructured time is required as well as being open to suggestions from teachers and peers.

Long-Term Orientation

According to Hofstede, how societies deal with Long-Term Orientation reveals how society deals with change. There is a tension with linking to the past where dealing with the risks of the future. Australia scored 21 on this dimension meaning that they prefer to hold onto traditions rather than accept change. Nations which score highly can adapt to long-term change in a way to prepare to the future. In the survey, the countries which scored the highest were South Korea, Taiwan, Japan and China with Puerto Rico as the lowest (Hofstede et al. 2010, pp. 257–8). Malaysia and Canada scored 41 and 36 respectively, which is higher than Australia but according to Hofstede, these are still viewed as short-term normative cultures. All three nations appear not to be comfortable or open to dealing with change, rather looking for quick results. In these contexts, if an arts educator wanted to develop an arts programs at a school, the most effective way would be to make a series of small changes each term as quick fixes rather than a long-term overhaul.

Indulgence

The final dimension is Indulgence which is the "extent to which people try to control their desires or impulses" (Hofstede 2016). This can often be conditioned when young children are socialised. A nation with a high score in Indulgence means that gratification, spending money, enjoying life and fun are valued. The society is optimistic for the future. A nation which scores low in this dimension are more restrained, more regulated and are less likely to socialise and spend money on entertainment. Australia and Canada score highly with 71 and 68 respectively, with Malaysia moderate on the scale with 57. In regard to the performing arts, an indulgent society would be reflected in the prevalence of art galleries, concerts, shows and festivals in which a society would invest time and money in these pursuits for entertainment. The culture of the society would reflect which art form or forms are valued. In a school arts programs, a nation which scored highly may offer lots of arts subjects, but they may be viewed as extra-curricular activities for students. A restrained society may not value The Arts, and spending time on these may be frivolous and may not offer these in schools. However, a restrained society with a strong artistic heritage may have arts programs in schools which are taken seriously. The secondary arts curriculum in Australia and Canada are quite comprehensive, offering opportunities for students to be engaged in a range of arts forms and practices. The Malaysian arts curriculum offers scope for students to study The Arts from select schools. All three countries have a rich arts heritage which is manifested in their professional visual and performing arts groups. The secondary arts curriculum is a reflection of society and what is valued for the next generation of artists.

DISCUSSION

Understanding cultural values for each country is complex and multi-dimensional. Hofstede's Six Dimensions of National Culture provide insight into what is deemed important, how individuals best function in their country and how they respond to change. The scores for Australia and Canada were similar in Power Distance, Uncertainty Avoidance and Indulgence, displaying that the power relationship in schools was relatively equal, can deal with some change and enjoyed the nice things in life. Australia scored highly in Individualism and Masculinity but low in Long-Term Orientation. How this would apply to an arts programs is that schools would value achievement of individuals and would be competitive but would hold on to traditions. Schools would value The Arts, especially when the programs were successful. Canada is similar to Australia but is a more feminine society and scored higher in Long-Term Orientation. Arts programs in schools would be more adaptable to change and the school community be more co-operative. Malaysia in contrast scored the highest in Power Distance showing a set hierarchy between students and staff but more collective than being competitive. An arts programs would be managed by the school leaders and there would be a collective culture within the classroom rather than promoting select individuals. The Arts programs in schools would be influenced by the cultural values of the nation and manifested in their curriculum documents.

Conclusion

Australia, Canada and Malaysia offer a secondary arts curriculum in their respective countries. Each of these documents has been developed to reflect the current educational priorities of the country and the future goals. These include the inclusion of indigenous cultures in a globalised society. In order to better understand the place of The Arts in education, Hofstede's Six Dimensions of National Culture were employed. This showed how countries may be perceived as similar, but due to their own subtle cultural ideologies and practice, arts programs would be manifested in different ways. The Arts are central to culture and society and have an important place in a nation's cultural identity. How this is practised and taught in the curriculum is dependent on schools, teachers, policymakers and the community.

References

Australian Bureau of Statistics. (2017). *Population clock*. Retrieved from http://www.abs.gov.au/ausstats/abs@.nsf/Web+Pages/Population+Clock?opendocument
Australian Curriculum, Assessment and Reporting Authority. (2011). The Arts. In *Shape of the Australian curriculum: The Arts*. Retrieved from http://www.acara.edu.au/_resources/Shape_of_the_Australian_Curriculum_The_Arts

Australian Curriculum, Assessment and Reporting Authority. (2016). *The Arts*. Retrieved from http://www.acara.edu.au/curriculum/learning-areas-subjects/the-arts

Cameron A. E. (1969). *The class teaching of music in secondary schools in Victoria 1905–1955: An investigation into the major influences affecting the development of music as a class syllabus in Victorian Secondary Schools*. Unpublished masters thesis, The University of Melbourne, Melbourne.

Canada. (2016). In *Wikipedia*. Retrieved from http://en.wikipedia.org/wiki/Canada

General Assembly of the United Nations. (1948). *Universal declaration of human rights*. Retrieved from http://www.un.org/en/universal-declaration-human-rights/

Hofstede, G. (2016). *National culture*. Retrieved from https://www.geert-hofstede.com/national-culture.html

Hofstede, G., Hofstede, G. J., & Minkov, M. (2010). *Cultures and organizations: Intercultural cooperation and its importance for survival*. New York: McGraw Hill.

Human Development Index. (2016). In *Wikipedia*. Retrieved from https://en.wikipedia.org/wiki/List_of_countries_by_Human_Development_Index

Kementerian Pendidikan Malaysia. (2015). *Kurikulum Standard Sekolah Menengah Pendidikan Muzik Dokumen Standard Kurikulum dan Pentaksiran*. Retrieved from https://cms.mrsm.edu.my/cms/documentstorage/com.tms.cms.document.Document_d7da9eb3-ac12c870-38675e41-fc664bf1/006%20DSKP%20Pendidikan%20Muzik%20KSSM%20Tingkatan%201.pdf

Malaysia. (2016). In *Wikipedia*. Retrieved from https://en.wikipedia.org/wiki/Malaysia

Ministerial Council on Education, Employment, Training and Youth Affairs. (2008). *Melbourne declaration of educational goals for young Australians*. Retrieved from http://www.curriculum.edu.au/verve/_resources/National_Declaration_on_the_Educational_Goals_for_Young_Australians.pdf

Ministry of Education. (2009a). *Ontario curriculum: Elementary. The Arts*. Retrieved from http://www.edu.gov.on.ca/eng/curriculum/elementary/arts18b09curr.pdf

Ministry of Education. (2009b). *Ontario curriculum: Grades 9 and 10. The Arts*. Retrieved from http://www.edu.gov.on.ca/eng/curriculum/secondary/arts910curr2010.pdf

Ministry of Education. (2009c). *Ontario curriculum: Grades 11 and 12. The arts*. Retrieved from http://edu.gov.on.ca/eng/curriculum/secondary/arts1112curr2010.pdf

Ministry of Education. (2016). *Annual education blueprint 2013–2025*. Retrieved from http://www.moe.gov.my/en/pelan-pembangunan-pendidikan-malaysia-2

Robinson, K., & Aronica, L. (2009). *The element: How finding your passion changes everything*. London: Penguin.

228   S. LIERSE

Victorian Parliamentary Papers. (1972). *Education Act*. Retrieved from http://
foundingdocs.gov.au/item-sdid-25.html

Sharon Lierse is Lecturer in Education at Charles Darwin University (Melbourne).
Prior to her appointment, she was an associate professor in the Faculty of Music
and Performing Arts at Universiti Pendidikan Sultan Idris in Malaysia, where
she was founder and managing editor of the *Malaysian Music Journal*. Dr Lierse
has also lectured at the University of Tasmania, and was Manager of Professional
Learning at the Australian Council for Educational Research. Her works have been
published widely and she has given conference papers around the world, including
keynote presentations in Europe and Asia. Dr Lierse specialises in arts performance
and pedagogy and excellence in teaching.

Conclusion: The Emerging Curriculum Agenda

Carmel Roofe and Christopher Bezzina

Life's purposes are often derived from the education system that a country provides for its populace. These purposes are also influenced by cultures of the global village and are often recorded in political agendas and policies that influence schooling within a society. Traditionally schools were seen as the main avenue through which ideologies were actioned. The metaphor for becoming assimilated was the cultural 'melting pot', instilling middle-class values to one and all, irrespective of ethnic, religious or cultural background. Roles for one and all were clearly defined. Expectations set for all to follow. Place, time and activities were closely tied with one another, very much determining what took place during school hours. As school ended we all went home and found our mothers waiting for us. Time and function were also closely joined. There was time to be at

C. Roofe (✉)
School of Education, University of the West Indies, Kingston, Jamaica

C. Bezzina
Leadership for Learning and Innovation, Faculty of Education,
University of Malta, Msida, Malta

Department of Education, Uppsala University, Uppsala, Sweden

© The Author(s) 2018   229
C. Roofe, C. Bezzina (eds.), *Intercultural Studies*
of Curriculum, Intercultural Studies in Education,
https://doi.org/10.1007/978-3-319-60897-6_11

school; time to spend at home, to work and play; and time to enjoy family time. However, with the increased access to technology and the rise of the internet, ideologies easily transcend borders, and place and time are no longer closely woven. Information has become easily accessible outside of the formal structures of schooling.

Our society has changed. When society changes, schools change, argues David Elkind (2000/2001). Our society has changed from modern to postmodern with our schools a far different social institution than it once was. The prevalent belief that schools have a common ethos, a set of values which are different from, and superior to others, and that all groups would accept and incorporate these values in their daily lives does not hold, at least not any more. Just a look at the local or international news shows how fragmented society has become where values and the roles of values in society and for society have become crucial. The postmodern period we are in has challenged our provincial notions of common values and defined roles and boundaries. The clearly demarcated social roles of the modern era have given way to the overlapping and less rigid roles of the postmodern era. Society is now faced with what Elkind describes as 'postmodern innovations' such as 'inclusion', diversity, 'multiculturalism', 'citizenship'. From our perspective, we would also add critical thinking and creativity that serve as a clarion call for the way we look at curriculum. We need to examine how the curriculum we develop within and across countries nurtures such principles, or are we losing the plot in order to fulfil state-mandated requirements? The narrow notions of testing that have become the hallmark of an education system must be replaced with practices that provide diversity in modes of learning and assessments that lead to quality education for all. The curriculum as the cornerstone for learning in schools should serve as the foundation for providing opportunities that awaken the critical consciousness of citizens to understand these principles while understanding themselves as individuals with their own unique identity.

The authors of the chapters in this book have provided the basis for what seems to be an 'emerging curriculum agenda'. This agenda is being driven by the theme 'social justice for all'. In this agenda, the curriculum is not seen as an end in itself but is seen as the foundation for cultivating the critical consciousness necessary for individuals to decipher truths and to draw conclusions about the world and themselves. Whilst the focus of this book is on the curriculum as a vehicle to social justice, we feel that issues that deal with social justice are much more than curriculum matters. We agree with Elkind's argument that curriculum is more about social acceptance than developing a programme to fit the curriculum; that multiculturalism is more about respect, respecting children as both unique human beings and part of a group. According to Elkind, this is 'one of the major adaptational problems posed to teachers by the new valuation of our common humanity' (2000/2001, p. 15). When we see such 'innovations' as social problems that are misread as issues that can be turned into subject matter to be taught in schools, we force curricular changes that do not achieve their intended aims. This book, through its various contributions, is a search for meaning and that teachers and teaching for meaning in the complex world of today is our challenge. Many teachers, including ourselves, grew up in education systems where teachers told their students what to think. Teaching for meaning implies and requires that teachers serve as mediators of thinking. They do their utmost to create opportunities for students to engage, debate and relate to the world in which they live. As Jacqueline Grennon Brooks beautifully put it, 'Living means perpetually searching for meaning. Schools need to be places that keep this search alive' (2004, p. 12). The Arts as discussed in this text represent an excellent starting point and an example of how the curriculum can help students to search for meaning.

The chapters in this book encourage educators, as learners, to challenge what is; to engage with students as learners, so that they too keep the search for meaning alive. Perkins (2004) argues that 'Education is not just about acquiring knowledge, but about learning how to do significant things with what you know' (p. 18). Teaching in today's world is indeed a complex and difficult task, one that goes beyond teaching facts and skills. The challenge involves connecting with students and showing them how to use knowledge in real-life situations. We have to challenge the misconception that teachers have to teach to the test. This is easier said than done given the drive for performativity that pervades societies. Various studies show that teachers can best raise test scores over the long haul by teaching key ideas and processes contained in content standards in rich and engaging ways, by collecting evidence of student understanding of that content through robust local assessments rather than a one-shot standardized testing and by using engaging and effective instructional strategies that help students explore core concepts through inquiry and problem solving (Hiebert et al. 2003; McTighe et al. 2004).

Data from the Trends in International Mathematics and Science Study (TIMSS) also challenge the premise that teaching to the test is the best way to achieve higher scores. TIMSS tested the mathematics and science achievement of students in 42 countries at three grade levels (4, 8 and 12).

The outcomes of TIMSS offer some additional insights worth referring to and that can serve as the basis for thinking beyond performativity. In an exhaustive analysis of mathematics instruction in Japan, Germany and the United States, Stigler and Hiebert (1999) present striking evidence of the benefits of teaching for meaning and understanding. In Japan, a high-achieving country, mathematics teachers state that their primary aim is to develop conceptual understanding in their students. Compared with teachers in the United States, they cover less ground in terms of discrete topics, skills or pages in a textbook, but they emphasize problem-based learning in which students derive and explain rules and theorems, thus leading to deeper understanding.

Various chapters in this book help us to appreciate the critical and central role that teachers play in creating aha moments. Our students need teachers who help them challenge the reality they face. People commonly think of creativity as the ability to think outside the box, to be imaginative or to come up with original ideas. The creativity we are referring to in this volume is one that shows the need for persistence and resilience, that choices come at a price, that life presents us with challenges and decisions that cannot be addressed superficially. As Beghetto and Kaufman (2013) argue, 'creativity requires work, effort and risk' (p. 14). When teachers prepare the context for creativity to flourish, students will be able to relate to their true selves as they do things and reflect about things openly without the fear of being misunderstood or ridiculed. But are teachers adequately prepared to create these aha moments? Certainly, this suggests a new set of skills that teachers should possess and therefore teacher training programmes need to be responsive in providing these skills. The curriculum in teacher training institutions must seek to prepare teachers to teach for meaning and to help students challenge ideas. A critical purpose therefore for the teacher training curriculum is to help trainees challenge their conceptions so that they themselves can experience what they will be required to do for their students.

Through what we do in schools is crucial it is not necessarily enough. As John Dewey argued, it is only when formal education in schools and informal education outside of schools come together, principles such as justice, equity and freedom will take on meaning as people engage in responsible citizenship making democratic behaviour routine. It is here that the statement 'education is life, life is education' takes on added significance. Jacques Delors argues that 'Lifelong learning is about work and life, success in work that benefits the community, and the future of our young people who will enter the labour market [if they are lucky enough we would add]. But, Delors goes on to state that 'on a deeper level, it is about knowing oneself better, ... gaining a kind of self-esteem to help us deal with the risks and constraints of life, and acquire the ability to take control of our own lives' (2013, p. 329).

It is here that the spirit of education seeks and finds meaning. Parker J Palmer in *The Courage to Teach* (1998) argues that when we bring forth the spirituality of teaching and learning we help students honour life's most meaningful questions. By spirituality, Palmer is talking about connectedness. He argues that

> "we can evoke the spirituality of any discipline by teaching in ways that allow the 'big story' told by the discipline to intersect with the 'little story' of the student's life. Doing so not only brings up personal possibilities for connectedness but also helps students learn the discipline more deeply. Learning does not happen when the subject is disconnected from the learner's life" (Palmer 1998, p. 9).

The chapters help us to connect with our own very existence; with the way we have related to education in all its facets throughout our journey. It presents to us an opportunity to stop at the crossroad and to explore and challenge our own assumptions that we bring to life and the possibility of creating realistically better ways of living with others. The major difference between schools, regions, countries lies in the way they organize the curriculum. This organization very much depends on the way educators look at learning both from a personal perspective but more importantly the way they relate together and with students. When teachers do get together to create democratic and collaborative processes, the curriculum comes to life and people engage in a journey (Jeffrey and Woods 2003) worth pursuing. This also requires repositioning of the curriculum as the means by which the changes needed to create a better society can occur. As demonstrated through research, all countries regardless of their wealth grapple with the same social and economic issues though to varying degrees. Designing curricula requires that we to consider the uniqueness of context. The various chapters in this volume show that issues of race and gender cannot be decontextualized. The schools, school leaders and teachers working together and alongside community members is needed. For, as Tatum argues 'We can't just aspire to be prejudice-free. We need to examine how racism persists in our institutions so we don't perpetuate it' (1997, p. 17).

The emerging curriculum agenda suggest that there needs to be collaboration between those working in schools and those outside in order to inculcate in students the kinds of values that are needed in society. A culture of collaboration within and across countries and agencies such as higher education and industry is needed to support and stimulate creativity and innovation. However, such collaborations must first seek to understand the context of each country then seek to find the most appropriate and best areas for collaboration. In this way, a balance is created that respects the uniqueness of contexts.

We contend that for lasting, sustainable changes to occur and for us to create the ideal world of inclusivity and social justice for all, the curriculum and teachers must be given priority attention in and across countries. The curriculum should be used as the means for reducing the disparity between those who are considered to be the 'haves' and the 'have nots'. It must serve as the means for the cultivation of critical consciousness necessary for a worldview that goes beyond the truths learned and experienced. This requires teachers who teach with a moral imperative. Teachers are critical to the effective implementation of ideas and so their own preparation should go beyond teacher training colleges to include ongoing professional development. Ongoing professional development should provide the space teachers need to reflect, debate and challenge notions about how they teach and how they help students to navigate the constant changes given their realities. Teachers are critical to the implementation of ideas, but if they are not adequately prepared to implement these ideas no matter how good, they will not be successfully implemented. Additionally, teachers need to be given the autonomy to make curricula decisions but they will not be confident to do so if the successes of their endeavours are determined only by test scores (Caena 2011; Frost 2008; Webster-Wright 2009).

We are conscious that the ideas presented in this text are by no means exhaustive. We have no doubt that there is similar work going on in other networks across the world and in single schools, where their moral purpose is steadfast and where inroads are being made to address injustices of all sorts. Hence, we encourage policy makers, researchers and educators to continue researching to unearth new ideas that advocate for quality education for all.

REFERENCES

Beghetto, R. A., & Kaufman, J. C. (2013). Fundamentals of creativity. *Educational Leadership, 7*(5), 10–15.

Brooks, J. G. (2004). To see beyond the lesson. *Educational Leadership, 62*(1), 8–12.

Caena, F. (2011). *Literature review. Quality in teachers' continuing professional development. Education and training 2020.* Thematic Working Group 'Professional Development of Teachers'. European Commission, Brussels.

Delors, J. (2013). The treasure within: Learning to know, learning to do, learning to live together and learning to be. What is the value of that treasure 15 years after its publication? *International Review of Education, 59*(3), 319–330.

Elkind, D. (2000/2001). The cosmopolitan school. *Educational Leadership, 58*(4), 12–17.

Frost, D. (2008). 'Teacher leadership': Values and voice. *School Leadership and Management, 28*(4), 337–352.

Hiebert, J., Gallimore, R., Garnier, H., Jacobs, J., et al. (2003). *Teaching mathematics in seven countries: Results from the TIMSS 1999 video study (NCES 2003–013).* Washington, DC: U.S. Department of Education.

Jeffrey, B., & Woods, P. (2003). *The creative school.* London: RoutledgeFalmer.

McTighe, J., Seif, E., & Wiggins, G. (2004). You *can* teach for meaning. *Educational Leadership, 62*(1), 26–30.

Palmer, J. P. (1998). *The courage to teach. Exploring the inner landscape of a teacher's life.* San Francisco: Jossey-Bass.

Perkins, D. (2004). Knowledge alive. *Educational Leadership, 62*(1), 14–18.

Stigler, J., & Hiebert, J. (1999). *The teaching gap: Best ideas from the world's teachers for improving education in the classroom.* New York: The Free Press.

Tatum, B. D. (1997). *Why are all the black kids sitting together in the cafeteria?* New York: Basic Books.

Webster-Wright, A. (2009). Reframing professional development through understanding authentic professional learning. *Review of Educational Research, 79*(2), 702–739.

Carmel Roofe is a lecturer in Curriculum and Instruction at the University of the West Indies, Mona, Jamaica. She is a member of the Institute for Educational Administration & Leadership-Jamaica and a Fellow at the Charles Darwin University, Australia. Her career in teaching spans both the secondary and higher education levels.

Christopher Bezzina is Professor of Educational Leadership in the Faculty of Education, University of Malta, and the Department of Education, Uppsala University, Sweden. He is both a Commonwealth and Fulbright Scholar and is currently Vice President of the Commonwealth Council for Educational Administration and Management.

INDEX

© The Author(s) 2018   237
C. Roofe, C. Bezzina (eds.), *Intercultural Studies
of Curriculum*, Intercultural Studies in Education,
https://doi.org/10.1007/978-3-319-60897-6

CPSIA information can be obtained
at www.ICGtesting.com
Printed in the USA
BVOW05*1302101017

497265BV00009B/19/P

9 783319 608969